Wildlife Wars

Wildlife Wars

The Life and Times of a Fish and Game Warden

TERRY GROSZ

Johnson Books
BOULDER

Published in the United States by Johnson Books, a division of Johnson Publishing Company, 1880 South 57th Court, Boulder, Colorado 80301. E-mail: books@jpcolorado.com

9   8   7   6   5   4   3   2   1

Cover design by Debra B. Topping
Cover photograph © Jeffrey Rich Nature Photography. Roosevelt elk in redwoods, Prairie Creek State Park, CA.
Author photo © James Bludworth

Library of Congress Cataloging-in-Publication Data
Grosz, Terry.
   Wildlife wars: the life and times of a fish and game warden /
Terry Grosz.
       p.   cm.
   ISBN 1-55566-245-5 (cloth: alk. paper)—ISBN 1-55566-246-3
(pbk.: alk. paper)
   1. Grosz, Terry. 2. Game wardens—California Biography.
I. Title.
SK354.G76A3   1999
363.28—dc21   99-34216
[B]   CIP

Printed in the United States by
Johnson Printing
1880 South 57th Court
Boulder, Colorado 80301

 Printed on recycled paper with soy ink

THIS BOOK IS DEDICATED TO Elliott Sutta, one of the most intelligent and complex world of wildlife professionals I ever met. He was always able to understand the big picture and respond to its trials, no matter what legal trail he had to take in order to guarantee its success. He was always there, supplying gifted counsel, supported by an ethic that loved challenge, and providing solutions that furthered the preservation of the resources of this great land of ours. To the man I admire as a wildlife professional, respect as a man, and love as a brother, I dedicate this book of stories from one westering man to another.

Contents

Preface

ORIGINALLY, I HOPED TO leave behind some form of written word as a record of my days as a California state Fish and Game warden, then as a U.S. game management agent, and finally as a special agent with the U.S. Fish and Wildlife Service. Initially, this dream of short stories was committed to loose stacks of paper in a forgotten corner of my office, which were someday to act as a reminder to my children and grandchildren of what their father and grandfather had done with thirty-two years of his life. However, as the work in progress grew and others shared in the reading of those loose stacks of paper, another dream began to grow. Today those dreams and paper stacks have metamorphosed into the book you now hold in your hands. This book traces my footprints across the face of time in the world of wildlife as I tried to protect those natural resources, our national heritage, if you will, against forces hellbent on their destruction.

In this book, and I hope others to follow, I have tried to describe the very essence and soul of the wildlife protection trade through the many faces of human conflict as my ship of life crossed many others on the great sea of our natural environment. I was very fortunate in my years as a wildlife law enforcement officer to have seen and experienced the end of the very best years of the California Department of Fish and Game. I was also fortunate to have witnessed the end of the very best years of the U.S. Fish and Wildlife Service. Suffice it to say that in over three decades, one sees many changes in the world and, as is to be expected, many are not for the better.

I was also fortunate to be blessed with a body that more or less held up to the rigors required by the profession in the form of long hours, lousy food (usually sat upon by my Labrador retriever), dangerous animals, inclement weather, poor supervision, budgets designed to not allow one to do the job one was trained to do, national politics skewed toward private interests, wildlife that would not cooperate, equipment purchased from the lowest bidder, unsympathetic government attorneys, juries that did not have an ounce of common sense, judges who had no sense of history, more long hours, crooked state politics, useless state and federal help, and many more obstacles.

I was also blessed with a wife who had a deeply unique sense of her husband and understood what he was trying to do long before he knew himself. Over those thirty-two years, she quietly assumed the position of second love and patiently waited until I retired to assume her rightful place as my first love. I also had two sons and a daughter who, like their mother, realized Dad was on a quest and, also like their mother, provided unmitigated support and love in order that my vision quest might be fulfilled.

I was also blessed over the years with some of the best staffs and officers in the nation to assist me in achieving the many goals I set for preservation of our natural resources. Most of these folks were of such quality that no accomplishment was impossible as long as you gave them a little time to figure out how to administer the program or run the bad guys to the ground. They were so good that I often teasingly told them if they ever got on my trail, they should expect a bullet. That would be the only way I could get them off the trail once they set their sights on their target. The American people truly owe those folks a debt of gratitude for what they did to preserve the natural resources of this land for those yet to come. It is a fact that the wildlife one sees today in this country is a tribute to those wildlife officers who came before and those who currently hold that position, representing the "thin green line," and their front-line staffs.

It might be surprising to learn that my career all started with the malicious tossing of a snowball. In 1954 I was a twelve-year-old boy living in Quincy, California, a town nestled in the northeastern Sierras about eighty miles west of Reno, Nevada. It was the dead of winter, and in those days the snow in that lumbering community was higher than the shoulders of Babe the Big Blue Ox. I was walking home from school that winter day and chanced to see a bunch of out-of-work lumbermen tossing snowballs at a covey of mountain quail huddled under a manzanita bush alongside the highway. The snow was so deep that the only place the quail could go was under some of the deeper stands of brush in order to find some ground to stand on. One of the men, called Gabby by the others, whanged a quail on the head with a snowball, killing it instantly. The men ploughed through the waist-deep snow to retrieve the dead, fluttering quail as the rest of the covey flew off into the ponderosa forest to safety.

Well, I was a ragged-assed kid in those days and was able to talk the men out of the quail so I could take it home to share with my family. However, once I had the quail in my hand, I turned around and walked back into town and straight to the local game warden's house. There was just something about fair play, deep snow, and starving quail that hit a nerve, even for a twelve-year-old hungry kid. The game warden was a stoop-shouldered man, the stoop having been caused by a poacher's rifle bullet, but a damn good man and an excellent game warden. Paul Kerr listened to my story, then loaded me into his patrol car and headed for Gabby's home. In those days everyone knew everyone in such small mountain communities.

Driving up in front of Gabby's house, Paul knocked on the door and was invited in. I often remember that in those days the law was a welcome and respected sight. Shortly afterward, Paul came out of Gabby's house, got back into his patrol car, and took me home. He had written Gabby a ticket for taking a game bird during the closed season and seized the quail for evidence. However, before he took me home, he took me by his back porch, opened up his evidence freezer, and pulled several packages of deer steak from it. He placed the meat in a paper bag, telling me to take it home for my mom to cook up for us kids. He also thanked me for obeying the law and turning in those who took advantage of wildlife in its deepest time of need.

I never forgot those words. Years later I went to college at Humboldt State in Arcata, California. In 1966 I graduated from Humboldt with a master of science degree in wildlife management. Shortly after that I took the California state Fish and Game warden's exam along with 1,300 other hopefuls. Forty-five of us were selected for the physicals, and ultimately twenty-five of us were selected as game wardens, of whom twenty-three were sent off to a training academy in southern California. Upon graduating from the academy, I was assigned to a warden's position in Eureka, California, and spent a year and a half there. In 1967 I was transferred to Colusa, California, in the heart of the Sacramento Valley, about eighty miles east of Sacramento. I worked in that area until May 1970, when I resigned my state commission and accepted a position as a game management agent with the U.S. Fish and Wildlife Service. From that day on, I never looked back.

This book, which I hope will be the first of several, deals with only a small portion of my state wildlife law enforcement career and experiences. Even though these events are true, they have been altered so that no one will be able to identify any of the real-life characters. I have even incorporated some blind alleys into the text to throw off the really astute students of wildlife law enforcement history, be they pursuers or pursued. The places described in the book are very real, but the names of the characters have been changed to protect any who remain living or their families. You may find many of these tales sad, disgusting, evil, funny, moralistic, or just plain and simply gross. However, they all come from the actual fabric of my life's adventures, and the events they depict are still ongoing in new forms and places.

Regardless of your reactions, bear in mind that these events actually occurred and that they are the adventures of just one officer. There are almost ten thousand like officers, state, federal, and provincial, across North America who could tell similar tales. That being the case, imagine the scope and degree of illegal activity and the actual soul and essence that meets such activity on a daily basis in the world of wildlife all across North America.

I hope that you will be able to read between the lines and realize the amount of destruction that takes place daily among *your* plant and animal communities, national and international. There are fewer and fewer natural resources over the horizon. In fact, for the most part they are going or gone. Also, I hope you will understand the dangers met by those wearing the badge and those left behind on the home front. They are tremendous, many times requiring the ultimate sacrifice.

Bear in mind that the business of extinction is alive and well. Let us hope and pray that we do not all go the way of the passenger pigeon. Then again, maybe that would be the way to go, and let Mother Earth heal and start all over again—perhaps this time with better results.

Acknowledgments

MY GREATEST DEBT in connection with this book is to my daughter-in-law Carrie Grosz, a tireless supporter of the work, a gallant transcriber of the rawest form of tapes, a gifted craftswoman of the English language, and a genius in the world of computers. This combination, along with her talent in gently guiding her father-in-law from the electronic dark ages to at least a benthic level of light in the world of computer electronics, ultimately enabled these stories of one man's thirty-two-year battle as a wildlife conservation officer protecting this nation's natural resources to be told.

1

Ishi-Pishi Falls

LEAVING MY HOUSE IN Eureka for work as a state Fish and Game warden one morning in 1966, I was acutely aware of the warmth on my back as the cold, early-morning Humboldt County mist met my face. Looking up into the typically foggy Pacific North Coast morning and appreciating the moisture for its effects on the redwood forests, I hurried to get into my patrol vehicle. I checked to make sure that the gear needed for the day's outing was present in the back seat of my "office," then turned the key in the ignition. As the engine on my Mercury Comet roared into action, little did I realize that I was heading for a unique survival chapter in my life as a wildlife law enforcement officer.

Picking up the radio mike, I called in to the dispatcher and notified her that unit 154 was 10-8, or on duty. Nancy, our dispatcher-secretary, acknowledged my call and matter-of-factly informed me that Captain Gray wanted to see me "right now." The tone of her voice told me that failure to meet with the captain promptly would do nothing but bring the "wrath of God" down around my ears. The start of a perfect north coast day had lost something of its promise. What the hell had I done to offend our Fish and Game captain? I mused. In those days the captain of a Fish and Game squad was viewed as if he were seated at the right hand of God. Crossing either of those two usually meant someone was going to pay the piper.

I ran my image of Captain Gray through my mind, as I had done many times since my entry into this Fish and Game squad. What a work of art! He was captain of the Pacific Coast Squad, which covered an area comprising Humboldt, Del Norte, and Trinity Counties and contained seventeen land and marine wardens whose job it was to enforce the California Fish and Game laws. He had been captain of the squad for years and was solidly backed in that position by his supervisor, Inspector Les Lahr, another old-timer and ex-marine, who had fought in the "Banana Wars," as he liked to tell it. Inspector Lahr and Captain Gray were two of a kind, for the most part, and to cross one was to cross the other, with usually foul results. Because Inspector Lahr had originally selected Captain Gray for the Pacific Coast captain's position, there was little wrong the good captain could do, and hence there was no way to appeal over Captain Gray's head. So not getting along with the captain meant a pitching deck in a Type 8 gale, if you get my drift. Captain Gray didn't like anyone with a college degree because he didn't have one (he didn't feel a game warden needed any schooling); didn't like anyone with a degree in wildlife management (a typical old-school game warden, he thought of someone with a wildlife degree as nothing more than a hated biologist); didn't like Germans (I never did figure that one out); and didn't like anyone larger than he (240 pounds). Well, that left me out on all counts, especially with my 320-pound, six-foot-four-inch frame.

In addition, Captain Gray enjoyed his alcohol and was usually into his "martini cups" by ten every morning, work or play. My biological father was an alcoholic, and this disease had caused the breakup of our family when I was just a small lad. As a result, I was raised by my mother, and times had been hard, to say the least. My memory of those desperate days did little to provide me with compassion for those who let alcohol ruin their lives and those of like ilk around them. My youth and immaturity often got in the way of my patience and common sense, leaving me little stomach for Captain Gray and his drinking. Basically, we became grandly intolerant of each other shortly after we got to know one another: Walt Gray disliked me for what my background represented, and I disliked him for his booze and behavior.

As I write these words, my first meeting with Captain Gray comes vividly to mind. I remember walking up to him my first day at work after I had completed my training course at the Fish and Game academy. Keep in mind that I had recently undergone all the required state testing for the position of Fish and Game warden and had been one of twenty-five selected from 1,300 statewide applicants to become a member of the next warden training class. Twenty-three of us had attended a law enforcement training academy in southern California. Out of a class of eighty diverse law enforcement officers from all over the state, I had been elected the class president and finished sixth in my class academically. The state of California had assigned me to Eureka, California, under the then unknown Captain Gray. That first work day, I recognized the captain by the two gold bars on his uniform shirt, walked over to him smiling and sticking out my hand, and said, "Good morning, Captain, I'm Terry Grosz, your new boarding and backup land officer."

I clearly remember his words and cold stare as he faced me. "Mr. Grosz, it's *Captain Gray* to you, and as long as I'm captain of this squad no goddamned biologist is going to work for me as a game warden."

Somewhat taken aback, I said, "Pardon me?"

"You heard me," he replied. "You are on strict probation for the first year and general probation for the next two after that. I don't expect you to be around after the first year." With that he spun around, walked into his office, and closed his door, thus ending the conversation.

I stood there stunned until I felt a firm hand on my shoulder. Turning, I found myself looking into the steel-blue eyes of Warden Joe Devine from the Arcata duty station. "Don't worry, Tiny; I will keep an eye on you and see that you remain gainfully employed." His smile told me that no truer words were ever spoken, and we became fast friends and remained so until the day he died. However, from that day on I got all the shit details Captain Gray could hurl my way in the hope that I would screw up or quit and he would be rid of me. But I came from good German stock, and it didn't work that way! I was his for the duration, like it or not.

As Captain Gray had indicated and I came to find out, the California Department of Fish and Game had a program whereby during your first year with the department your supervisors could let you go for almost any job-related infraction. After that you remained on probation for the next two years, during which time it was a little tougher to let you go, but they could still dismiss you without a whole lot of fuss. With that possibility in mind, I was pretty careful not to let anyone grind me under and did what I had to do in order to survive professionally. In a little over one year I had become number one in the squad for citations issued, had a prosecution rate of 100 percent, and was the number-one pistol shooter among all seventeen officers, among whom were some pretty fine shooters, such as Warden Herb Christie from the Fortuna duty station.

∾

But at this point I was still only a few weeks into the job. Coming back to reality and the moment at hand, I acknowledged the dispatcher's request and, wondering what Gray had in mind for me today, drove to the main Fish and Game office in Eureka. Entering the captain's office, I stood at attention, said, "Good morning, Captain Gray," and waited for him to acknowledge the presence of a lesser mortal.

After a few minutes the important activity of cleaning his fingernails was concluded, and he looked up at me with a grin. That grin meant only one thing: that he had something on me. Sure as hell, here it came. "Terry," he said, "what the hell are you doing out there for a living?"

I said, "Pardon me?"

"Your ticket load is a disgrace. You haven't written enough tickets since you arrived to pour pee out of a boot."

Though I knew just the opposite to be true—not only was I the number-one ticket writer in the squad but I had a 100 percent conviction rate to date—I just looked at him and said, "Yes, sir."

He continued to stare at me through those ever-bloodshot eyes and then said, "I got just the detail for you. Hoopa—that's it, Hoopa. Maybe a few days out there will bring you to your senses and get your ass in gear."

Again not able to stay with the man, I said, "Pardon me, sir?"

"You are going to the Hoopa area to work those bastards snagging the sturgeon in the Klamath River near Ishi-Pishi Falls, that's it; that's where you're going. Maybe with a whole lot more effort in that area, you will bring in a citation load that is more representative of a game warden in my squad. Use the undercover truck, and now get your ass out of here!"

I answered, "Yes, sir," whirled, and left his office.

Passing Joe Devine, a senior warden of thirty-plus years who had turned out to be a great friend and father figure, in the hall, I said, "Joe, got a minute?"

He said, "Sure, what do you need, Tiny?"

I explained my assignment of working undercover on the Klamath River to go after sturgeon snaggers. Joe couldn't overlook the tinge of excitement in my voice. After all, this was the first real, non-crap detail Captain Gray had given me—or so I thought. But Joe, looking me dead in the eye, sadly shook his head. "Tiny," he said, "Gray just signed your death warrant!"

Not really believing what I was hearing, I said, "Come again?"

Joe took me by the arm and, looking over his shoulder at Gray's office said, "Come with me." We went downstairs into the state parking garage, where Joe filled me in on the history of what used to be part of his old district when he was a younger Fish and Game officer.

"Tiny," he told me, "that area he is sending you into is never worked today by less than two wardens at a time because of the isolation and physical danger. You have to drive through the Hoopa Reservation, where the last law is located, then on to Weitchpec [another twelve miles farther into the bush], then on to Orleans [another sixteen miles], and then finally on to Ishi-Pishi Falls [another eight miles to where the road, in those days, ended at the Klamath River]. The only law out there is God, and he is in short supply in that neck of the woods. Additionally, the undercover truck Gray wants you to use is known to everyone out there, and Gray's source of information on the sturgeon snaggers is a crook. Knowing Gray, he probably has already told his buddy out there that you are coming and more than likely has supplied him with your physical description.

"The nearest medical help, if you can call it that, is at Hoopa on the Indian reservation, and the overall area you will be working is full of loggers, Indians, and construction workers, who I think are currently building a bridge across the Klamath River. You'd better let me talk to Gray and see if he will assign another officer to help you. Hell, you're just out of the academy and don't know your ass from a hand axe."

Knowing what Captain Gray's reaction would be if a subordinate approached him with a suggestion for an operational change, and starting to feel excitement over the impending danger (not to mention the delusion of immortality I was clearly beginning to develop), I said, "Joe, you'd better let this one alone. Gray gave me this assignment, and if I don't follow through, it will give him ammunition to make my life impossible under the first-year probationary rule."

Joe knew I was right, but I could tell he didn't like what Gray was doing to a green officer, especially a newfound friend and potential ally against the captain. The look on Joe's face and his body language put me on the alert, which gave me the edge and probably saved my life over the next month or so.

Without another word, I walked over to the parked Fish and Game undercover truck, crawled under the dash, and removed several ignition wires while Joe smiled knowingly and approvingly. Walking back to Joe, I put my arm around him and thanked him for the fatherly advice and warning. As I walked away, I turned back to tell Joe I owed him. His answering smile told me, "Naturally." I then went back upstairs to the captain's office and knocked on his door. I was instructed to come in, and a look asking what the hell I was doing there crossed Gray's face. Before he could say anything, I said, "Captain Gray, I know you wanted me on the road posthaste in reference to this sturgeon-snagging detail, but the undercover truck is deader than a hammer. I've tried everything I know, but something is wrong with the ignition system, and from the sound of this assignment I need to be going now."

Gray acknowledged this turn of events with a nod, so I continued, "If the state will pay mileage I will take my own pickup and use it for the undercover rig if that's all right with you, sir."

Gray, wanting me out of his sight, nodded again, and out the door I went before he could change his mind. Finding Joe again in the wardens' office, I asked him for the name of a gunsmith who wouldn't gouge me on the purchase of another pistol. Joe gave me a hard look, then mentioned a place near where I lived, and I went out the front door with a spring in my step that came only when I was charging into a lion's den. I could tell from Joe's approving expression that I might just make it yet as a law enforcement officer.

Twenty minutes later I pulled into the backyard of the gunsmith in Eureka that Joe had recommended. Stepping from my patrol vehicle, I walked quickly across a small lawn into a no more than ten-by-ten-foot wooden shack behind a residence. Some gunsmith and shop! I thought, my immature mind quickly judging the situation. Walking up two steps and into a small, dark room smelling heavily of Hoppe's gun oil and stale cigars, I was struck by the clutter of things arrayed around this tiny space called a gun shop. My eyes quickly adjusted to the darkness of the room, and I spotted a man about seventy years old sitting in a rocking chair behind a small wooden counter. Lying on the old fellow's lap was a pre-1964 Winchester on which he had been working until my rather large size had blocked out the light when I entered through the open doorway. Looking up from the rifle and over half-rimmed glasses, the old man asked if I was Terry. Somewhat surprised but correctly figuring that Joe had called to pave the way, I said, "Yes, I'm Terry, and I need a good second pistol without a large price."

Getting up from his chair and laying the Winchester down as if it were someone's kid, the smithy opened a drawer under the counter, pulled out a Colt Commander .45 ACP semiautomatic pistol, and shut the drawer before I could see any other choices. Laying the .45 down on the counter, he looked at me with eyes that betrayed a world of sights and experiences they had known long before they rested on me. Understanding what was next, I picked up the pistol, removed the magazine, and racked back the slide to ascertain whether it was loaded. The weapon was empty, and I returned the slide to the closed position, reinserted the magazine, and carefully let the hammer down so as not to damage the firing pin.

Looking at the old man out of the corner of my eye, I could tell he approved of my safety precautions. When I clasped my palm and fingers around the handle, the gun fitted my hand as if it belonged there. I asked how much, and without a moment's hesitation and in a tone that identified the price as fair, the smithy said, "Ninety dollars." Since that was at least $30 less than any other .45 ACP I had priced, and I needed a weapon that would put someone down for keeps when needed, and he was Joe's recommendation, I responded, "Sold." I worked out a payment schedule, purchased a box of 230-grain full-metal-jacket cartridges, and went out the door, anxious to be on my way.

Returning home, I packed the gear I felt I would need on this detail, gave my wife and bride of three short years a "sweetened" version of what I was off to do so she wouldn't worry, told her to call Joe Devine if she needed to get hold of me, and headed down the road in our new Jeep pickup into what was to become a character-developing adventure.

Leaving Eureka, I drove around Humboldt Bay north to Arcata, out Highway 299 to Willow Creek, then from Willow Creek to and through the Hoopa Indian Reservation and down the narrow, twisting mountain road to the little town of Orleans. Talk about the Twilight Zone—this was really the end of the line. It wasn't the end of the world, but you certainly could see it from here through the tall Douglas firs. My new home was a small town at the road's end that comprised several houses, a Forest Service subdistrict office, a gas station–garage–general store–post office all in one, and the Ishi-Pishi Bar. Aside from a few outbuildings of nondescript character, that was about it.

Never having worked undercover before and really just weeks out of the academy, I wasn't sure where to start. The cold facts of reality were beginning to sink in, but I knew the law; knew where the fish were; understood what snagging was; and had the authority, badge, and two guns. Not knowing what else I would need, I cast my eyes toward the unknown. Boy, was I green! Parking in front of the general-store complex, I got out of my vehicle and with all the confidence I could muster walked into the place as if I owned it. Moving to an area that contained fishing gear, I did a little looking around and then went to the counter and selected several sets of massive handmade treble hooks that were advertised as a "snagger's delight" by a middle-aged shopkeeper who was taking more than a usual interest in my actions.

A quick look at the hooks showed me that they clearly exceeded the maximum distance between hook points as prescribed by Fish and Game code (Title 14). I followed up this purchase by selecting two hundred yards of monofilament line rated at 180-pound capacity. Damn, it was unreal. This store sold almost nothing but illegal gear designed to take the mighty green-and-white sturgeon out of the Klamath River by hook or by crook.

As I shopped I noticed that the storekeeper continued to quietly watch me. His eyes weren't really looking at me, but he was watching closely nonetheless, I being a stranger in town and all. Finally, with all the illegal fishing gear and other needed items in hand, I approached the counter, laid my selections out for his perusal, and asked, "How much is the damage?"

He scanned the gear and offhandedly said, "Going fishing?"

Feeling this was my chance, I answered, "I think so."

He looked up at me and repeated, "You think so?"

"Well, I'm not really sure. I've never snagged sturgeon before, but I hear it's fun, so I'm here to give it a try."

He looked at me again without really looking and inquired, "Where you from?"

"Arcata. I just got out of college and will be teaching elementary school this fall, and I just decided to have a summer of fun before I have to go to work." Not really having any kind of deep cover, I used the schoolteacher routine because my wife was a teacher, a damn good one, I might add, and I had learned some of the ins and outs of her profession from her. A schoolteacher also seemed like someone who wouldn't appear threatening to a bunch of outlaws, so a schoolteacher I was.

My items were sacked up and the storekeeper asked, "You know how to use this stuff?"

I answered, "No, but I'll watch someone else and then give it a try."

Looking over my shoulder, he asked if that was my Jeep pickup parked in front of his store. I nodded. He said, "Nice truck."

"They sure are, not to mention fast, and it has a really good engine."

He asked, "Would you like to make a little money hauling things in it?"

I said, "Well, that depends. Not rock or logs—it's still pretty new, and I'd like to keep it that way. What did you have in mind?"

He said, "How about fish?"

I laughingly told him I was going to haul lots of fish in it if I could ever master this snagging thing.

He laughed too and said, "That's what I'm talking about. Would you like to help some friends of mine haul some fish?"

I answered, "As long as it doesn't tear my truck up, you bet. Who are these fellows?"

"Never mind. Just be in the Ishi-Pishi Bar this evening about seven P.M. and ask for LeeRoy. He'll fill you in."

"Sounds good to me, but in the meantime, do you know of any places where I can go on the river and try out some of this gear you just sold me?"

He laughed and gave me directions to a spot on the Klamath River above town where I might find others who were snagging sturgeon as well. I spent the rest of the day exploring my new home and found an area up by Fish Lake where I could camp out and not be discovered by the locals once I had found a way into what was going on. Making sure all evidence of my profession was concealed in my Jeep, I drove down to the Ishi-Pishi Bar as evening approached.

I entered the bar about seven and walked over to the barkeep. I told him the storekeeper had sent me over to meet a guy called LeeRoy, and that was all I knew. He examined me carefully without saying a word, then, apparently satisfied for whatever reason, nodded toward a noisy table in the back of the room. I ordered two pitchers of beer, loaded up with glasses, and headed over to the table.

I approached the group at the table and said, "I'm here to see this fellow LeeRoy."

The men fell silent for a moment, then a little mousy fellow said, "Is that beer for him?"

I answered, "Well, it's for him and his friends."

With that the mousy fellow stood up, extended his hand, and said, "I'm your man. What's your handle?"

Putting the beer down, I extended my hand and responded, "Hi, I'm Terry." Introductions were made all around. I was asked to sit, and the beer was passed from empty glass to empty glass.

All the men around the table were from the construction crew working on the bridge going over the Klamath. They worked four days on and then had three days off, and on their days off, they went fishing. Two more pitchers of beer and the "fishing" turned to "snagging." *Bingo.* I bought still more beer and continued to become a better and better friend.

The lads admitted to snagging dozens of sturgeon and smuggling them to their Yurok Indian friends, who smoked them and sold the smoked meat for $2.50 a pound. The Indians took half of the profits, and the construction workers got the rest. From the loose talk around the table, I gathered that they could sell all the fish they could catch to the tourists; hence the extensive snagging forays by those members of the construction crew they trusted. It also seemed that they had a slight problem in that one of their own who owned a pickup had recently been fired and left the area. With him went their means of transporting their snagged sturgeon, and they needed another "mule."

With a big grin, I stood up and said, "I'm your man. Strong as a mule and have pickup, will travel."

They all laughed and said they needed to talk to Dan but were sure it would be all right.

I said, "Who is this Dan fellow?"

Several of them said, "Shhhhh, he'll hear you." LeeRoy pointed to a huge mound of a man sitting at the bar and told me, "That's Dan." Dan was about six-foot-three, three hundred pounds if he was an ounce, and wore a once-white T-shirt and blue jeans. Strapped around his waist was a .44 magnum Ruger Super Blackhawk pistol, and he had on knee-high fringed leather leggings with a real-McCoy Bowie knife shoved down inside one leg, with just the handle sticking out. His long, dirty-blond hair went to his shoulders, and he had arms as big as most people's legs. What a horse, I thought. Taking a fresh beer in his hand, LeeRoy got up, walked over to Dan, and began to talk quietly with him. Dan turned around, looked at me, and then turned back to talk some more with LeeRoy. Soon LeeRoy came back to our now quiet and expectant table with a big grin. Looking at me, he said, "You're in. Dan said to be upriver tomorrow. I'll show you where exactly on a map later, and we'll go to work."

LeeRoy slapped me on the back and added, "Let's get some more beer and celebrate!"

I agreed, and the two of us went to the bar, where I ordered four more pitchers of beer. I also ordered the mixed drink that Dan was drinking and watched the barkeep give it to him. He didn't move or thank me for it, just drank it down straight away. God, what a horse, and a really dangerous problem if pissed, I thought. The lads at my table continued to drink, and my large bulk was now serving me well. Since I could hold more beer than just about anyone else at that table, I kept pouring the beer down my newfound friends' throats and watched them get tipsy. As they grew drunker they became more loose-lipped, and I got more and more information about their snagging operation—names of retailers, other poachers, everything! Man, talk about the luck of the Irish: I was on a roll and into an organization of poachers without hardly even trying. I thought, this undercover stuff isn't so bad or hard to do after all. In a few moments round two would commence, and boy, did I learn a hard-and-fast lesson about this type of work.

LeeRoy slowly reached over, took hold of my forearm to get my attention, and pointed to a tall, thin, one-armed man who had just entered the bar. LeeRoy said, "Don't ever screw with that guy. He would just as soon as kill you as look at you!"

I looked over at the man and noticed that he had seated himself next to Dan. Turning to LeeRoy, I said, "Don't worry. I don't want any trouble; all I want is to catch a few fish." With that, I went to the bar and got two more pitchers of beer. The men at my table continued to drink until about fifteen minutes later when I heard someone behind me at the bar get slapped.

All of us turned and saw Dan and the one-armed guy facing off. I heard Dan snarl, "If you had two arms, asshole, I would kill you for that. No one slaps me and gets away with it."

The one-armed man looked Dan right in the eye from about one foot away, said, "Don't let that stop you, asshole," and pointed to the front door. Out the door both of them went, and no one followed. It was as if this fight were something no one wanted any part of. That feeling again told me just how dangerous this Dan fellow was and what a hold of terror he had over his compatriots.

The clock ticked, scuffling noises came from outside the front door, and still no one moved. It was the goddamnedest thing I ever saw. The bar was quiet as a tomb, and since everyone else just sat still, so did I. In a few moments Dan came casually walking back through the door and in a voice not to be argued with said, "Let's go."

Everyone, and I do mean everyone other than the bartender, got up and followed him out the back door of the bar to where most of the vehicles were parked. Since my Jeep was parked in front, I went out the front door and stumbled over the moaning carcass of the one-armed fellow. He had been slashed to ribbons and was bleeding like a stuck hog! His eyes were open and looked like hell, but it was clear that he was not on his way to his eternal reward because most of the wounds didn't look that deep, so I kept moving to my Jeep. Damn, what the hell was I to do? I was an officer of the law and sworn to uphold the laws of the state of California. I hadn't seen Dan strike any of those blows, but I was sure as shootin' that they were the work of his knife. As I stood next to my Jeep trying to figure out what to do, my thoughts were cut short as the members of the construction crew sped around from the rear of the bar and LeeRoy hollered, "Get out of there, Terry." Since the one-armed fellow seemed likely to live, I turned, got into my Jeep, and got the hell out of there with a mental picture of how I would testify against Dan sometime down the road. There was no law in town, and medical help was about twenty-five miles away, so I knew the one-armed lad would have to make it with the help of the townspeople who were already starting to gather. As I sped toward Fish Lake, I figured I would just have to get Dan later and would do so when I wrapped up my sturgeon-snagging case.

After a somewhat sleepless night, I drove down to the place LeeRoy had shown me on a map the previous evening to hook up with my newfound snagging friends from the construction crew. Finding their cars parked above a large, slow-running deep hole on the river, I walked down to see what I had to do. I met LeeRoy about halfway down the forested mountainside as he stepped out from behind a large Douglas fir. It was apparent that he was acting as lookout for any game wardens who might be in the country. As he beckoned me over to his hiding place, I could tell he was nervous and wanted to talk.

He said, "Damn, Terry, sorry about last night. Just remember, you didn't see anything or hear anything, and don't mention it today in front of nobody."

"No problem, LeeRoy. That's a dead issue—uh, sorry."

He just laughed and said, "Go on down and see how we're set up, and get ready to work."

I worked my way down the last forty or so yards to the river, and there before me was a rocky ledge that overlooked about a fifty-yard-long sandbar jutting obliquely out into the Klamath River. The river was at least three-eighths of a mile wide here, with a current that would get anyone's attention. Lying directly below me next to the bank was a hundred-yard-long pool of quiet water directly off the river's main flow. It was a perfect area for tired sturgeon to pull out from the main current and rest before renewing their migration upstream. Standing on the sandbar were eight construction workers, each with a four-foot ocean rod with a Penn nine-aught reel loaded with 180-pound monofilament test line. Attached to each of these homemade snagging outfits, as near as I could tell from where I stood, were three sets of illegal-size treble hooks with half-pound weights attached to the lines just above the hooks to get them down on the bottom where the sturgeon were lying as they rested. As the hook sets were dragged along the sandy river bottom with vigorous jerks, any that moved over the backs of sturgeon were instantly lodged in the flesh of the fish, and the fight was on. Damn, what a commercial production! To get to the sandbar one had to inch along a narrow, rocky ledge that ran along the rock face edging the quiet pool. Once far enough along the trail, one had to jump down about four feet to the sandbar and there commence fishing.

A shout brought me back from my analysis of the area to a scene seldom seen by anyone but commercial poachers. One of the lads had snagged a huge sturgeon, and the strength of the fighting fish was dragging him off the sandbar even though the man must have weighed over two hundred pounds and had his shoulders thrown back at an angle and his heels dug into the sand. Two of his buddies quickly reeled in their lines and ran to his aid. As each man approached, he wrapped his arms around the waist of the lad being dragged off the sandbar and into the Klamath River by the sturgeon's massive weight and length. This move would be repeated by more men as the fight dictated. Basically these fish, which averaged three hundred to six hundred pounds, would move sideways into the current once hooked and let the fast-flowing river help them in their battle for life. All three men were now getting dragged off the sandbar. Realizing they had hooked a fish that was too large, probably over eight hundred pounds, and that their chances of landing it were zero, one of them took his cigar and touched it to the line, which separated like a rifle shot. The sturgeon was free—carrying a set of snag hooks and lead weights in its back, but free. Back on the sandbar there was laughter, and the fellow who had just lost his fish rebuilt his snagging outfit and commenced to fish once again.

Trying to memorize who was doing what for my testimony later, I was cut short by a quiet voice behind me. Turning, I looked into Dan's cold blue eyes. He extended his hand and said, "I'm Dan. What's your name again?"

I told him, "Terry."

He quietly looked me over and then asked, "What did you see last night?"

Without even a pause I said, "At least fourteen pitchers of beer."

Dan looked at me for a moment, then threw his head back and roared with laughter. Then he reached for my shoulder, turned me around, and said, "There are six sturgeon down there." He pointed to some sturgeon tied together in the water alongside the sandbar. "Have the guys give you a hand hauling them up to your Jeep, and here is a map showing where I want you to take them. All you have to do is just drop them off and come back for more. If you get caught, you are on your own. At the end of the week you get a split in the take the same as the other men, plus a little more for the use of your Jeep and the gas." Handing me the map in question, he strode off to where his men, who had observed our discussion and suspected its gist, were beginning to haul the snagged sturgeon up the riverbank toward my Jeep.

For the next two hours we hauled sturgeon up the mountainside to my waiting truck. Once loaded with at least three-quarters of a ton of fish, off I went to the location on the map. On my way through town to the Indian fish smokers, I passed the Ishi-Pishi Bar. It was about eleven in the morning, and the one-armed guy was long gone. Blood had spread around where he had lain, and I could see the big bluebottle flies covering the blood pool. Not daring to slow down, I proceeded to the Indian smokers' setup a few short miles out of town and dropped off my load of fish. The smokers didn't say anything, just took the fish, and I left. This ritual was repeated three times that day. No wonder the sturgeon were struggling to maintain their numbers in the Klamath River against the siltation from adverse logging practices, illegal commercial snagging, and all, I thought. My first day's actions made me all the more determined to apprehend every one of these men, regardless of the odds I would face trying to arrest all concerned. It is nice to be young and foolish at the same time because the foolishness doesn't usually compute.

This routine went on for the next two weeks during the construction crew's days off. In between I would go home and report on the poachers' activities. My first report created quite a stir with the captain, and needless to say, several meetings with other officers in the squad were held until a battle plan was devised. They decided

I would continue working undercover until I had all the evidence we needed to convict all the snaggers. Then a large crew of wardens would go in and round up the men, including Dan, and we would prosecute the lot. The plan was simple, or so it seemed, and I was pleased with it. But as a result of the knife fight the Humboldt County sheriff decided, even though the one-armed guy had skipped town, to send a temporary deputy to Orleans to get things under control. That's when the whole affair started to go to hell in a handbasket.

When I returned for the third time, the poachers were pretty tense. It seemed that the new town deputy had been talking about how the Fish and Game might come to town and clean out the operation unless the snagging stopped. With that information rattling around, the Yurok Indians were nervous, as was the snagging crew. I continued to play Joe Dumbhead and hauled the big fish as before, but now I had other men riding shotgun to ensure that everything went smoothly when I delivered the illegal fish to the Indians.

Several days later the whole covert operation got backed into a corner, and I was forced to play out my hand without the help of the rest of my squad. As I hauled a load of fish one afternoon, LeeRoy met me halfway up the mountain at his usual stakeout location and said, "Have you heard the news? Dan is leaving."

"No," I said, stunned. "Why is that?"

"Oh, he's afraid someone will turn him in for stabbing that guy the other night, and since he has two prior felonies and doesn't want to go back to the big house he's getting out of the area to work on another construction project where they don't know him."

"When is he leaving?" I asked.

"Today about nine o'clock, just as soon as he can find the boss and get what pay he has coming," LeeRoy muttered sadly as he helped me carry a particularly heavy sturgeon the rest of the way up the hill to my pickup. Arranging this last sturgeon under the tarps in the back of the Jeep so no one could see what I was transporting, I thought, Damn, I'm going to have to apprehend all these guys by myself without help from anyone. There were thirteen people involved in this fishing ring, counting the two Indians smoking and selling the fish and the storekeeper. I had the goods on all of them except the storekeeper who had sold me the illegal fishing gear, which was not itself a violation. A violation did not occur until the illegal fishing gear was used contrary to California state law by the person who had purchased it. Because the storekeeper was on the outside of the ring, acting more as a facilitator than anything else, I vowed to let him ride this time and to net him sometime later down the road when things weren't so hectic. I knew that once I nabbed the men who had been doing the snagging, the Indians would disappear into the reservation. That prospect didn't really bother me, though, because I knew I could work with the Bureau of Indian Affairs and eventually round up those men for illegally selling the sturgeon. Proving the sale would be easy, for I had purchased over thirty pounds of smoked sturgeon from these lads off and on during the days when the operation was in full swing.

Snapping back to the immediate problem, visions of ten tough construction workers against just yours truly, I realized that even though I was a strapping lad weighing in at over three hundred pounds, once they figured out who I was and what I represented to their immediate futures, I would be in all kinds of trouble. Wait, I told myself, I can get the new deputy who recently moved into Orleans to help. Man, that thought was like a heavy weight being lifted from my shoulders. Waving to LeeRoy as he headed back to his lookout, I drove into town, thankful that my shotgun rider for the day had a bad hangover and had chosen to lie on the cool, wet sand of the sandbar by the snagging hole.

Arriving in Orleans, I parked my Jeep carefully behind the deputy's house trailer to prevent anyone seeing me with him. I had heard that the new deputy was a little guy but well built. He was a sergeant and had been an amateur boxer, so I knew I had the help I would need to corral this bunch of outlaws. Well, not all the help I would need—but this was a damn good start and would have to do. Besides, at my size I could hit pretty hard if I had to. A couple of well-placed punches and the odds would be better than ten to two, I thought as I walked to the front door of the trailer and, after looking over my shoulder to see if anyone had noticed my presence, knocked on the door.

I heard a scratching around inside the trailer as if someone were getting up and a voice saying, "Just a minute." After more moving around, the door opened to reveal a rather small man, hardly a drop over five-foot-six but with a muscular, wiry frame. "Yeah, what do you want?" was his salutation. Not wanting to waste any time standing around in the open, I identified myself as an undercover game warden, giving him my name and displaying my badge, and told him quickly about my covert detail. He looked at me in disbelief. Continuing, I told him about Dan's planned departure and that like it or not, I had to bring the detail down at this very moment and needed his help.

I was stunned by his response. Without mincing a single word, he told me he would lend me his shotgun but would not help. He said he was in this town by himself, and if he wanted to survive he had to be careful whom he helped. Fish and Game was not an agency he wanted to help because of the rampant wildlife violations in town and local attitudes about those kinds of violations. I couldn't believe what I was hearing, but I wasn't letting him off the hook that easily. I tried to convince the deputy that the fellow who had recently stabbed the one-armed lad, the situation that had brought him to town, was leaving Orleans and that little activity on Dan's part sure as hell wasn't a Fish and Game violation but a penal-code violation, which was certainly in the deputy's ballpark. The deputy said, "Did you actually see this fellow Dan stab the one-armed guy?"

I answered, "No, but who else could have?"

Without budging an inch, he said, "You didn't see it actually happen, so how can you say that?"

I could see that I was getting nowhere with this lad, and looking him straight in the eye I said, "I can't stand here in broad daylight all day and argue with you. I am making a request from one law enforcement officer to another for assistance; will you help?"

"It's not in my area of responsibility. Since you got into it, call your own people for assistance." With that he closed the trailer door, and I angrily returned to my Jeep. Not caring whether anyone saw me now, I took my .44 Smith and Wesson magnum, which was my service weapon, from behind the seat and strapped it on my right hip. Reaching under the seat into my kit bag, I took out the .45 ACP Colt Commander I had purchased from the gunsmith in Eureka and strapped it on my left side. Jamming extra cartridges into my right pocket for the .44 and sliding an extra full magazine for the .45 into my left pocket, I fired up the Jeep and headed for the fishing hole. I was furious. I'll be damned, I thought, if I let an attempted murderer get away, not to mention not making a try for those men who had been illegally killing and selling all those sturgeon. Ah, youth … one against ten. Those appear to be fair odds to a man in his early twenties and pissed, I guess—at least they did that day.

Parking the Jeep where I usually parked, I checked my weapons and extra ammunition and started down the mountain toward the snagging hole. Meeting LeeRoy, the lookout, in his usual hiding place, I walked right up to him and said, "LeeRoy, I'm a California state Fish and Game warden, and you are under arrest." His face showed utter shock. Continuing, I said, "Furthermore, if you make one sound I will kill you here and run so no one will ever know who did it. Do you understand me? If so, nod your head, but remember, no sound or a bullet, your choice."

That poor little bastard wet his pants right then and there. He couldn't even speak, only nod, which he did. I guess I may have come on a little too strong, but this was my first case of any magnitude, and I had an urge to piss as well! Handcuffing a terrified LeeRoy to a small pine tree, I gagged him with a piece of his shirt, put his driver's license in my pocket, and headed down the mountain for the other nine lads. Arriving on the overlook at the head of the trail that wound along the rock face to the sandbar, I observed that they were all busy trying to snag sturgeon. Good, I thought, I still have the element of surprise. Dan was the closest to me, just sitting and watching the others; the rest were scattered along the sandbar, engrossed in their snagging activities.

Unsnapping the catch on my .44 in case I had to take fast action on the lethal side of things, I held up my badge and told everyone in a loud, clear voice, "State Fish and Game warden. Everyone is under arrest for illegal snagging activities. Reel in your lines, bring your poles and snag gear, and come on up."

No one moved! They just looked at me in disbelief. Goddamn, that was a lonely feeling. Having nothing better to do, I repeated my order, and the whole sandbar erupted this time. Every snagger threw his fishing gear into the river, thereby, in their minds, destroying the evidence. The gear was later retrieved, and a charge of littering was added to their lists of what not to do in front of a large game warden. Then, as if on cue, they all ran for the ledge that led to my position, either to fight or to flee. This was not good: nine against one, and all at the same time! The first to reach the ledge was Dan. All I could think of was his handiwork several nights earlier with the one-armed fellow. With that in mind, when Dan's head came up over the edge of the ledge as he tried to pull himself up, I kicked him right between the eyes. He groaned and instantly fell back onto the others, who were also scrambling to get up on the ledge, and they all crashed to the ground in a heap. Dan's inert form falling to the earth took all the fight out of the rest of the men, and they stood quietly on the sandbar below me, still looking at me in disbelief. I ordered all of them to hand me their driver's licenses, which they did. Securing those bits of identification in my shirt pocket in case some of them tried to escape later, I resnapped the strap over my pistol so they could clearly see that I was armed. I told them that since the odds were somewhat in their favor, I would kill the first man who so much as tried to do anything other than what I told him to do. The looks in their eyes told me they had no problem understanding what I had just said.

"Good," I said. "We now clearly understand each other. One of you crawl up on the ledge, and then one of you can hand Dan up, since he doesn't appear to be too chipper." One of the stronger men hoisted himself up onto the ledge and looked long and hard at me and the open forest beyond. "Remember what I said," I uttered quietly. The look faded, and he turned and lifted Dan up onto the ledge and then to a resting place beyond on the forest floor. One by one the lads hoisted themselves onto the ledge and then gathered in a clump near Dan's unconscious form, awaiting instructions. "Let's move on up the hill to my Jeep," I commanded, "and several of you grab Dan and bring him along." Moving up the mountainside, we picked up LeeRoy, who was still handcuffed to the pine tree. I removed his handcuffs and placed them on Dan, since I considered him the most dangerous. The cuffs went only one click on Dan's wrists! That should give anyone familiar with handcuffs an idea of the size of this fellow. With that, up the mountain to my waiting Jeep we went.

When we arrived I had the lads load Dan into the passenger side of the vehicle, making him as comfortable as I could. Closer examination revealed what appeared to be a broken nose, possible broken bones around the eye socket, and one eye fairly bloody from the high-speed encounter with my boot. I just remembered kicking him hard enough to put him out of the game. Who knows, if his head had come off maybe it would have flown clear across that river. Now I had the worst of the lot under control, and to hell with being a nice guy. Reaching behind the seat of the Jeep, I pulled out one hundred feet of five-eighths-inch nylon rope and tied it to the front bumper. I picked LeeRoy out of the lot sitting in the road in front of the Jeep as I had told them to do and tied a slipknot noose around his neck. He went ballistic! He screamed and jumped around, claiming I was going to hang him. Now, how the hell can you hang someone from the front bumper of a vehicle when he is standing on the ground? Brother. I guess I might have frightened him a little more than I needed to.

I repeated that process until I had everyone but Dan tied to that nylon rope. Then I told them to walk forward until the rope was tight and they were all strung out in front of my Jeep like a human sausage. I told them they were going to walk to town in that fashion because I had only one set of handcuffs, and I was going to turn them over to the deputy sheriff. I also told them that if the rope went slack I would put the Jeep in reverse and drag them until there wasn't an ounce of meat left on their hind ends. Their call! The collective look I got back told me they were a beaten lot, and that it would be all right from now on. I had chosen the rope instead of trying to place the whole lot in the back of my Jeep to protect myself; I wasn't letting them any closer to me than was absolutely nec-essary. With that, I started up the Jeep and we began our three-mile march into the town of Orleans.

Upon our arrival in town an alarm went out among a few of the local outlaws to rally the boys and get the son of a bitch who had all the lads on a rope like firecrackers. Ignoring the growing crowd, I pulled up in front of the deputy's house trailer. Honking the horn, I was dismayed to find him gone. The angry crowd was becoming louder, so I laid my .45 on the dash of the Jeep and told the lads on the rope to remember what I had told them: they should keep their friends at bay, or those on the rope were going to have thin hind ends.

I realized that I couldn't stay in town without creating an in-creasing "hoorah," so we started a long march down the highway to-ward Willow Creek, the next wide spot in the road. Just outside Or-leans I met a speeding California highway patrol officer, obviously responding to a report of the crazy guy with the men on the rope. He passed me and executed a power turn behind my vehicle. He flew up behind me, and on went his red lights and siren, alerting the entire world and God to the saga on the highway. Relieved, I stopped the Jeep and stepped out of the cab only to be met with a 12-gauge shotgun and a terse command to assume the position. I did as I was told and was disarmed before I could say a word. Then the officer turned me around and said, "What the hell are you doing?"

I told him I was a game warden, had all these lads under arrest, and couldn't get any help, so I was bringing them in the only way I could since I had only one set of handcuffs.

He stared at me as if there were no tomorrow. "Identification, please," came the next command with the shotgun still focused on the center of my chest.

Once properly introduced by my badge and credentials, I ex-plained what had happened and who my prisoners were. He couldn't believe what I had done but was relieved to find another officer instead of a nut at the end of the human pack string. Un-doing my rope from the prisoners' necks, we loaded as many as we could safely squeeze into his patrol vehicle and then put the rest in the back of my Jeep along with my evidence sturgeon.

He said, "If they try to break out the rear window I can shoot from here, and if they want to jump I'll collect them with my push bumper, so let's go." Off we went without incident to the jail in Willow Creek, where, after gathering all the information I needed, we separated, the lads happy to be rid of the Fish and Game madman and I just as glad to be rid of them. Throughout the later legal proceedings, my "rope trick" kept coming up, but the county prosecutor was able to blunt that concern. Everyone was eventually found guilty, and each man drew $1,500 in fines and spent thirty days in the county jail. Dan was also found guilty of assault and battery, not to mention a parole violation, and the last I heard he was finishing up his time in prison from previous charges. The Yurok Indian salesmen disappeared and had not yet been apprehended when I left California in 1974. The store owner was never prosecuted for his role in the snagging ring because the county prosecutor didn't feel I had a good enough case to wrap him up. But several weeks later, while back in the area patrolling overtly, I caught the store owner on a back road with a loaded shotgun, shooting from a motor vehicle on the road. I was able to arrest him on charges of taking bandtailed pigeons during the closed season and use and aid of a motor vehicle to take migratory game birds. The no-help deputy was soon relieved from his Orleans duty, and the Humboldt County sheriff began to make plans to provide a full-time officer for the area.

Several months later a public-spirited fisherman passing through Orleans observed a handmade "wanted" poster offering a $700 reward for killing the "big game warden." Checking around, he found the same "Wanted Dead" poster in every establishment, including the post office. The FBI was notified, and agents visited the town and took down the poster in the post office. I later learned that the postmaster lost his job for violation of some federal law for placing unauthorized posters of such a nature in a federal facility.

The sturgeon snagging stopped, but I continued to work that area overtly for several months after my covert operation just to show the lads that the long arm of the law was supreme. I think that because the thrill of the chase had been so strongly manifested in one very young game warden, I stayed in this zone of activity longer than would normally have been expected. There is nothing quite like hunting your fellow human, especially when one is young and foolish.

I learned more about survival in the six months I worked that area than most officers learned in six years and was grateful for that experience. It served me well in the many years that followed in my wildlife law enforcement sojourns, not to mention keeping me alive as a result of some of the survival tactics I had to learn in my time there. Captain Gray had done me a favor through an unseeing management directive. For that I was eternally grateful.

I later found out that the Ishi-Pishi Bar really did have a gallon jug behind the counter full of money for anyone who killed the big game warden. If you divided the alleged $700 in that jug by my weight, I didn't even fetch the price of good hamburger! Damn— I would have thought I was worth at least the price of chuck steak.

2

A Carload of Indians and a
Trunkload of Fish

DURING AN EARLY PART of my career, as part of my cross training I was assigned to work under a senior warden named Hank
Merak whose duty station was Willow Creek, California. Hank had
a reputation as a very hard worker: his ethic was seven days a week,
twelve-, fourteen-, sixteen-, and even eighteen-hour days. I appreciated that kind of attitude because I had come to enjoy, even rel-
ish, the long hours and attendant challenges my similar commitment had to offer. Hank's assigned district required that kind of
energy, and anything less meant disaster for the many resources it
contained. His patrol area included some of the toughest mountain
country in the state. *Rugged* wasn't the word; *rocky* and *straight up and
down* were more like it. His *flat* would be *steep* in any other warden's
jargon. His rivers were full of king and silver salmon; the mountains
were full of black-tailed deer, black bear, and mountain lions; the
Hoopa and Yurok Indian Reservations sat in the middle; and all this
was surrounded by loggers and every kind of wildlife outlaw imag-
inable. Throw in 100-degree heat, rattlesnakes galore, and all the
poison oak you could care to crawl into far enough to remain concealed and yet view the bad guys, and you should have a picture of
where I happily spent many hundreds of hours learning the tricks
of the trade from one of the state's best.

One of the reasons Hank requested assistance was to try to crack
an illegal commercial salmon operation that was driving him nuts,
not to mention cleaning out the salmon runs on the Trinity River.
Hank had a confidential informant who had told him there was a
small group of Hoopa Indians legally gill-netting the Trinity River
but illegally selling their subsistence catch to the commercial fish

houses in Eureka. Any use of gill-netted salmon other than subsistence use was illegal under California laws. The informant advised Hank that "the Indians take the fish over the mountains to Eureka for illegal sale to the fish houses, not by the state highway route but over old logging roads." He continued, "The Indians have a very special car they use to transport the fish on these runs to the commercial fish houses. It is an old four-door Buick with a huge, powerful engine. They have removed all identifying parts associated with the car so that if they are caught and decide to run and leave the car it can't be traced back to them. The car has large, heavy-duty tires and beefed-up springs in the rear to better haul the loads of salmon placed in a special metal box in the trunk. They have a driver who is very reckless and a 'shooter,' an Indian who would just as soon kill you as look at you, who rides with all the shipments of fish." To Hank this description sounded like the odds were just about right, and it was a challenge he couldn't leave alone. Realizing that an attempted capture might lead to a fight with somewhat uneven odds and that he might end up packing fish out with his bad back, Hank thought a partner, especially one the size of the new recruit, might be just the ticket. Fortunately or unfortunately, yours truly was about to get sucked into Hank's challenge—but I loved it!

Once the assignment was official and Captain Gray had sent me off to work with another warden he didn't like, I felt that I had finally come of age. I was being given good, challenging details away from the captain and with wardens who could teach me something about the world of wildlife law enforcement, not to mention how to survive our leader. Driving to Willow Creek that first morning, I was struck by how rugged the north coast country really was. Heavy logged-over undergrowth was punctuated by very steep mountains, followed by many river systems at the bottoms of almost impassible canyons. The terrain and the impending work associated with it lent an extra challenge to the detail. Arriving in Willow Creek, I followed directions to Hank's house and met the man I would grow to admire and with whom I would spend a lot of frustrating time trying to catch those breaking the law in what amounted to a wilderness with a nineteenth-century preservation mentality. At Hank's home I stepped out and stretched my tired frame. As I started to look around, my eyes caught a figure watching me from the shadow of a garage. The man was giving me the kind of look-over given by gun-fighters of old. Walking over to the stranger, I asked, "Hank?"

"The one and only," the man with the piercing eyes responded. Hank was tall and thin. He possessed a hawkish nose similar to mine but sure didn't have the body to match. His reflexes were very quick, and his eyes didn't miss any detail left by those he pursued. I discovered later that he was a man of extreme fairness, but once you crossed over the line, no matter what the odds, you had a fight on your hands with one who was as tough as a horseshoe nail. During that first meeting, Hank continued to look me over. He seemed to be satisfied with the initial review, but I could tell that he would wait to form his final opinion based on my handling of matters. That was all right with me; proving myself was the way I had been raised, and I could compete in that kind of arena very well. Hank said, "Come on in and meet my wife, Vickie, and the kids."

Vickie was a typical game warden's superwife. She was patient with the public and basically raised the children, ran the house, killed the snakes, and took very good care of her family. In addition, she was an excellent cook, and many a meal fit for a king did I eat at their home. After dinner that first night, Hank and I sat out on the back porch waiting for nightfall and discussing the immediate salmon-poaching and -sale problem, the people of the area, what he expected of me, and the dangers to look out for. It quickly became apparent that Hank was not one to run from danger. He was a fighter no matter what the odds and expected me to back him in any and all altercations. Nightfall found us on the Trinity River checking Indians legally gill-netting salmon, making sure they complied with state and tribal laws. That night ran into many other similar evenings, with the two of us growing closer as time passed. During that fall of the late 1960s we spent many hundreds of late hours staked out in the mountains of Hank's district, looking for this carload of Indians with their trunkload of fish—not to mention all the other illegal events one came upon when working in the back country at night.

Hank's vacation was coming up, and he didn't want to leave the stakeout after all the hours we had spent in the bush. However, Vickie insisted, and Hank left on his travels, grumbling all the way. I thought I might get a little relief from the many unproductive night hours I had spent on this detail, a vacation of sorts, if you will—but I was sadly mistaken. One day after Hank left on his vacation, Bill Williams, the Klamath warden, called and told me to meet him at Hoopa the next day.

It seemed that Bill, a hell of a hunter of men, didn't want to lose any benefit from the work Hank and I had already done and was slipping into Hank's adjacent district to continue the project. I was a little surprised, but the idea was fine with me. Bill was one hell of a good officer and a gentle, soft-spoken man, and I truly enjoyed working with him. His sneaking over into Hank's district made me a little uneasy, but as a rookie I found that I was destined to lead a life of following orders, not giving or questioning them. We picked right up where Hank and I had left off, with long, hot, dusty hours in the backcountry at night, and during the process I was surprised at Bill's stamina. He was a lot older than I but had just as much drive as I did. Years later I discovered how that combination comes to be. The good Lord has a job for a game warden to do protecting his creation. When wardens grow old and slow, He sees to it that those people still have the energy to go the distance. Today, at fifty-seven, though old and slow myself, I find I can still outwork many of those who are thirty years younger than I.

One morning about three A.M. found us staking out a high mountain pass, surrounded by "snakes" of logging roads running in every direction through the second-growth timber. Through this maze of logging roads ran one heavily traveled dirt road that eventually wound itself down into the city of Eureka, some thirty miles away. Our patrol vehicle was parked just above a steep turn, so anyone traversing the road would sweep around the curve and be upon our rig before the driver of the oncoming vehicle realized we were there. If that person were on the wrong side of the law, we could fall upon the culprit posthaste, and escape was not an option. We had been so parked since nightfall and were sitting on the roadbank behind our vehicle, visiting and listening to the night sounds around us. Our dinner had been the usual game-warden meal, cold C rations. We were drinking iced tea from our thermoses to keep awake, and our talk had slowed until we had both drifted off into our own thoughts.

At first it was hard to be sure, but eventually we heard the grinding of an automobile engine laboring under a heavy load as it inched up toward our high mountain location. We could see by the sweep of its headlights as it navigated the steep logging road switchbacks below us that it was coming our way! To a game warden, there was no reason for anyone to be out on those roads at that time of the morning unless they were up to no good. It was time for action. Bill positioned himself at the bottom of one switchback about thirty-five yards from where he placed me, at the top of the next turn in the road. That way, if they drove by him they still had to get by me, with Bill "eating up" their rear. Oh, to be a rookie game warden at a moment like this. By God, what a thrill!

The car slowly ground around the last turn by our parked vehicle, and as its headlights hit our patrol car, out stepped Bill. Bill, like me, was in uniform and easy to recognize as a Fish and Game warden. He strode out into the middle of the dirt road, shone his flashlight into the driver's eyes, and shouted, "Halt! State Fish and Game warden!"

There was a pause that seemed to last for hours; then I heard the car's engine roar to additional power, heard the spinning of tires on the dirt road, and saw Bill suddenly leap out of the way. As I stated earlier, Bill was an older man and not too fleet of foot. To avoid being run down, instead of running he dove off to one side of the road. But the onrushing car was too close, and it hit his legs, throwing his rag-doll form into the ditch. The car, gaining speed, was now coming my way. At that point, this rookie game warden decided he'd better get his crap together or he too would soon be lying in a ditch. That moment certainly had all the trappings of a dangerous situation—I found myself standing in the middle of the road, in full uniform, holding up my hand, while my hind end did strange things! I guess I couldn't blame myself for having a tight tail end, especially in light of Bill's notable lack of success in stopping the fleeing automobile just moments before. ...

I remember looking through the windshield as the car approached and observing a lot of people inside, maybe four or five. I heard someone in the car yelling, "Kill him, kill him, kill him." The unmistakable form of a head, arms, and a rifle that looked like a Model 94 Winchester came out the front passenger side of the onrushing vehicle. I heard the *clackety-clack* of a lever-action rifle indexing a round into the chamber and assumed I was the target of that lad's intentions.

Being rather large of frame and with a more than sufficient center of mass, I decided that now was the time to apply all the training the state of California provided before this chap with the rifle let all the air out of me. I removed my .44 magnum pistol from the holster, holding my five-cell flashlight alongside and aiming it in the driver's eyes, took dead aim at the driver of the onrushing vehicle, now about forty feet away, and shot at his head. The windshield exploded, and the automobile started to move erratically back and forth across the logging road. However, it continued to advance rapidly, and the lad with the rifle was still trying to get a bead on me as the car wove violently. When it was about twenty-five feet away, I aimed dead center for the radiator, which I knew would lead my bullet to the engine, and let another round from the magnum sail on its way. *Whomp* went the 250-grain bullet as it hit the engine block. The heretofore smooth-running engine suddenly sounded as if it had a bad case of the trots. Apparently, tomorrow wasn't an option for that engine.

Stepping off to my left to avoid being hit, I calmly indexed another round into my pistol to take care of the lad with the rifle. Not realizing how close I was to the edge of the steep-banked logging road, I found myself dropping over the road's edge and carried several feet down the bank. Quickly regaining my balance, I turned back to face the vehicular threat, realizing at the same time that my "trip" over the bank had lowered my perspective by several feet so that I was now looking at the center of the fenders and doors as the car passed by on the road above. Looking up, I saw that the chap with the rifle was still trying to change the shape and form of what God had given me, so up went the magnum, and as the car went by I set it off for the third time, right through the center of the front passenger door. *Ka-boom* went what at the time was the world's most powerful handgun.

Boy, did the crap hit the fan with that entry of a high-speed lead projectile! The barrel of the magnum must have been very close to the side of the car as it raced by because I got a faceful of paint chips, unburned powder, and flames. My ears went dead to sound, not to mention the fact that I couldn't see for all the flying debris. In fact, for a second I thought the chap with the rifle had shot me through the head. But my training paid off. As the car went on, I could feel the recoil of the magnum as each succeeding round was fired and sailed into the side of the offending vehicle. Being that close to the scene of battle, I could tell from the screams and human movement that I was surely getting everyone's attention. The car quickly passed me, careened off the right side of the road, and went crashing into the canyon below with a loud roaring and gnashing of metal against the rocks and trees. By now my hair, what little I had in my crew cut, was standing straight up as if it wanted to see better.

I hurriedly jumped back up on the road and after a few moments of frantic rubbing could finally see out of my right eye, or master eye. God, it was a great feeling not to be blind but able to see again. This was my first shootout, and needless to say, I was more than a little nervous. Running down the road toward where the car had gone off the edge, I tried to reload my pistol from the two drop pouches on my gunbelt. Since I had expended all six rounds into the front and side of the vehicle, I thought it only proper that I arrive on the scene capable of taking care of myself and any of the bad guys who still had a little fight left. Drop pouches surely were properly named. I think that of my twelve extra cartridges, I got only six into the cylinder while running down the road. The rest were scattered along the road as I ran to where the vehicle had gone over the edge. About that time I saw Bill staggering along the road toward me on what turned out later to be just badly bruised legs, yelling, "Kill the sonsabitches, kill the sonsabitches."

Good, he was OK—I could tell by the way he was giving me instructions on how to treat my fellow human. Reaching the edge of the road, I shone my flashlight down over the edge, trying to locate the vehicle and its occupants. The air was still full of dust, and I had to wait a few moments for it to clear. Fearing the worst, I saw that the car had gone down a long taluslike slope on its wheels and struck a huge Douglas fir dead center. The hood was up, the trunk lid was up, all the doors were open, and in the distance I could hear people clattering down the rocky slope and off into the cover of night.

I waited a moment for Bill to arrive and asked him, "How you doing, partner?"

"I hurt like crap, but I guess everything is OK," he wheezed. I looked him over, and what he said appeared to be true, so I headed down the rocky slope to the vehicle to see if anyone needed help or if anyone was left alive to arrest.

"Cover me," I yelled.

As I cautiously approached the car, it dawned on me that my instructions to Bill may not have been the best choice at a time like this. At that range, with a shotgun, how in the hell was he going to provide cover for me? Hell, we are all going to die if he starts shooting, especially in his mad-as-a-hornet state of mind, I thought. Oh well, I guess if he has to shoot we will just let God sort out the survivors.

Arriving at the car, I found it empty. There was blood all over the front seat behind the steering wheel along with glass from the shattered windshield. There was a bullet hole in the windshield in line with the driver's head, but no body. I guess the flying glass did the damage that produced all the blood, not the bullet. There were also bullet holes in the engine and through the front passenger door, one in the door post, one through the back door, and one in the trunk area that had "killed" a gutted and iced salmon. Looking into the trunk of the car, I found about five hundred pounds of salmon in a specially designed, open-topped stainless-steel fish box. The fish were all iced down, and every one of them had net marks across the opercula, a sign that they had been taken by a gill net.

Well, here we were, with a vehicle without license plates, vehicle identification number, or any other way to trace it. A trunkload of fish, a bloody car, and not a body to be seen. It seemed that the lads driving the car had left to go change their shorts! That was fine by me. In Bill's frame of mind, if anyone returned they were likely to be murdered! Seeing that there was nothing else I could do, I spent the rest of the night transporting gill-netted salmon up the hill to be loaded into our patrol car for disposal. Several times while catching my breath I chanced to look at the bullet holes in the door of the car. In both cases, the hole was about leg high and the bullet had lodged in the opposite-side door. There was no way those chunks of lead should have failed to hit someone. I think someone was really looking out for those guys that night.

We never did get those bad guys. Closer examination of the vehicle in daylight showed a machine composed of many parts, none traceable to any one owner. The informant left the area for good shortly after the incident for the sake of his personal health, and the fish stopped going over the mountain to the fish houses in Eureka. Hank returned, and because Bill had been working in Hank's district without really asking permission, Bill ordered me to keep what had occurred on that mountainside to myself. Not wanting to create a rift between the two senior officers, I did as I was told. The users of the vehicle never raised the issue of that night, and because of the hasty departure of his informant, Hank never found out that we had tangled with those men on that mountain. He continued to work the area in the hope of catching the lads running the salmon, and I went my way to other assignments.

In 1978, as a special agent for the U.S. Fish and Wildlife Service, I was assigned to the Klamath River along with a gang of other special agents to stop the Indians from illegally running their gill nets in those waters. Basically, the Indians felt they had a right to run their nets along the entire length of the Klamath River, from the mouth to all points upstream. It appeared to be nothing more than greed and ego destroying their heritage, and most seemed to not give a damn about preserving the fish population and the river. The U.S. Fish and Wildlife Service Division of Law Enforcement was pressed into action to hold the line until the biologists and senior managers could determine what the Indians should legally be allowed to do. It didn't take long for our lads, though outnumbered and initially poorly led, to clean up forty miles of river and allow the salmon an escapement that far surpassed any that had occurred before. I was assigned as the riverine operations officer on that detail for two weeks, and it didn't take me long to see that the work done to protect the salmon was a real tribute by those special agents who served in protecting that segment of our national heritage under the worst of conditions. Once the Fish and Wildlife Service officers regained the Klamath and the Indians realized that to cross swords was to invite a knot on the head, things quieted down and opportunities arose to view the overall situation. One of those opportunities allowed me to fly over the area looking for gill nets missed by our lads on the ground or in the jetboats.

Just for kicks, I had the pilot fly me over the place where I had had my first shootout as a state Fish and Game warden in the 1960s. Sure as hell, there sat the old Buick with the hood, trunk, and doors still up and open. The tires and part of the engine were missing, but otherwise there she still sat in all her past glory. A memento, if you will, of times gone by, of a game warden's first shootout, of a carload of Indians and a trunkload of fish.

As far as I know, the illegal flow of salmon didn't start moving again through the mountain passes for some time after that event. According to Hank, word on the reservation was that the Indians all of a sudden started running the fish to Eureka at night down Highway 299 instead. I wonder if those men got religion or whether it was the 250-grain, .44 magnum bullets tearing through the car doors, skimming past sweating bodies and out the other side at 1,400 feet per second. It is amazing what can be achieved by using just a little "mettle"—or should I spell it "metal"?

I guess I will never know.

3

Gold Beach

THE SUN OF ANOTHER DAY lifted its rays over the mist-shrouded Pacific Range, giving the magnificent redwoods below an ethereal crest. As the sun's golden fingers continued to race across the treetops and down the ridges to the sea, they fell upon a tired face expectantly scanning a dirt road half hidden by a long bluff created many millions of years ago. Though I was tired, I thanked God for another day and then just stood there for an hour and enjoyed the morning. The steady rolling thunder of the Pacific Ocean surf beating against the beach sands to the west and the pleasant smell of the salt spray told me I was a small part, but very much a living part, of His creation. Around me were rolling sand dunes covered with tall salt grasses, wild strawberry plants hugging the ground, a few stunted red alder trees, driftwood from past violent storms, and a hundred or so quietly resting and feeding Roosevelt elk. This variety, the largest living species of elk in North America, is found on the North Pacific Coast and a short distance inland from northern California all the way to Vancouver Island.

Surveying my small part of the world on that day, I wondered if I would make a difference. The elk were safe for another day, but night would come again, and so would the most efficient and savage predator on earth. Then how would my charges fare? That thought slowly moved through my mind, mixed with the clutter that came from limited sleep and the invading damp chill from spending a night as a lone sentinel in the sand next to the surf. That thought of death to come from humankind vanished as quickly as it had appeared, like the foam from a receding wave on the beach. My stomach was telling me it was time to eat something before the little guts were eaten by the big ones. Surveying my latest field of battle and satisfied that all was well for now, I picked up my gear and shook off the ever-present sand.

I slowly walked, letting my stiffness work itself out, to a hidden patrol car parked among a copse of brush and stunted red alder trees along a small creek that was finishing its run to the ocean. My muscles spoke to me as they were wont to do after a long period of inactivity coupled with the damp that comes from lying in the wet sand. Surveying my resting elk one more time and satisfied of their well-being, I headed from my stakeout point to the highway and then south toward home for some much-needed sleep.

Letting my mind wander as the miles sped by, I ran through the scenario that had brought me to my area of the beach and the elk herd I was trying to protect. Steve Logsdon, one of my fellow graduate students at Humboldt State College in Arcata, California, had always complained that poachers kept killing the Gold Beach herd of Roosevelt elk that made up part of his master's degree study group. At that time there wasn't much I could do other than helping him clean up the animal parts left as a result of that poaching for academic study of sorts, but I never forgot those episodes. After graduation and my subsequent acceptance of a commission as a California state Fish and Game warden assigned to that same north coast area, I had the tools and time to address the problem. Shortly after I returned from the Fish and Game academy, I found myself heading to the home of Dr. Archie S. Mossman, a brilliant mammalogist, an outstanding wildlife professor at Humboldt State College, and a close friend.

I met this old friend in front of his home, and we warmly shook hands. "Terry!" called an excited voice from the house, and out stormed Archie's diminutive wife, Sue. Into my arms she went as I gave her a hug and greeting. Sue was also a dear friend and an exceptional academic herself. After a few pleasantries, in response to my serious questions Archie told me that the poachers were still killing the Gold Beach herd of Roosevelt elk as if there were no tomorrow. In fact, the latest kill, a seven-point bull, had been discovered just a week earlier. The animal had apparently been wounded by a poacher and had crawled off to die in agony among his living

brethren on the beach. The poachers, scared off when a couple of
kids who had parked in the area instantly turned on their headlights
upon hearing the report of the rifle, had made no attempt to follow the animal. The bull died without making a sound, as most
wildlife does, ultimately bloating and rotting where he fell.

That report from the kids, Archie's informants, coupled with my
next window of opportunity, led to my staking out the Gold Beach
area of Humboldt County. This unique and beautiful area is a narrow strip of land between the Gold Beach bluffs and the Pacific
Ocean just north of the town of Orick, California. The entire area
was within the boundaries of Prairie Creek Redwoods State Park,
and its resident herd of elk, like the land base, was strictly protected
by the state of California. The elk, like the ancient redwoods, are
magnificent. They are the largest elk in North America and once
roamed all through the Pacific coast forests during their historical
period of greatness. Today they are just a remnant population of
what was once part of the magnificent redwood ecosystem. Thanks
to humankind's destruction of habitat and overharvesting of the animals, both legally in historical times and illegally today, they have
been relegated to a fraction of their former greatness. The Gold
Beach herd is unique because more often than not it frequents the
beach area instead of the dark timber characteristic of a climax
coniferous redwood forest. In that uniqueness came danger from
the muzzle of a rifle because of the herd's accessibility in the sand
dune area and the remoteness of its home from the eye and ear of
those sworn to protect the elk.

That is where I personally and professionally came into play. I
love the earth and the wild things living on it. As a young warden
I wasn't what one might call a "tree hugger," but I had a newfound
respect for what nature had to offer as I began to mature in my job
and as a person. I had cultivated that respect partly because of the
wonderful wildlife education I had received at Humboldt State
College, partly because of the silver star I now wore on my chest,
and partly because of the responsibility that star required of me in
providing resources for the enjoyment of those yet to come.

I had caught my over-limits of fish and killed my over-limits of game throughout my younger days. Those kills were never wasted, but all in all my actions were wrong. With the weight of the silver star came the realization of what I owed and what was due. I guess one could say I was doing penance for my earlier days.

Pulling into my driveway in Eureka, I was met by my bride, Donna. She unsuccessfully tried to hide her concern and relief as I ·tiredly stepped from the patrol car, only to fly into my arms for a bear hug such as only I could give. I believed God had never made a woman quite like this one, and I was very fortunate to have her as my mate. I sometimes think God had taken her aside and told her that if she took that heathen under her wing, she was assured a place at His right hand. I don't think she knew what she was letting herself in for, but I ended up with the grace of her presence in my life. Refusing an offer of a large home-cooked breakfast, I grabbed some homemade bread (made for me every day of my life by my bride) and slapped some peanut butter on it; that would have to suffice for the moment (typical game-warden fare!). Off to bed I went, with visions of poachers on Gold Beach falling into my grip the following night.

❧

The sun began to set below the perennial fogbank offshore, throwing its red fingers skyward as a last act of defiance. Turning my eyes landward, I again scanned my quietly resting, or in some instances feeding, elk herd. God, what an evening. The smell of salt was in the air; the crashing of the surf came to my ear; and the pungent smell of elk drifted from nearby and mingled with the damp smell of the earth, all served up with a mild, moisture-laden offshore breeze. The coolness that is the Pacific Northwest began to manifest itself as I drew my jacket more tightly around my neck. Here we were again: the elk and I against an unknown assailant, a predator who would return again. The assailant knew the time, the place, and the method. All I knew was that the assailant was coming, sometime. The odds seemed just about even. The poacher had the upper hand on timing and I the upper hand on patience—not to mention the bracelets for his hands when he reached into the cookie jar containing the elk "cookies."

The last vestiges of daylight finally disappeared into the velvet dark routinely found in a temperate rain forest such as most of Humboldt County is, and with it came the circling of the herd in the tall salt grass around me. It was a great feeling being alive, being there in the field, and being trusted enough by the elk that they felt secure in gathering for the night close to the very type of animal trying to do them harm. Moments like that remain clearly fixed in my brain years after these events occurred. Darkness manifested itself now like a heavy, moisture-laden velvet cloak as I lay back against a large sand dune and waited for the anticipated evening's fireworks. This was the ninth night I had lain in wait for the lad or lads illegally killing these magnificent animals, and tonight my gut feeling told me an event was in the offing.

Around midnight a light fog drifted in and settled around my position. The degree of fog was not enough to deter anyone wanting to kill an elk; in fact, it would likely have just the opposite effect because the fog would provide a little more cover for the shooter, not to mention dampening the sound of the shooting. By two A.M. all was very quiet, and the inky darkness was so complete that I could put my hand in front of my face and feel its heat on my nose before I could see its outline.

The elk had settled down and were now resting all around me. Their pungent smell, soft whistling calls, and sounds of rumination were my world for the moment. The stiffness from my damp soil "bed" was beginning to tell on me, but I remained still. I didn't want to scare or arouse the sleeping elk; besides, what better decoys could one ask for when trying to trap an elk poacher? I thought as I tried to fight off the ever-present urge to sleep.

About three-thirty, a pair of headlights swept into the area from the south side of the beach below my position. Without hesitation, they continued north along the dirt road that paralleled the bluffs along Gold Beach, past me and out of sight of my position. It was four A.M. before the headlights returned, and I suspected it was just some young couple out to take advantage of the darkness. The vehicle proceeded south along the dirt road before me, passed my position, and again drove out of sight. A large bull, nervous of the interruption at that time of the morning (probably because he had been shot at before), stood up, and in so doing awakened part of the herd. The animals' activity was normal, and I continued to snuggle deeper in my warm coat until I saw the headlights slowly coming back north along the dirt road.

This time I went into full alert! This car could very well contain my shooters. They could have gone north on the dirt road just to check out the other end to see if any game wardens were staking out the elk herd. After driving through the area where they wished to shoot and not finding anything that would cause them trouble, they had returned, or so I supposed. I was no longer cold but shook with anticipation of the moment that was likely to come. I didn't have to wait long. When the vehicle was even with my elk herd, it stopped, and *zip,* out came the pencil-thin blue-white stream of a powerful spotlight. It swept the area where the herd had been sleeping, and instantly the elk were all on their feet. I should have realized the inherent danger at that moment, but my fixation on capturing the poachers blinded my common sense. The intoxicating effect of hunting your fellow human beings sometimes, just like real drugs, masks your sense of danger. That's what happened to me that morning. The light continued to sweep over the elk herd, finally illuminating a large bull. The elk, uncomfortable with the light in his eyes, lowered his head and tried to move away from the offensive beam, only to have it follow him every step of the way.

In the meantime I was lying on the ground in an attempt to stay concealed, stripping off my coat and trying to get ready to run these lads down on foot if they shot an animal and entered the field to claim their prize. What a prize they would get, I said to myself, all six-foot-four, 320 pounds of flying tackle from the local game warden! A six-by-seven (western count, that is, an animal with six antler tines on one side and seven on the other—thirteen points by the eastern-count method) bull raised his head, and *boom* went the report of a rifle. The orange ball of flame fairly leaped from the vehicle in the direction of the standing elk. A *ka-thump* told me they had hit the animal, and solidly. Before I could see what happened to the large bull who had just been shot, it happened!

Being a rookie, I had not planned for the next few seconds' worth of events, a danger I was about to learn the hard way. Elk exploded from the grass around me. They were crashing in every direction, trying to get away from the light and the sound of the rifle. A huge cow jumped right over me in her frantic effort to escape, her hoof taking the cap clean off my head like a bullet. Next I collided with a frantic calf trying to follow its mother, knocking me to the ground and stunning me for a moment. Finally understanding the exploding danger around me, I got up from the ground and ran for a dark form I recognized as a tree, hoping to use it as a shield. Another fleeing elk slammed into my side, sending me sailing through the air for about ten feet. I hit the ground, rolled, and came up running as my survival instinct told me to keep moving. *Zip* went another bullet in the direction I was running, and it wasn't too damn far away, either! Those knotheads, I thought, the urge to kill has them shooting at anything and everything! I dove to the ground as another bullet zipped across my bow and again bounced up running, not wanting to be trampled by fear-crazed elk flying for their lives. *Zip* went another bullet, followed by a heavy *thump* as an elk running directly in front of me went down hard in a flurry of flying sand, grass, and pieces of driftwood.

The pungent smell of "paunch" (escaping stomach gases) told me that animal was a goner. But not quite. Up she came, and out of fear and pain charged me. In the dim residual light of the spotlight as it swept the field in search of another quick victim, I saw her kick out at me with her front hooves. As I ducked, her hoof hit my right shoulder a glancing blow, knocking me into the red alder I had been running toward. Knocked sideways and off balance at a dead run, I sailed into the tree, hitting it at a damn high rate of speed. The impact knocked the wind out of me with a loud *whoosh* and sent me glancing off to one side into a large pile of driftwood. My shoulders hit a log, my head snapped back into another log, and then the lights went out!

I came to at daylight and saw a small bird looking down at me from his perch on a driftwood log. Boy, my head hurt like there was no tomorrow, and my eyes wouldn't focus for more than a moment at a time. Closing my eyes seemed to help, so I kept them closed while I moved my hand to the large knot on the back of my head, only to remove it quickly because of the pain even light touching caused. There was no blood on my hand, but considering the velocity with which I had hit that driftwood pile, I thanked my lucky stars my head wasn't split open. I lay there for a few more moments, letting my eyes focus and getting up the courage to see if I could stand and walk. After a bit I could see that the pain wasn't going away, so I rolled over and, using my arms to push off, staggered to my feet. Hanging on to a log end in the woodpile, I steadied myself so I could survey the field of battle and, with any luck, not fall. Some battle! The place was deserted. No bad guys, no elk, and one very sore and dizzy game warden were all that remained. The fog was drifting in, and I just let the cool, moist air bring me back to the state of a semifunctioning human being.

Damn, my head hurt. Every step I took was hell, not to mention the fact that I could hardly lift my gun arm. At first I couldn't remember why, but then it came back to me: the kick in the right shoulder from the wounded elk that had nearly taken my head off. I was lucky I had the sense and the grace of God (who loves fools, little children, and game wardens) to duck. After another thirty minutes or so of just getting adjusted to my painful world, I began to move slowly around the area. There was a large gut pile not fifteen feet from where I had lain next to the driftwood pile, all that remained of the cow who had kicked the stuffing out of me as she was beginning her dance with death. It was amazing that the lads had gutted that elk so close to where I was lying and had never seen me there among the tall grasses. They were very cool customers if they *had* seen me and, realizing that I was out cold and not a threat at that time, continued to collect their ill-gotten gains in spite of my inert carcass.

Further examination of the grassy resting area revealed another gut pile next to a small dead bull that had been deemed unworthy of collection. Not seeing anything else related to the previous night's poaching damage, I gutted the small bull, propping open its legs so it would cool out, and then walked over to the dirt road to see if I could pick up any spent shell casings for evidence. My head was not as bad as it had been, but I still could not turn it too quickly or bend over without a lot of pain. I continued my search, but nothing remained except a set of vehicle tracks heading south and out of the park and some drops of blood on the sandy road, the only remaining trace of the night's sad events.

Realizing I was a spent unit on this case, I headed for my patrol vehicle and drove out to the state park headquarters. I informed the park rangers of where the elk was lying in the grass so they could collect it and donate the meat to a needy family. I didn't tell them of the previous night's events, first because I was not happy with my performance and second because I suspected everyone in the killing of the Gold Beach herd—and what better killer than one on the inside!

❧

I caught a lot of poachers in that area during the following year but was never sure whether any of the men I apprehended were the lads from the night I had had to use my football skills to avoid being taken out by the animals I was trying to protect. I did learn an important trick of the trade: on all future stakeouts I stayed the hell away from the center of an elk herd. After that incident, I would set up across the road from the elk. That way, when the lads stopped their vehicle to shoot, I was on the opposite side from where they were looking and could move right up on them before they even realized I was there. Most of the time, when they shot I would be kneeling unseen just a few feet from the side of their vehicle and would let them go out into the field to retrieve their kill. When they returned, usually dragging an elk, guess who would be between them and their method of escape?

Several times the sharper killers would shoot from the car, then drop off one poacher to gut the animal while another sped away in the vehicle to reduce the chance of detection and apprehension.

That method was fun because it gave me a chance to stalk the lad in the field and, in every instance, walk right up on him just as his interest was totally absorbed in the gutting of his prey. It was even more fun having that lad, handcuffed, of course, call his buddy from the just-returned vehicle to come out and help him. More than once I scared the living hell out of the man coming from the vehicle when I rose out of the three-foot-high grass no more than two to three feet away as he approached.

After several such successful poacher-apprehension ventures in the Gold Beach area, the illegal elk killing slowed, then stopped outright. In that period of my life I had learned several lessons that would serve me well throughout my career—and in the process had used up one of the lives allotted to me as a person and a game warden. I learned that many times the game you are trying to protect will not cooperate with you. In fact, sometimes it will try to kill you, not by intention but simply because the will and instinct to live is so strong. I accepted that fact because that instinct is what the world of wildlife is all about, namely, survival of the fittest. However, when operating in this wildlife-survival arena, one must also consider the human factor. Human beings are animals and many times act savagely like animals. But they are animals who have lost almost all of their basic wild instincts other than the instinct of the final act of killing. The loss of such senses often betrays poachers because those holding the "thin green line," through instinct, training, practical experience, and their own partial reentry into the world of wildlife, turn out to be the better hunters. The good ones in our line of work are just like some domestic cats: they possess the genes of old, which allow for field survival and a fairly easy return to our wild nature. When one hones these skills as a conservation officer and learns to read the wild, it is just a matter of time until those who poach but don't reclaim their heritage of wild skills will find themselves stalked by a far better-equipped human being bent on catching the most dangerous game.

So, for those reading these lines who walk on the "dark side," keep in mind that it is just a matter of time. ...

4

Chili for Breakfast

THE SUN WAS FINALLY beginning to burn off the light fog that
was lying over the sea west of Eureka, California. Lieutenant Ken
Brown, a marine warden for the state of California, gave a glance
seaward to acknowledge that fact, then busied himself with cali-
brating the patrol boat's radar and pumping the bilges. I finished the
deck chores and went below to stow our food and gear. The *Rainbow,* a thirty-five-foot twin-screw, gasoline-powered, navy-gray Fish
and Game patrol boat stationed in Eureka, was to be our home for
the next sixteen hours, or however long it took to get the job done.
For Ken, the boat commander, a stint at sea was a joy. For me, the
boarding officer, it was hell, pure and simple.

I was a rookie game warden for the state of California, having
been hired right out of college after graduating from Humboldt
State College with a master's degree in wildlife management. After
sixteen weeks at a police academy, I had returned to the area where
I had spent five of my seven years in college to start my career in
wildlife law enforcement. Part of my duties consisted of filling in as
a boarding officer on the state's resident patrol boat, which was used
to help keep the large Pacific North Coast commercial fishing industry in check. My job consisted of boarding commercial fishing
boats at sea to make sure they stayed within established fishing limits, fished only during prescribed seasons, used legal gear, were
properly licensed, and fished within the prescribed zones set aside
for their particular commercial activity. I loved the work, the challenge, the danger, and even the sea. What I hated was the fact that
I got motion sickness at the drop of a hat.

Being afflicted with a weak inner ear meant nothing but misery
every time I went to sea. In fact, I was so bad that every time I even

46

started to work on our patrol boat in the marina, knowing we were going to sea shortly thereafter, I got seasick—not a little sick but major-broadcast puke-six-feet sick. As long as we were moving I was OK. But let us stop the boat, with all the pitching and yawing and loss of horizon, and I was one sick lad. Then throw into that situation my duties as a boarding officer, which really made my day complete. I had to jump from ship to ship at sea in order to be able to do a firsthand check of the boats and their crews for compliance with state conservation laws. Then I had to descend into the bilges of those ships to check their catches, breathing the smells of their greasy cooking, rotting sea products from the last catch left over in the bilge, and diesel fumes—and up would come everything I had inside me, including my gizzard! Then, with a sickness born in hell, I would have to jump from the commercial fishing vessel back onto the small, pitching deck of my patrol boat with legs made from the best rubber going. Damn, I'm getting woozy just thinking about those days.

The Pacific Coast Squad of game wardens in which I worked in-cluded lots of World War II and Korean War veterans, and none of them, being such good friends and all, spared me advice on how to avoid seasickness. Many of them were ex-navy and had lots of ideas that were "sure-fire" stoppers of that affliction called motion sick-ness. Eat lots of bread or crackers before going out to sea; eat pick-les before going out to sea; eat a big meal with lots of grease before going out to sea; don't eat anything before going out to sea; and so it went. I followed their advice to a tee, trying to avoid a misery that knows no bounds, and all I did was continue to puke my guts out on each and every trip. On one particular trip, when I believed for a moment that I had puked up my gizzard and watched my lips land on the stern, the seas were running fifty feet if they were running an inch. With no horizon and a slow speed to avoid beating the boat to pieces, all I did was lie on the stern and let the sea water roll over me, not because I wanted to but because I was so sick I couldn't even crawl! Good old Ken tried to keep the speed up and stay in the troughs of the waves to reduce the motion, but all to no avail.

My motion sickness finally got so bad that I made arrangements to visit a hypnotist to see if he could do something for this malady. I had tried every kind of medicine known to humankind by that time and succeeded only in numbing my brain and everything else except that part of me that made me throw up. The hypnotist was my last stop. If hypnosis didn't work, there was nothing to do but gut it out. But before I actually visited the hypnotist (an expensive treatment I really couldn't afford), a revelation came to me from an old friend, Hank Merak, who had served on an LST (a landing ship tank, a round-bottomed vessel that pitched and yawed even at anchor in the harbor and hence became universally known as a "seasick special") during the Korean War. Hank was a fellow officer from Willow Creek. We had served a lot of long hours together in the wildlife wars, and I knew he wouldn't lie to me. Upon hearing about my problem, Hank said, "Hell, Tiny, try chili for breakfast— the hotter the better." Well, a drowning man will grab even a spear if thrown to him. Hank told me the cook on his LST, when he knew a storm was coming, would cook up huge pots of the hottest chili known to humankind and make the crew eat it. Hank said the antidote worked so well that he never saw a man seasick on his ship, even during a typhoon off the coast of Japan. Needless to say, I was ready to try anything to stop feeling so rotten all the time when at sea; in addition, if I felt better I could do a better job as a boarding officer and maybe slow down some of the sea pirates fishing the waters off the north coast.

I am here to tell you, there is nothing worse than being a prey to motion sickness. In fact, when I got home after my sea duty, if I got into a high-speed chase after a poacher in my patrol car, say that evening, many times I had to stop and puke if I swung around the turns too fast. Often the malady would last up to three days after my last turn at the wheel on sea duty. When one gets that sick, one will try anything. Looking back today, Lord knows I wish I had not tried that chili idea. But as I said, a drowning man will …

Ken had called and informed me that we had a sea detail the next day assisting Warden Devine. I thought, Oh no, but it was my job and both men were close friends, so, closing my mind to the seasickness that would come, I said, "When and where?"

"Meet me tomorrow, three in the morning, at the office, and we'll take it from there," Ken replied. With that, he hung up, and I went to my home and prepared a sea bag full of gear for the detail. Hell, I was already starting to get seasick! The next morning, after I transferred my sea gear to Ken's patrol vehicle, we stopped off at a twenty-four-hour restaurant in Eureka for breakfast. Ken decided he was going to order ham, eggs, and potatoes. I, with Hank's words of wisdom ringing in my ears, surveyed the menu, and sure enough, there it was: *chili*. When the waiter returned I ordered a big bowl of chili without a moment's hesitation, and Ken looked at me with eyes raising the question of seasickness. I told him about my conversation with Hank, but I could tell he wasn't convinced. Well, a little doubt wasn't going to stop me: the fellow soon to be dying at sea unless he found the miracle cure was me!

While we waited for our breakfast to arrive, Ken discussed our current assignment. It seemed that a drag boat (a type of commercial fishing boat that drags a large net, shaped like a sleeve, along the bottom behind it, scooping up every fish within the width of the net's opening) operated by one of Eureka's finest outlaws was fishing within the two-mile-closure limit imposed by the Fish and Game Commission. This two-mile limit extended seaward from the shore and had been established to protect the stocks of bottom fish from being entirely depleted by shortsighted members of the commercial fishing industry, of whom there were many. Our target's method of operation was to wait until it got damn good and foggy, then sneak into the two-mile-closure area and drag his net until he had a load of fish. He would then lift his net and run back out to sea, past the limit, before the fog lifted as if he had been there all the time and no one would be the wiser, especially Fish and Game enforcers.

Because of the danger of running aground in the fog or hitting one of the many large rock outcroppings prevalent along the north coast, radar had to be used during any drag-boat fishing activity. The radar served two purposes: first, the obvious one of staying off the rocks. The second purpose was to help the poacher spot any other boats that might be approaching. Poachers running outlaw boats didn't want other commercial fishing boats to see what they were doing; they kept the secret of their success close to the vest so they could continue to make high profits. In addition, if Fish and Game wardens didn't actually see the outlaws poaching, then they couldn't write citations for violations of the law or suspend fishing licenses.

However, in cases involving greed or ego, someone is always watching. Commercial fishermen tend to watch each other like a bunch of feeding vultures. If someone is making a killing, they all want in, and away they go to the fishing grounds of the fisherman who is successful. Soon the area is fished out, and they start watching each other's movements again. In this particular case, several honest fishermen had noticed this suspected drag-boat skipper consistently coming in with full loads of high-quality bottom fish while everyone else was doing just so-so, no matter where and how they fished. Suspecting something a little fishy, a group of fishermen supplied a fair amount of booze and soon had members of the successful boat's crew spilling the beans. Even with the story out in the open, the commercial fishermen getting stiffed refused to talk to the Fish and Game authorities. It took a paid informant working in a cannery to supply the information we were currently relying upon. Our plan was simple. We would take the *Rainbow* and work up along the northern part of Humboldt County, seaside, and attempt to trap our illegal fisherman as he fished within the boundaries of the closed zone. The *Rainbow* was a small vessel, and with the right amount of fog and a little luck we were hoping we could get close enough to catch him with his nets down. If so, there was no way for him to escape without pulling up his nets or leaving them. Either way, the speed of our boat made catching this lad a sure thing. To assist us in this endeavor, Joe Devine, the Arcata game warden, would sit high up on the surrounding cliffs and let us know when the drag boat entered the closed area. This combination of forces is fairly easy when you have high ground and an informant. Sometimes when one is above the fog, as Joe would be, one can see downward better than those in the fog can see around them. Nothing could go wrong with the plan—unless of course you threw in the chili factor.

Speaking of chili, here came our breakfasts. The waiter gave me a look of disdain as he delivered my bowl of chili and crackers. However, when one is big enough to eat hay, it is amazing how little those of lesser size will say about their innermost thoughts. Remembering what Hank had said about "the hotter the better," I ordered some hot sauce to go with my food. The waiter gave me the "genuine nut" look for eating chili that early in the morning, but he complied. The chili smelled great, and it was. I like to cook and consider myself a fair one. But let me tell you, whoever cooked up this homemade chili had the world's best recipe. It was full of the best darn meat, and plenty of it. The chili sauce was perfectly thick as well as tasty, and the beans were done just right. It was so damn good I ordered another serving and added the last of the bottle of hot sauce to my second bowl. Ken finished his breakfast and said, "Terry, that smelled so damned good. How was it?"

"Ken," I said, "it was the best I have ever eaten."

"Well, if that's the case, I'll have a bowl," said Ken as he gestured the waiter over to our table. "Bring me a small bowl of that chili, if you please," he said. The waiter gave both of us the "goofier than thou" look and headed for the kitchen. Ken relished his chili as much as I had. He was going to order another bowl, but our time was getting short, so off we went to the marina, the *Rainbow,* and our trip north for a hoped-for successful meeting with our illegal drag boat.

At the marina I began preparing for our sea detail. As I worked on the boat, I waited for the telltale sweating, crappy feeling in my stomach, and clammy hands. Nothing happened. I felt fine for the first time in over six months of sea duty. Casting off the vessel, I stood ready to assist as Ken deftly maneuvered out into the channel. By now I had usually felt really terrible in times past. Today I felt fine. Damn, for once I really felt pretty good. Out the channel toward the buoy marking the sandbar at the mouth of Humboldt Bay we went, and still no bad feeling. Ken looked at me with the "how do you feel" look, and I just grinned and gave him a thumbs-up. Ken gave me that "wait until we really put to sea and then we will judge just how you feel" look. I had that same worry, but maybe this time, I thought, I had the bull by the horns. Turning into the wind as I had in times past to avoid getting sick, I thought maybe just once Ken would have a shipmate who wasn't deathly sick all the time. Swinging past the bar and out of Humboldt Bay, Ken turned the *Rainbow* north, advanced the throttle until she was up on step, and then handed me the helm so I could get more boat-driving experience.

For an hour or more we swiftly moved to the north, slicing through the wave troughs with the bow and surfing the crests. Boy, was life nice when you could enjoy it from the vertical position instead of lying horizontal on the stern of the boat! The sun was beginning to rise, and what a sight it was. The ocean was flatter than a flounder, with only slight swells. There was a slight offshore wind, and when the sun's rays hit the water at a slight angle it was like sliding through a pond of liquid gold. We spooked several bunches of sea ducks, mostly scoters, from their resting places, and it was fun to watch the heavy-bodied birds fly gracefully above the swells. The air to the north of us began to fill with swarms of feeding gulls, and the sun began to warm our right sides and faces. Man, this is what real sea duty is all about, I thought. Then a crab-trap marker buoy loomed ahead, breaking into my daydreaming, indicating a crab pot had been set in the closed zone. Ken took the helm as I moved forward with a bow hook to retrieve the float. Ken pulled alongside the marker, and I hooked it cleanly with the bow hook on the first pass. Walking the float to the stern of the boat, I hooked the crab-trap rope to the windlass and attempted to raise it so we could confiscate it. But the trap was sanded in and wouldn't come up. Ken gave me the finger-across-the-throat signal, so I took out my Buck knife and cut the rope.

As the rope settled out of sight beneath the waves, I tossed the float into a basket belowdecks and Ken resumed our travel to the north and, we hoped, our drag-boat "friend." Then it dawned on me. We had sat there for several moments, rolling back and forth while retrieving the float, and I had not gotten seasick. That realization must have hit Ken at the same time because he looked at me and said, "Love that damn Hank and his chili suggestion." I just grinned and logged in the annals of my mind that I owed Hank a good bottle of whiskey for his suggestion. It not only had saved my life, as far as I was concerned, but would make me a better boarding officer. Bad guys, better grab your last parts over the fence because here comes a real boarding officer who is big enough to eat not only hay but chili at three o'clock in the morning and do all the above before sea duty on the North Pacific! I thought.

Ken again handed me the helm as we headed north toward our hoped-for meeting with the drag boat. Life was good. We had our fog bank way to the north, the boat was running like a Swiss watch, and I felt like the world was finally a great place to live, especially at sea. Then it happened! *Way down* in my guts, I heard a faint rumbling. Not bad, mind you, but definitely there. Just a little gas from the beans, I thought, attempting to disregard the feeling. Then more rumbling. I still felt pretty damn good, so I continued to ignore the noise from beneath my "engine room." Suddenly the rumbling took on the authority of a Mack truck. It was now *very* apparent that I was going to have to take a dump or suffer the shame of a badly messed pair of pants. I called over to Ken and asked him to take the helm while I went below. He appeared to be lost in thought, and I called again. Snapping out of his preoccupation, Ken responded and walked over to take the helm. Damn, I thought, it was not like Ken to be lost in his own world like that. He usually was right on top of things when at sea. But the rumbling in my guts told me to hurry or suffer the consequences, so belowdecks to the bathroom I went. The bathroom on the *Rainbow* was nothing more than a narrow slot, maybe four feet in length and two feet wide at the most, with a small toilet at the end. Well, picture me, a six-foot-four 320-pounder with a three-foot-wide stern section trying to squeeze into a two-foot-wide entrance to a toilet. Oh yes, the toilet. It was a real jewel as well. The toilet seat was ten inches wide at the most, with a handle alongside that was used to manually pump the waste out the side of the vessel and into the sea.

Well, how in the hell was I going to push a three-foot-wide fanny through a two-foot-wide slot and place that fanny on a ten-inch toilet seat in a pitching and yawing boat? Easy. By now the rumbling in my guts had taken on a life of its own, and if I didn't let it out, I was a goner. In I went, wedging my tail end onto that seat, and with relief let go a load of the worst case of gas and diarrhea I'd ever had. Instant relief. Then it dawned on me. If I stayed there with the smell and loss of horizon, I would get seasick. In fact, some of the telltale signs were already starting to manifest themselves.

Not wasting any time, knowing what might be coming next, I pumped the waste over the side (or so I thought) with the toilet handle, squeezed out of the toilet chute, pulled up my pants, and started back up on deck. On the walkway I met Ken, who was coming down in a hurry as if he had a Mack truck problem as well.

"Gangway," he mumbled as he brushed by me, obviously en route to the same place I had just vacated. With my usual graveyard humor, I told Ken, "I already warmed up the seat for you." Scrambling up on deck, I took the helm in the absence of the skipper and checked all the gauges. I could hear Ken's efforts clear up where I was, even over the sound of the twin engines steadily churning our way northward. Before I could enjoy the moment of Ken's dismay, my guts started rumbling again, this time with a vengeance greater than before. As Ken came back up on deck, still pulling his pants up, I passed him on the way back to the toilet again. When I hit the seat that time, the force of the gas and semisolids leaving my body damn near lifted me clear up off that toilet. Brother, something was wrong here!

About that time, Ken shouted, "Terry, get a move on, here I come again." I got up off the seat and hurried out of the bathroom. Ken passed me going into the toilet before I even had a chance to get my pants up. Meanwhile, the *Rainbow* continued merrily on her way north at twenty knots without anyone at the helm. I ran up on deck and grabbed the helm. My guts again told me to head for the toilet and that to miss a step would bring dire consequences. Heading down the steps, I met Ken coming out of the toilet, still pulling his pants up. He had apparently heard me coming and knew the consequences of trying to sit on that ten-inch toilet seat while I tried to plant my tail end there as well. He had abandoned the toilet to avoid a messy collision. "Ken," I said, "we caught something at that goddamned restaurant."

"No shit," he said. "No pun intended, but I think we got a bad case of salmonella." Now I knew why he had been lost in thought earlier. Like me, he had been trying to figure out the rumbling deep in his guts. For the next forty or so minutes we both made liberal use of the toilet, passing each other many more times in that two-foot-wide entrance. Or as close to passing as we could come in a space that narrow!

Finally, after cleaning ourselves out entirely, we both stood at the helm with our pants unzipped and unbelted in case we had to run for the toilet. There was absolutely no body control. Once the urge started, you had better be moving. As if we needed any more problems, I was now starting to get seasick. I looked over at Ken and through greening lips told him, "Your crap really stinks." He laughed a strained, weak laugh and told me I wasn't a bed of roses either.

"Thank God that stuff was pumped overboard. Man, that stuff was really terrible," he said. I agreed as I headed for the radio, which had come to life with Devine's voice. Joe advised us that our lad was where we thought he would be and wanted to know how far we were from contact. I told him we were just a few miles away and would switch from the tower to car-to-car on the radio in about ten minutes. Joe was smart in not giving out any information over the Fish and Game radio as long as he was transmitting over the tower. Many of the fishermen had radios that could receive our transmissions, so we had to be careful. However, the outlaws could not receive our car-to-car transmissions; hence the switch once we got within line of sight of each other.

Joe agreed, and as we began to approach the fog bank to our north, Ken switched on the radar. There, as pretty as you please, was a blip on the screen in addition to the known rocks identified on our navigation charts. Our target was clearly only about one-half mile offshore and, given his speed, had his nets down and was fishing. Ken headed as close as he could get into shore in order to confuse our target's radar with the shore background and reduced our speed to that of a stalk. Then he went below to map out the coordinates of our fisherman for later use in court, while I took the helm.

My seasickness was in check, but I felt like crap. I knew I wasn't far from being the only hay burner soon to be puking his guts out into the North Pacific. I knew that once we stopped moving I would be puking for the first five minutes until I was cleaned out, then stuck with the dry heaves for the rest of the day. Oh well, I puked up my liver and gizzard the last trip, there couldn't be much left to feed to the fish, I thought darkly. Contacting Devine on our car-to-car frequency, I let him know our location, and after a brief moment of silence he announced that he could just barely see us down through the fog bank. He told me, "Your target is just about three-eighths of a mile ahead of you and to the westward." This confirmed our location of the target on our radar, and seasickness or not, we had this chap. The only problem was that I had forgotten the chili factor.

The fog swirled around us as we moved slowly northward toward our prey. The crash of the surf could still be heard, reminding us of the danger as we slowly moved around the rocky outcroppings in our quest to apprehend this chap and his crew. Ken came back up on deck. The next thing I knew, I felt a rumbling under my feet, heard a soft *boom-whoosh,* and turned in time to see our hatch cover land on the end of the stern. Smoke began to pour from the engine-room compartment and out the open hatch! Our eyes simultaneously swept the gauges to see that the starboard engine was dead and the last temperature reading was in the red zone. Something had gone badly wrong. We still had one engine functioning, but for how long we didn't know. Ken and I looked at the radar and confirmed that we were dangerously close to the rocks and the surf's edge. That was no place to lose the helm or the engines. Ken had to stay on the radar and wheel or we would be on the rocks for sure. I grabbed a fire extinguisher and jumped through the open hatch into the engine-room compartment. Jesus, what a sight. First of all, during our episode with the trots, Ken had forgotten to pump the bilges. I was standing in water deeper than the ten-inch tops of my Wellington boots. Furthermore, that water had a brown scum floating on it that was none other than our earlier attempts to rid ourselves of what troubled our guts.

Later examination revealed that the pipe from the toilet to the outside environment had broken just above the exit hole. Instead of pumping the effluent overboard, we had been pumping it into the bilge! Damn, what an awful smell. In addition, a small fire on the starboard engine bulkhead caused by an overheated engine (in typical state fashion, our engines were designed for brackish water, not sea water) was sending smoke from burned paint, plastic, insulation, and oils into the air. If I hadn't been seasick before, I certainly was now, and instantly. Vomiting as I walked through the warm bilgewater covered with a scum of human effluent toward the fire, carrying the fire extinguisher, I must have been a real sight. Some ablebodied seaman I made! Quickly putting out the small fire, I sloshed, walked, and vomited my way back to the hatch opening through the smoke and the heavy methane smell.

There was no doubt in my mind that the methane generated from our waste, mixed in the warm bilge water, produced enough gas to cause an explosion. How do you write that one up or explain it to the U.S. Coast Guard? Ken continued to steer our vessel away from the rocks and out to sea. As the *Rainbow* turned seaward and sideways, the radarman on the target vessel got a clear look at us, and the men on the drag boat began to pull their net for an unencumbered escape run into the fog to the north.

Devine, still watching from the cliffs, said, "What are you guys doing? He's getting away! What the hell are you doing; why are you guys leaving?"

Ken explained that we had lost an engine and were heading out to deeper water and the safety it offered. Joe acknowledged the response and said he would move north with the suspect boat and try to get a solid identification for courtroom use. In the meantime, Ken told Joe, if we got the engine fixed we would attempt to continue our pursuit of the offending ship just as long as Joe could keep it in view. With that, Devine moved north with the drag boat and we moved west, cleared the rocks, and set out an anchor. Examination of the offending engine revealed wiring burned beyond emergency repair; a trip home to the repair shops was in store. We called Joe and let him know. Joe told us he had lost the fisherman in the fog, and with that we called the detail off. We never did get enough firsthand information to prosecute that chap for fishing in the closed zone that day.

For the next twelve hours the *Rainbow* limped south toward

home, and I puked all the way. I got so sick that once I tried to go belowdecks and lie down in one of the bunks. I was so weak I couldn't even crawl up the eighteen inches from the floor to the bunk. That was it, I told myself, no more of this activity for any reason. Once back at the docks in Eureka, we tied the vessel up to her moorings, and then Ken and I headed for the restaurant where we had eaten our deadly breakfast. Once there, it was all Ken could do to keep me from killing the cook, not to mention ripping off his lips and feeding them to the nearest magpie. Needless to say, the manager reimbursed us for the cost of our breakfasts, and the restaurant was closed down for a week by the health department shortly after it received Ken's official report. A small reward for my puking throughout a sixteen-hour day.

Several days later Ken and I made a report to Captain Gray, our supervisor. The captain listened intently and seemed more interested in my well-being than in the operation. Several days later I found out the true meaning of his so-called concern. He had assigned me to the *N. B. Scofield,* an old LST converted by the state of California into a research vessel, as part of my mandatory cross training. Captain Gray didn't like game wardens with wildlife degrees, "goddamned biologists," he called them. He thought he had finally figured out a way to get me to quit. Needless to say, the German rose up in me, and the captain and I had quite a discussion—one in which I apparently shared my feelings with everyone on that floor of the building. Suffice it to say that my sea duty ended that day, and I did not have to go on the *N. B. Scofield* for research training. It seemed that my master's degree work would suffice.

I have enjoyed every day of my career since then. I have been at sea very little since that day, and that is just fine with me. If I have to go back to sea to further the battle for this world of wildlife, I will. But you can bet your bottom dollar, it won't be with a breakfast of chili under my belt. By the way, Hank never got that bottle of whiskey.

5

The Big One That Didn't Get Away

WORKING AS A TRAINEE state Fish and Game warden in Humboldt County, California, I teamed up with several senior officers, including the Fortuna warden, Herb Christie, to patrol the many miles of rivers and streams holding the fall runs of silver and king salmon. Hundreds of fishermen, some good and many in the outlaw category, pursued their fishing avocation during that season along the numerous pools and riffles frequented by the salmon. Many fishermen believe it is hard to beat the fine eating a fresh-run salmon with sea lice will provide. In addition, sport-caught, smoked salmon brought many hundreds of dollars into the pockets of those inclined to break the conservation laws to steal and sell from nature's pantry.

In those days the limit for all salmon species sport-caught on the Pacific Ocean or in the interior waterways was three. For some reason, when the salmon arrived in the offshore waters or the interior river systems it seemed as if just about everyone involved in fishing for this species lost not only their common sense but their ability to count as well. Over-limits, double trips (catching a limit, taking the fish home, and coming back for more the same day), snagging, use of gill nets, use of explosives, fishing at night, spearing on the spawning riffles, and the like were all too commonplace. Most Fish and Game wardens just sucked it up and redoubled their efforts to hold the line on the waterways in order for the salmon to get a reasonable escapement for future runs. Since the migrating fish were confined to the river systems, that was the area where most officers concentrated their efforts. It was here that the fish were finally to mate, spawn, and die. The success of future fishing depended on the salmon being able to procreate in such numbers that another run would be forthcoming several years down the pike. Hence, the officers would flock to the historic spawning areas and through their enforcement efforts allow that miracle of nature to work its magic.

Most people don't realize that for every thousand eggs laid, only two fish will survive to spawn at a later date, two, three, or four years down the line. With those odds, the officers did not have much problem working long hours in dangerous areas, often alone, to give the salmon a hand. Since my warden position was to act as backup to three senior wardens on their days off, I found plenty to do. A sixteen-hour day, seven days a week trying to protect the salmon along the many hundreds of remote miles of river system in three large California counties was just about all I could handle. In fact, I ran myself ragged, along with a lot of knotheads breaking the laws, and loved it.

During that particular period Herb Christie and I teamed up to try to catch the illegal salmon snaggers and night fishermen who plied their ugly trade along the Eel River in his district. During those days one could fish from one hour before sunrise until one hour after sunset. The rest of the night belonged to the fish so they could rest and continue their migration without disturbance. However, as I said, many fishermen lost their common sense when the salmon arrived and broke the conservation laws at will in order to catch the wily salmon. In the Fortuna area, Herb and I worked evening after evening to catch chaps using illegal snagging gear or fishing at night with their illegal Glo-Pups (a fishing lure that, when the light of a flashlight was directed at its surface, glowed in the dark waters for a few minutes after being cast out and was almost irresistible to salmon). Herb and I spent many evenings trying every trick of the trade we knew to hold the "thin green line" against outlaws of every kind. The bad guys, on the other hand, spent evening after evening trying to elude the local game wardens and, to be frank, were doing quite a good job. Keep in mind that those plying the illegal trade knew when and where they were going to violate the conservation laws. We knew only that the outlaws would be after the salmon somewhere along the many miles of river system.

Our goal was simple: to try to allow the salmon some rest as they proceeded upstream to take care of their ancestral duties. The snaggers too had a simple goal: to fill their freezers with the rich red meat a salmon took four years to put on its bones and could lose in a moment if snagged or illegally hooked after dark.

One place in particular drew all three players—namely, illegal fishermen, game wardens, and salmon—and that was a spot called Singley Pool. Singley Pool was a three-hundred-yard-long pool of deep, slow-moving water on the Eel River that was bordered on each end by long, exhausting riffles. After running the lower riffles, the salmon would slide into Singley Pool with relief and rest until their strength returned. Sometimes the salmon remained in this pool for several days before obeying the genetic commands that drove them on to their foreordained deaths. Therein lay the problem. A known or historic concentration of salmon will draw in the human predators, and this area drew in the good, the bad, and the ugly in record numbers.

Herb and I spent many an hour trying to work unobserved on the Singley Pool area in order to keep track of and maintain legal order among its many anglers. It was a tough proposition, no matter how we cut it. To get to the pool area proper, we had to cross a large, open dairy pasture in clear view of the outlaws for at least four hundred yards before we got to the fishing area. After many false charges we came to the conclusion that there was no easy way to make a successful approach and catch the lads in this fashion.

Frustrating a game warden like that is dangerous. The warden comes to think he is really being challenged, and with that, out of the ashes will come an idea guaranteed to give the bad guys a gut ache—not to mention a thinner wallet after citation time.

On one of Herb's days off, as I was driving into Eureka after a morning checking ocean fishermen in the Trinidad area, an idea on how to work the Singley Pool hit me like a ton of bricks. Turning my patrol car around, I drove out to where an old college friend called High Tide, whose real name was John, lived. Knocking on the front door of his fishing shack, I heard a voice yell, "Out back." I walked around the shack and came upon my friend dressing out four nice king salmon, about thirty pounds each. He was in the process of carefully removing the roe (egg sacks) from the females in order to make fish bait from them for use at a later date. When he looked up, High Tide's eyes told me he had not been expecting his friend the game warden.

"Morning, High Tide," I said.

He continued to look at me as if he were not happy to see me just at that moment. Turning his back to me in an attempt to shield what was lying on the cleaning table, he mumbled, "Morning." At the same time he carefully tried to slide one of the fresh salmon under a piece of tarp on the cleaning table. How the hell one slides a thirty-plus-pound salmon out of sight right under a game warden's nose I don't know, but it was a nice try.

"Where did all the fish come from?" I asked.

Turning back toward me, High Tide looked me right in the eye and said, "I caught them this morning on the Mad River just above the freeway bridge."

"All of them?" I asked.

"You know damn well I caught all of them," he replied, somewhat exasperated.

"All four, John?" I asked.

"Would you and Donna like one?" he inquired, his voice pitched higher than usual.

Laughing, I said, "John, I'm going to have to take all four of them since the limit is only three."

Turning back to the cleaning table, he turned off the hose that had been washing down the cleaning table and stuck his fillet knife in the dirt at his feet. "Can I at least have the roe?" he asked.

"Sure, John," I answered. "I don't need the guts for evidence on a fish seizure." He beamed, retrieved his fillet knife from the ground, and finished cleaning the fish. While he worked, I went back to the patrol car, retrieved my citation book, and walked back to High Tide and the objects of our attention. So as two friends visited, one cleaning fish and the other writing the one cleaning fish a citation for possessing an over-limit of salmon, the morning progressed. Once the salmon were cleaned, I placed evidence tags on them and High Tide and I sacked them up and placed them in the trunk of the patrol car. After we washed our hands, High Tide signed the citation and I gave him his copy. He folded the citation and put it in his shirt pocket.

"Why are you here?" he asked. Good old John, he knew me well enough to know I was always working an angle.

"John," I said, "I need to borrow your wetsuit."

He was aware that I wasn't a diver, or at least much of one, and asked, "What the hell are you up to now, Terry?"

I told him, "Don't ask, and I won't have to lie to you."

He smiled, knowing damn well I was up to no good, went into the back room of his fishing shack, and fetched me his wetsuit. It would be a tad small, but High Tide was the biggest of my friends who owned a wetsuit, so it would have to do. His big, sheepish grin told me all was well on the over-limit issue. I had caught him fair and square after he had done a dumb thing, and he knew it. I'm sure he caught the awkward grin on my face as well, but when there's only one game in town, everyone must play by the rules.

After a few words on the use and care of the suit, I was out the door and heading south to the Eel River. Passing Humboldt Hill, where I lived, I stopped by my home, put the evidence salmon in the state evidence freezer, and then picked up a few more needed items, including an old welder's glove my dog, Shadow, had dragged in from somewhere in our neighborhood. Then away I went.

I parked my state patrol car a mile or so below Singley Pool in a thick grove of red alder away from prying eyes and taking my gear, including the wetsuit, slowly walked upstream, moving carefully around any fishermen I discovered along the way. My timing was perfect: I arrived at the long riffle below Singley Pool at dusk. I waited for the honest fishermen to leave, then changed into the wetsuit, hid my uniform and gun under the riverbank, and slid into the cool waters of the Eel River to test my latest idea. Walking, crawling, and swimming my way upstream through the rough edge of the riffle, I entered the lower end of Singley Pool at about nine P.M. I rested for a bit to get my bearings in the protective cloak of night and tried to see if anyone was fishing for salmon close by. Sure enough, above me and about one hundred yards away was a small bunch of men illegally fishing after hours. The glow of their cigarettes gave them away in the inky night. An old saying of Warden Joe Devine's went through my mind. When the two of us had worked together at night and discovered outlaws by the glow of their cigarettes, Devine always used to say, "If you were in New Guinea, you would be dead now." He had been a soldier in the South Pacific during World War II, and I guess he was referring to the Japanese snipers. Boy, old Joe sure was right. Every time someone lit up or pulled on a cigarette, I could see it very clearly. Quietly moving upstream, I stopped just opposite the four lads fishing for salmon in violation of the laws of the state. At that point I was no more than thirty-five yards across the river from them and looking my prey right in the eye.

They were having a grand old time, knowing the game warden, dumb enough to drive across the extensive pastures adjacent to the fishing area at night, would give his position away with his headlights or the sound of his car and provide plenty of warning. So they weren't a bit worried, and their fun continued as different members of the party occasionally looked over the riverbank to see if anyone was driving across the pasture in question.

I stayed in the water about thirty to forty minutes watching these lads fish, gathering the information needed to prosecute each of them for fishing after hours. They were using the Glo-Pup lures, holding the flashlight to them in the palms of their hands to hide the light, then casting them out into the water for the unsuspecting salmon. The Glo-Pups were sailing by my head and landing right and left of my new position up to my neck in the river. When one landed not more than two feet away from my crocodile position, I quickly reached out with my gloved hand and grabbed it. I felt a hard jerk from the lit cigarette attached to the fishing rod. *Zzzzzzzz* went his reel as he jerked harder to really set the hook in his "salmon."

"Goddamn," hissed a voice, "I got a big one, a really big one."

Chuckling, I thrashed around in the water, all the time pulling and jerking on the lure. Soon I heard one of the others saying, "Get the net, get the net." Almost breaking out in a roar of laughter at this point, I kept my cool and kept pulling hard on the lure, splashing occasionally as a foul-hooked fish (one snagged somewhere other than its mouth) will do. It was too dark for the poor chaps to see me, and for all they knew they had a monster king salmon on the line—well, a monster at least.

Zzzzzzzzz went the reel again, and I heard a voice say, "Get a net, hell, get a gun. This son of a bitch is the king of all the king salmon. I bet he will go one hundred pounds." Three hundred twenty, I thought, grinning as I let myself be dragged toward their shore.

Imagine the fun I was having. God, it was great. For once the game warden had the upper hand, uh, glove, that is. Is this chap going to get a surprise! I chuckled to myself. I really had to work hard at not laughing aloud as my feet finally touched the river bottom next to the eagerly waiting fishermen. Still working toward my "fishing buddies," I kept up my thrashing and hell-raising in the water, hoping all the members of the fishing group would get close together to help the lad on the other end of the pole. If they did, it would make it easier to capture all of them in one fell swoop if I had to get physical.

As I "fought" my final few feet to shore, the lads were really getting excited. One lad said, "This is the biggest fish I ever caught; it must weigh at least one-fifty!"

Another fellow said, "Get ready, here he comes." Well, they had that right: here he comes. Standing up, I turned my flashlight on and shone it directly into four expectant faces, and they weren't disappointed in their surprise at the size of their "catch." Shaking off my welder's glove with the lure firmly attached, I said, "Good evening, gentlemen. State Fish and Game warden. You are all under arrest!"

You can't imagine the looks on their faces, illuminated by my flashlight. Two of the lads were frozen in their tracks upon seeing this thing rise from the river. The fellow with the fishing rod bent double from the hook caught in my glove dropped into the river as if he had been hit with a hammer. He started to wheeze, choke, and grab at his chest as if he were having a heart attack. I had apparently scared him so badly that he peed his pants, dropped into the river, and, being scared so badly, couldn't get his breath upon being confronted with this apparition from the river. I couldn't imagine what went through his mind when he expected a salmon and instead ended up with a huge man dressed in a wetsuit. The fourth fellow took two steps back and sat down hard on the riverbank, unaware that his wide tail end had just crushed his own fishing rod. Needless to say, it was an outstanding evening long remembered by all, especially by the one who had caught the big one that didn't get away. I gathered up all the fishing gear and issued them all citations for late fishing after the lad who had dropped into the river recovered. Then I thanked the gentlemen for being gentlemen, walked back out into the black of the Eel River, and quietly disappeared as I drifted to the opposite bank and out of sight. My little group of fishermen just stood there on their bank of the river as I crawled out of the water on the opposite side, trying to figure out what they had done to God to make Him so mad.

It wasn't long before word went out that the game wardens were swimming in the rivers at night, catching those who dared to violate the fishing laws. As a result of this night action, for the next month Herb and I couldn't make a salmon case along the Eel River if we tried, especially in the Singley Pool area. Herb's nature was such that he didn't say much about my little venture, but I could tell from the occasional approving look in his eyes that I had done well.

Fishing is truly a magnificent sport. No one holds an edge unless they cheat. But in cheating, you run the risk of discovery, and therein lies the problem. You never know what you will catch if you break the law long enough. But if you break the law while fishing, you may hook the biggest of fish—and it may be the one that doesn't get away.

6

The Gunnysack

ONE JUNE I WAS PATROLLING on foot along a small salmon-spawning stream off the Mad River in Humboldt County at midday. I was there to provide protection to the spawning salmon that had recently returned from the ocean to their ancestral home. Basically, my job as a state game warden was to identify the spawning grounds and make sure unscrupulous wildlife thieves were not in those areas spearing, snagging, or gaffing the fish as they tried to spawn. On that particular day I discovered that the stream was devoid of salmon on the lower reaches but loaded with them higher up. As I continued my rounds the coolness from the forest and stream and the intense quiet made a moment to remember. I always enjoyed the out-of-doors, and this moment helped to cement that love. A few bird calls added to the quiet, and the damp, rotting floor typical of a temperate rain forest made me move as softly as an early American primitive. Using that stealth, I quietly walked up on riffles that looked like good spawning areas, and the mad rush of the salmon across those riffles to deeper pools at either end for security told me the fish had already crossed humans in these reaches and had nothing but bad memories as a result. Piles of fish guts in the bushes and spear marks on the sides of some of the spawners told me these fish needed some top cover, and I was just the lad for that type of assignment—or so I thought. Noting that I was not far from several lumber mills in the Blue Lake area, and knowing the penchant of many of the lumber workers to slide around and bend the Fish and Game laws, especially by spotlighting deer and spearing salmon, I decided a little more work in this important spawning area might be in order.

Hiking another mile upstream, I happened on a black bear feeding on salmon and was able to leave without the bear ever knowing

I was there. On the way back I watched a pair of river otters killing and sharing a spawned-out male silver salmon. They too did not seem aware of my presence as I faded back into the cover of the forest. Circling widely around the areas most important to spawning and keeping the quiet needed for success, I hotfooted it for home. I figured I would take the rest of the day off and let the night find me on the salmon-spawning grounds, alone with nature and what it had to offer. I also figured that if humans entered that scene in my presence and did not honor the ritual currently being performed by the salmon, then I would count them as a bonus.

The next three nights found me on foot patrolling those areas of the stream I had identified as loaded with spawning salmon. I was dressed in black, wore tennis shoes for extra speed, and silently stalked the edges of the stream looking for any errant humans spearing or gaffing the fish. It was great sport, quietly moving over the damp forest floor and creeping up to the areas most likely to lure in the most dangerous game, as humankind is sometimes called. I used no light of any kind, just my senses and quiet, deliberate movement. I figured I would not disturb the fish, and if I ran across any man I wanted to be on him before he realized he was being stalked. That way, I figured, when I grabbed the offending soul, the scare would go a long toward keeping him off the salmon-spawning streams for a long time to come. Being grabbed by a six-foot-four, 320-pound man in the dark when you believed you were alone had to have an effect on the soul, or at least on the sphincter. That thought of protecting the salmon and possibly finding a lad along the stream who needed finding provided the spice for my detail.

About midnight one evening as I was making the rounds, I quietly slid up on one big, long riffle that earlier had held at least one hundred spawning salmon. Sneaking up to the edge of the bank that overlooked this feeder stream, I slowly drew my frame up to its full height and, standing alongside a grand fir, stood there in the cool and quiet of the night, watching the salmon play out the ritual that had been part of their destiny for eons. I could hear them running up the stream, hear the splashing as one male ran another off from his territory, and hear the females working to clear out redd, or spawning, sites with their tails, all going on under a full moon over the forest canopy. Fingers of light shafted down into parts of the forest and stream itself. At that moment parts of my world were black as a bucket of dark velvet, while others were draped in silver as only the moon can do. It was absolutely beautiful, not to mention very restful. I sat down under the tree, resting my tired back against the deep moss on the bark, anticipating a few quiet moments with my fish. I had sat there for about ten minutes, completely absorbed in the drama being played out below me in the stream, when all of a sudden I realized I had company! Across the stream, not thirty feet away, stood a huge form. Now, I am a rather large fellow, but the outline on the other side of the creek was even bigger then I, and by a very large margin.

I sat there fascinated by the ability of a person that large to move through the temperate rain forest understory in the manner of a tiger. After a few silent moments, this man–mountain moved into the middle of the stream among the salmon, carrying what appeared to be a long-handled fishing spear. The stream exploded with fish reacting to this intruder as the unmistakable sound of a metal spear striking the rocks reached my ears. At that point the instincts that came with being a game warden, a hunter of humans, took over, and I silently rose to my feet, using my tree for cover. I waited until this man successfully speared a fast-moving salmon, removed it from his spear once he reached the bank, and deposited it in what appeared to be a gunnysack after knocking it on the head to reduce its struggles. Good, I thought, I now have enough evidence to rack his old hind end in court in Arcata. My judge hated those who took the salmon in such unfair ways, and I couldn't wait to get this mountain of a man in handcuffs for his appearance before "the man."

Waiting a few moments on the bank for the fish to settle down, the poacher stepped back into the stream for another salmon. Since I had the evidence I needed to prove my case beyond a reasonable doubt, I didn't see any reason for this chap to keep on killing such a valuable resource, so I checked my gun to make sure it was fastened tightly in the holster. Knowing there might be a footrace or fight, I didn't want the pistol to fall out or be loose enough for this chap to grab it and use it against me. Stepping out from my place of concealment, I turned the beam of my flashlight directly on him and observed a huge man in bib overalls with his back to me, standing in the middle of the stream. Even from behind his massive red beard was readily apparent, sticking out on both sides of his face.

I thundered, "Hold it right there! State Fish and Game warden. You are under arrest."

The man instantly put his hands up into the cold, damp night air, still holding the spear, and began to plead with me: "Please, mister, don't shoot! I've got three little kids! Please don't shoot."

Feeling confident that I had this situation well under control, being immortal and all, I walked down the bank into the creek to handcuff the lad. He didn't move, just kept his back to me with his hands and spear held high.

Mistake number one. What he was doing was keeping the light out of his eyes and echo-locating me as I approached, splashing through the stream. He knew exactly where I was and exactly what he was going to do. Looking back over that incident today, after thirty-plus years of experience, I now know that I should have had him walk backward to me rather than walking up to him. As I drew near, I told him to hand me the spear. Mistake number two. Instead he slammed the butt of the spear backward, catching me right between the eyes. The blow knocked me down into the water, stunning me so completely that all I could see was purple, green, yellow, and orange flashes racing around in my head. I quickly struggled up and out of the water to defend myself against any other attack, which turned out to be unnecessary, for he was running toward the bank of the stream from which he had come. I drew my pistol to shoot and then realized I couldn't see well enough to take aim because I was still temporarily blinded by the impact of the spear. Needless to say, I was steaming! I should never have lost a man that large, not to mention one with the destructive potential to the salmon resource that he had shown.

My eyes eventually cleared, as did my head. All I had to show for my efforts was a knot between the eyes, a wet ass, and a severely deflated ego. Home I went with my knot and a small cut that was

not enough to alarm my wife. I told her I had walked into an overhanging limb in the dark. I did not tell her that I had screwed up
badly. I walked away from this encounter a wiser man, and determined that if I were faced with a like occasion in the future, the
outcome would be very different!

Several days later I talked this episode over with the senior warden in charge of the district where the incident had occurred. He
was a good friend and teacher of young game wardens who had
been assigned to that area for more than thirty years. After hearing
my story, he looked at me and then commenced to really chew out
my ass. He said, "That's the trouble with you college kids; you're
dumb as a box of rocks. You're a goddamned German hardhead, and
that's dumber still." He went on to tell me that in the "big war" he
had been in the South Pacific killing all the Japanese there, and he
had had plans to go next to the European theater and kill all my
countrymen for creating a goddamned big world ruckus, but he ran
out of opportunity because the war ended. I didn't know what that
had to do with the current situation, but that kind of violent xeno-
phobic commentary was Joe's way of showing affection. Damn,
with the hind-end chewing he gave me, he was saying he loved me!
After five more minutes of friendly abuse, he looked me over once
again and, satisfied that I would live, asked me to repeat the story
and not leave anything out.

I patiently told the story again, and I was sure I detected in his
eyes a look that told me he not only knew who the bad guy was
but how and when to get even. Joe was quiet for few minutes and
then said, "Tell you what, I'll call you in a couple of weeks and show
you how to handle this kind of situation so it is not repeated in the
future, by either party." There was no more explanation than that,
and I sure missed the clue at the tail end of his sentence.

I said, "Okay, but I want to go along with you and make the
arrest."

I noticed a strange look overtake Joe's Irish eyes again, but he
said, "Sure, no problem."

Just by the way he said it I could tell something was not right,
but I couldn't put my finger on it. Friendly mistake number three.

Two weeks to the day later, Joe called me and said to be at his house at six o'clock. When I got there, Pam, his lovely wife, had prepared a spaghetti dinner that I hadn't planned on, but I went ahead and ate anyway. One doesn't get my size by turning down good grub, and Pam was one hell of a cook. About nine o'clock we went out and checked for some reported illegal fishermen along the Mad River, citing most of them for fishing after hours, and then the two of us just generally dinked around. All the while I was getting more and more anxious to get going and get to the bottom of what Joe had in mind. About midnight Joe said, "Let's go," and man, I was more than ready.

Joe had been in his district so long and had developed his intelligence system to such a fine point that he knew exactly when to roll a wheel and when not to bother. Once we were on the dirt road next to the stream, we drove without lights almost to the same riffle where I had tried to apprehend the giant. I noticed when we quietly got out of the patrol car that Joe reached into the back seat to pick up a rolled-up gunnysack and brought it with us. I didn't think much of it except to assume he might plan to use the sack to carry back any evidence salmon we might seize. We quietly moved up to the edge of the stream adjacent to my riffle and lay down. Joe laid the gunnysack along his right side, and we waited.

About twelve-thirty A.M. we heard somebody quietly moving along the creek on the other side of the spawning riffle. Soon the noise broke out into the half-moon light, and it was the man-mountain, the same fellow who had thumped me between the eyes with the butt of his spear. I whispered to Joe that he was mine and started to get up so I could run off that bank, zip across the stream at a high rate of speed, and put a tackle on him that would break him right in half. Joe rested his hand on my arm and whispered in my ear, "That's the trouble with you young guys; you don't have the sense to just lie still."

I whispered back, "What the hell are we going to do?"

He said, "Watch."

I lay there on the cool streambank, watching my target, hoping I would get a chance to put a tackle on him that only his gizzard would appreciate, all the while aware that Joe was rustling that damn gunnysack. The next thing I knew, the whole damn world blew up. There was a tremendous explosion and a bright flash rolling off our bank toward the man-mountain that totally ruined my night vision. The next thing I heard was the target of my affections in the middle of the stream screaming louder than the devil himself.

I went up in the air about ten feet! In those days I had a crew cut, and it was standing straight on end! Then there was another roar and flash and more screaming from the man-mountain as he thundered out of the creek and went crashing through the brush like a bull moose.

Man, by now I didn't know what the hell to do. I had placed my hand on the butt of my gun and didn't know if I should draw, run, or shoot. About that time Joe solved my problem by yelling, "Run!" I was still standing there as if my feet were growing in the soil as Joe ran by. He slowed down just long enough to grab me by the shirt and get me going in his direction. It's amazing how fast you can run when you don't know why you are running, but everyone else is! We jumped in the patrol car and were out of there in a flash.

Bouncing down the dirt road like there was no tomorrow, I said, "What the hell happened?"

Joe pointed toward the back seat of the car, and lying next to the gunnysack was a 20-gauge auto-burglar double-barreled shotgun. He had loaded two shells with rock salt and seen to it that man-mountain was the backstop.

"Man," I said, "isn't that illegal?"

"I don't know," said Joe, "but nobody is going to know except you and me, and I don't plan on telling anyone." Another of those senior-warden things, I thought as my mind madly spun around the night's events. Joe headed for home, refusing to answer any more questions, and dropped me off at my patrol rig. "Nothing to nobody," said Joe. His tone was one I had not heard before but sure had little trouble understanding. We parted company, and I thought about the events of the evening all the way home. For the next four days I continued to stew about that night, but then I began to chuckle as I replayed the incident in my mind. Man, I bet that chap will think a long time before he goes salmon spearing again, I mused. What a shock. Pain right out of the darkest night just as you are having fun and filling your freezer with salmon. I began to laugh about the giant's misfortune until the tears came. That should teach him to whack a game warden in the head even though the dumb-ass game warden deserved it, I thought. Whoops, I just drove by a guy attempting to snag a salmon. That brought me back to reality, and off I went to address that problem.

On about the fifth day after our little "hoorah," Joe called and asked me to assist him in serving several warrants, and I told him sure, be right there. I met him a few minutes later, and out we went on Highway 299 to one of the area's mills called the Blue Lake Lumber Company. He pulled into an area of the mill where green lumber was pulled off a conveyor belt and stacked on pallets so it could air dry. Much to my surprise, there in all his glory pulling this "green chain" was my man-mountain, still wearing bib overalls but all wrapped up in swaddling gauze to control the running sores on his body from the rock salt. What little hair I had went up, and I was ready to fight again. But good old Joe laid a restraining hand on my arm and said, "Just listen and try to learn something that will serve you down the line." I hauled in my hackles and followed Joe's lead.

We approached man-mountain, and Joe called him away from what he was doing. Joe said, "I understand you ran into a little trouble the other night." The giant sort of glowered at Joe and then told him exactly where he could go and where he could stuff it.

Joe moved his five-foot-eight-inch, 155-pound body right up into the giant's face and told him, "That's the trouble with you; you want to screw me—you need to save that for the other sex.

"But," he continued, "let me tell you something. I pinched your grandfather, your dad, all your brothers, and half your cousins! I'm here to tell you that if I catch your blubber ass on my river with a spear again or clobbering one of my friends, it will be the last knowing thing you will ever do. Do you understand me?"

Man-mountain was at least two feet taller than Joe, but he just hung his head and answered, "Yes, sir."

Joe said, "That's good; now there will be no more problems on my river. Now, shake hands and the issue is done." They shook hands, and the giant extended his hand to me as he had been ordered. All I wanted to do was break his head, but the look in Joe's eyes told me a handshake was all that was in order, so I took his hand. After that there were no more words spoken as we turned and walked away.

I just shook my head and said, "I don't know how you do it, but you really do have a way with people."

Joe turned to me and responded, "Terry, don't ever forget, no matter their size or station in life, they come with two legs same as you and me and crap down between their boots same as you and me. There ain't no one who won't listen to reason, providing you back it up with two ounces of rock salt or the like." The way he looked at me told me that theory applied to thick-headed rookie game wardens of German descent as well.

I never forgot those words, and although I never had to resort to two ounces of rock salt, he was right. People are only what they are—some bigger than others, some meaner than others, but underneath they are all the same, if you get my drift.

7

Gut Feeling

IN THE EARLY FALL of 1966 I was a new state Fish and Game warden stationed in Eureka, California. As I went through the various steps, both academic and practical, of learning my new profession, I still found time to maintain old ties with college friends because I had only recently graduated. Donna, my wife, and I especially enjoyed the company of a fellow graduate student named Butch and his wife, Mary. Over the months, as this relationship developed into a strong friendship, we would get together on weekends, play cards, eat, and just have a merry old time that didn't require a lot of money. In those days such things were a whole lot simpler than they seem today.

One Friday evening Butch and Mary came over for dinner and an evening of cards. As usual, Donna had fixed an excellent meal, and the four of us were having the time of our lives playing cards and visiting. Then, along about midnight, I got an uneasy feeling. It's hard to explain that feeling, but it was one that came from deep inside. I could sense something about to happen, but that sensation was barely on the edge of reality and I could just as often pass it by as pay attention to it. I know that sounds funny, but some people can predict things about to happen, and that is what the feeling was like—not strong but with enough presence to make me uncomfortable, mentally and physically, if I ignored the feeling. My mother had the ability to foresee or predict events, and maybe I had that same gift, I sometimes thought.

However, up to that stage in my life I had not often experienced such things and was reluctant to say anything to anyone about the phenomenon. So I ignored this particular feeling and continued to have fun with my wife and guests. However, the feeling just kept getting stronger, becoming an almost physical presence, as the evening turned into early morning. Thoughts of putting on my uniform and going to the Snow Camp area above the town of Arcata kept overriding any thoughts of having a good time with Butch and Mary and ruining my concentration in general. Every time I got into a complex part of the card game, these feelings would sail right in and destroy my focus. That happened several times. The idea was always the same: that I should be in the Snow Camp area working illegal deer hunters. The sense never varied in strength or theme throughout the earlier part of the evening, and as the clock ticked on it was becoming more urgent, or so it seemed. I continued to try to ignore the feeling, but it persisted, and I guess it finally showed because Butch asked, "What is the matter with you? You're costing us the card game because you aren't keeping your mind on what's going on around you."

Looking at the group, I said, "I really feel like I should be up on the mountain. Something illegal is going on up there, and I should be there. I know it's weird, but I have had this damn feeling most of the evening that I should be up at Snow Camp. It's like a premonition, and the feeling is so strong it's almost physical." After letting those words slip out of my mouth, I felt like a fool.

There was a kind of embarrassed silence from my wife, and after a moment Butch said, "Nah, you're just dreaming." Seeing the discomfort this premonition was causing Donna, I dropped the subject and continued to play cards for another ten or fifteen minutes. By then the urge to get up on the mountain in the Snow Camp area was really fierce. I somehow knew that something illegal was going on up there, and I was being "called" to be there. Silly or not, that was how I felt, and the feeling obviously was not going away.

Finally I said, "That's it, Butch, I'm going up on that mountain come hell or high water."

"Terry, this is hogwash," Butch responded. "There is no scientific explanation for having a feeling that something wrong or illegal is going on miles from here. Damn, you just graduated with your master's degree and should know better than to believe in premonitions."

"Well, I'm going. If you want to come, let's go. The ladies can sit here and visit, and you and I can take a swing through the area and at least satisfy my curiosity. The Snow Camp area isn't far from here, and it shouldn't take long to run out the area."

Butch looked at me and answered, "I can't believe a grown man, especially a Humboldt State–trained man, would believe in this kind of crap."

"I can't help it; something is going on up there and I need to be there. Believe it or not, it's bugging the hell out of me, and I have to go see for myself."

Butch, seeing the determination in my eyes, threw up his hands and cards in disgust and said, "All right, I'll go with you, but we sure as hell are wasting our time." Butch was a straightforward kind of guy, one who didn't cotton to much that he considered extraneous to the business of life. In fact, because of his dogged, commonsense approach to life, his nickname at college was Pertinent Poop.

I hurriedly crawled into my game-warden uniform and shoehorned my six-foot-four-inch, 320-pound frame into my Mercury Comet patrol car, and off we went. A short time later we arrived on the west side of the tremendous deer area known locally as Snow Camp. The whole area was surrounded by ranches and lumber operations and was covered with second-growth forests, remnant redwood forests, and high-mountain grassy prairies. Snow Camp had a reputation as a favorite site for local employees of the lumber industry, or "brush okies," as they used to be called by members of the enforcement fraternity, to illegally hunt the Columbian black-tailed deer that foraged over the previously logged-over terrain.

Turning onto a narrow dirt road that led up the mountain and into the Snow Camp area, I noticed a heavy smell of dust in the air through my open window, not the kind you smell just after a car has driven down a dusty road immediately in front of you but the kind that hangs in the air from a car long past. The feeling was now stronger than it had been before, and it was as if it were leading me to the center of the source of its energy. I know that notion sounds stupid, but I was being dragged into battle without any idea why. Stopping the car, I turned off my headlights, and Butch and I sat there in the dark for about ten minutes to let our eyes adjust to driving with just a small sneak light that was fastened to the underside of my front bumper. As soon as we could see with this type of illumination, off we went, up past an abandoned farm and around a curve that led us by one of several old abandoned apple orchards that were favorite haunts for the local deer population. The whole time Butch kept after me for being goofy to believe premonitions and the like. I sat there and took it, just as I was taking into account the intense feeling that something was about to happen, and happen fast.

Coming slowly around the last curve by the top of one old orchard, I was surprised to meet another vehicle coming down the road without lights. We couldn't have been more than forty feet apart when both of us reacted. The instant the driver of this vehicle, a pickup, saw me, on went his lights and he zoomed past my vehicle with a vengeance, missing us by no more than a few inches.

"Holy crap," yelled Butch as he quickly pulled his arm in from the open window to avoid being hit by the onrushing pickup.

"Hang on," I shouted, knowing a high-speed chase over mountain roads was the next thing in order. I was on a narrow part of the dirt road and couldn't whip into a high-speed power turn, as I had been taught in the academy. So I raced up the road until I found a wide spot, spun a power turn, and came back the way we had come, with red light and siren waking up the night. The chase was on, but after about three miles of sliding around on the narrow, curving dirt mountain roads, the target of my affection pulled over and stopped, as did I.

Quickly stepping out of my rig to avoid being killed where I sat in case of a gunfight, I became aware of the tremendous amount of dust in the air created by our two sliding vehicles. I waited a moment for the dust to clear so I could see everything that went on in the vehicle I had just stopped. Approaching the driver's side of the pickup, I could see two very nervous individuals looking at each other as if a bear had just bitten them both in the hind end. I quickly scanned the bed of their pickup and immediately saw the reason for their longing expressions—two freshly killed does! Their

nervousness was understandable, as the killing of female deer outside the hunting season was a major Fish and Game violation in
California.

Standing behind the driver's door, I identified myself and asked
him to step out of the pickup, walk around to the front of the truck,
and place his hands on the hood. The driver did so without a pause.
With him under control, I looked into the cab and ordered the passenger to leave the vehicle in a like manner and do what his partner was currently doing. The lad scrambled out of the truck and
placed his hands on the hood. Neither said a thing, and it was pretty
obvious that they were both scared to death. Reaching into the
front seat, I picked a loaded .22 pump-action rifle up off the floor
and pulled a still-warm spotlight from under the passenger's seat.
Walking around the front of the pickup and standing behind both
chaps, I advised them that they were under arrest for the illegal possession of two does and that they were both going to the local
"bastille" in Eureka. I emptied the rifle and laid it and the spotlight
on the ground behind me, then gave the lads specific instructions
on how to spread-eagle, which they did. I searched them and handcuffed them together for transport.

With the urgency of the moment over, I realized I had forgotten
my partner, Butch, or Pertinent Poop. Ushering my two prisoners
back toward the patrol car, I could tell from Butch's wide-eyed look
that his recent experience of chasing a rapidly fleeing vehicle down
a dirt road had left its mark. Looking into his eyes, I could that see
he was reliving the whole episode from the "gut feeling" I had had
earlier to the placement of wildlife criminals in the back seat of my
patrol car for transport to jail. The grin on his face read thrill, pure
and simple. I think I identified another look in his eyes as well, that
expression of a hunter of humans. But on second thought, I dis-
missed that notion as a misreading. Without further ado I loaded
one of my deer-killing chaps into the front seat of the patrol car and
his partner behind him in the back seat. I had Butch sit in the rear
seat behind me and told him that if the lads started anything he
should keep them off me until I could get the car stopped and deal
with the problem.

"We ain't going to cause you any problems, mister," came a weak voice from one of my prisoners. I had to grin. They were right. I weighed in at probably fifty pounds more than my two prisoners combined. Without a word, Butch and I headed for Eureka, and then it hit me! The gut feeling I had had earlier was gone! There was nothing but a calm, almost a void. I chalked the gut feeling up to experience, one I would watch for and use in the future if given a chance. The poachers were transported without any problems to the county jail, where they were booked. The two deer were hung in the state evidence locker for later use in court and subsequent distribution to the needy, and the rifle, ammunition, and spotlight were secured in an evidence locker for later forfeiture. Butch and I happily headed back to the ladies. Arriving home, we had a tall tale with which to beguile our wives to make up for their ruined evening.

It was too late to continue our card game, so Butch and Mary left, but not before we decided we would get together the following night and pick up where we had left off. The next night Butch and Mary showed up about seven P.M. and had dinner with us, and the card game commenced. Throughout the game, the previous night's "hoorah" was the centerpiece of the conversation. Butch just couldn't get over what had happened, from the gut feeling to the apprehension of the two lads with the deer. We had lots of laughs, and the men beat the hell out of the ladies in cards (as we always did).

About eleven P.M., my bride decided it was time for refreshments and brought out her homemade tarts, which were not of this world and one of my very favorite treats. I helped her serve the coffee, and then, *wham,* I got that feeling in the pit of my stomach again! Just like that, *ka-boom!* Knowing what the odds were against its being true two nights in a row, I kept my thoughts to myself and passed my gut feeling off to a heavy but good dinner. The strategy didn't work. I was getting a strong sense that I needed to be up on that same mountain again. In fact, the feeling was telling me to head for Snow Camp!

I said to Butch, "I'm getting that feeling again, like I need to be back up on Snow Camp."

Butch looked long and hard at me, then said, "Let's go!" I could again see that quick, almost gunfighter look I had observed in his eyes the night before. I thought, How can that be? Butch is a self-acclaimed dyed-in-the-wool biologist, not what I would call game-warden material. The feeling waved over me again, and I quickly forgot those thoughts. This time there was no arguing—get in Butch's way now, and you would be stepped on! Brother, what a change a couple of arrests can make in a chap. I got into my uniform, and out the door and into my patrol car we went. The women could not believe what they were seeing in their two grown men.

Butch and I roared up through the back road toward the Snow Camp area and, for the second night in a row, turned off on the same dirt road. Stopping the car, I doused our headlights, and we sat there letting our eyes adjust to the velvet dark of a forested night. We rolled our windows down and let the night roll in, bringing its smells as well as its coolness. There it was, the smell of dust in the air. Someone had recently been on this seemingly deserted back-country road. I looked over at Butch and put a finger to my nose. He nodded, and the look in his eyes told me he also smelled the dust. Good, he might make a game warden yet, I mused as I slid the patrol car into gear and turned on my sneak light. We slowly and quietly proceeded up the mountain road past the abandoned farm, past the orchards, and on along the road for about another mile.

Turning a corner by an old wheat field, I spotted a pickup truck parked in the middle of the road not thirty yards away, with its headlights on and both doors flung open. As we drew closer, I saw two lads run out of the brush along the side of the road by their pickup, jump into the truck, and turn off their lights, hoping they would not be observed. I figured they had heard the soft crunch of gravel under my tires as I slowly worked my way toward them. Well, the jig was up. On went my headlights and red light, and this time, as I moved up to their vehicle, I blocked the road so there would be no escape. I quickly stepped out of my vehicle, sprinted through the headlight beams, and moved to the driver's side of their truck.

"State Fish and Game warden," I thundered and at that moment noticed by the light of my flashlight that both men had a lot of fresh blood on their hands, pants, and shoes. I asked them to step out of their vehicle, quickly checked them for weapons, turned them around so they were facing me, and took a good look at them. These were two of the sickest-looking chaps I ever saw. Suspecting what had happened, I instructed both of them to hand me their driver's licenses, which they did. Then I removed a .22-caliber bolt-action rifle from the front seat of their vehicle and a spotlight from the floor that was still plugged into the cigarette lighter. It was apparent that these lads were scared to death. Neither one was bigger than a pint of piss, and both were scarcely more than twenty-three years old.

Towering over them, I thought I would try something that could perhaps be added to my budding pool of field law enforcement experience. "Lads," I said, "I want you to go back out into that brush patch and bring me the deer. Remember, I am holding your driver's licenses, and if you run I'll have warrants for your arrest by morning." The hard look I gave them was not lost on the two, and there was no argument as they headed out into the field under the watchful eye of my patrol-car spotlight. They soon brought out a freshly killed deer. Dragging that doe to the side of my patrol car, they dropped it and then looked to me for more instructions. My gut feeling was still there, so, again looking them both in the eye, I told them to go back and get the other one. Now, keep in mind that Butch and I had not actually seen these men do anything. I would have found the deer myself by just backtracking the lads. However, it was more fun to let the killers hang themselves.

The two looked at each other as if the bear from the evening before had bitten them in the hind ends too. A quick look at Butch, who was standing by the open passenger door of my patrol car, confirmed that he was enjoying this little drama being played out along the roadside in the middle of nowhere. Again there was no argument, and back the two chaps went to get another deer, which they dragged out and laid alongside the first one. My gut feeling was now gone, but I asked them in a hard voice, "Are there any more?"

They replied meekly, "No."

"Butch, take my extra flashlight and go take a look." Butch went and looked around, only to find that their answer had been honest.

I advised the two lads that they were under arrest for the illegal possession of two does, then searched them, handcuffed them, and transported them to the jail in Eureka, just like the two men from the night before. Again, all the evidence was cared for and secured.

Until then, Butch had been a dyed-in-the-wool biologist, or a researcher type. But it was apparent that he had really enjoyed these last two evenings, and he didn't lose that look in his eyes that told me he was hooked on this sport of hunting your own kind. Soon after that evening we lost touch for a while, and I didn't know how deep the feeling had gone until he called me about a year later and told me he was now working for the state of Nevada as a game warden in the Elko district. Brother, what a turnaround! He went on to tell me how much he had enjoyed those two evenings and that he had decided that he agreed with my philosophy that it was better to act now through law enforcement than to wait several years for the biologists or researchers to do the wildlife management work. Butch said, "Catching those poachers really reinforced for me the true meaning of your wildlife management philosophy, and that is why I am a game warden today."

"Butch," I asked, "did you ever get that gut feeling like I used to?"

"Yes, I have. I follow it up every time, and it's amazing—about 80 percent of the time there is something wrong and I'm lucky enough to be in the middle of it." He went on to thank me for that little lesson in life and said, "I now trust my gut feelings, and it has paid off many times, not only in catching somebody but in saving me from danger as well."

I saw Butch and Mary only twice after that, but both seemed to be enjoying their life in the great state of Nevada. I have gotten that gut feeling many thousands of times since those evenings so long ago. I too have found its accuracy to be unerring not only in giving me advance notice of an upcoming event but in reducing my personal danger as well. For over thirty-two years my gut feeling has put many not-so-nice people behind bars or at work to pay off fines for wildlife violations. Who says God is not on the side of game wardens?

In the end it just goes to show what I know about genetics and game wardens. When God creates game wardens, He gives them a bent gene. It might take a while for that gene to manifest itself, through the heat of battle or even through such a small event as the smell of dust in the air, but if you have the gene, you will come to know it. It also seems that when the November moon is full, another game warden is born somewhere, and many an outlaw pays the price. Come to think of it, it was November when Butch, Mary, Donna, and I played those card games and I got that gut feeling. *Hmmm.*

8

I Just Wanted a Fish for My Sick Wife

ONE HOT SUMMER AFTERNOON I was patrolling the Klamath River in the old Fish and Game undercover truck in an attempt to apprehend any chaps inclined to illegally snag salmon and sturgeon. For the information of anyone not so inclined, *snagging* means dragging large, weighted treble hooks over the backs of fish resting in deep pools, setting the hooks, and dragging the prey to your net and freezer. In many parts of the land, such as California, this type of fishing is illegal because its efficiency acts to drastically reduce the populations of some fish species. Also, in many people's minds snagging is an unfair and unsportsmanlike practice. The country I was in that summer afternoon was full of wild, deep-running rivers, most of them full of salmon and two species of sturgeon and surrounded by populations of lumber workers and Native Americans, many of whom thought that obeying the conservation laws of the land was something they didn't need to do. Hence my fateful presence on the river that day, which was to change me and my way of doing business with people for the rest of my life.

The cool canyon air felt good flowing over my sunburned left arm as it hung out the window of the Fish and Game truck. I moved along State Highway 96, executing the turns of the twisting mountain road as it followed the beautiful, crystal-clear Klamath River meandering below me. My thoughts were lost in time as I surveyed the steep cliffs, extensive evergreen forests, cliffside waterfalls, ferns, and the river below, with its beautiful salmon riffles and pools interspersed with stretches of outstanding spawning beds, all unfolding before me.

Swinging around one particularly sharp turn, I chanced to see a man far upriver finishing a series of jerking and retrieving motions with his fishing rod, indicating that I had a potential illegal snagger working the fish, most likely salmon. Driving by in such a manner as not to arouse his suspicion, I pulled off the highway and down to the river on the first dirt road leading to the sandbar where I had seen my snagging suspect. Turning off onto another sandy road that paralleled the river, I was heading toward the pool where I thought my suspect was when all of a sudden I realized I had driven right up to where he was fishing, and there I was in plain sight. Damn! Nothing like screwing up a good case, I thought as I pulled off the road and into an open place where he could see me. Since I felt I had lost the edge on this chap, I went through the exaggerated motions of retrieving my fishing gear from the back of the truck so he could see I was just a "fisherman."

That part of the ruse behind me, I started slowly walking toward him, all the while appearing to examine the river closely as if looking for a good fishing spot in the pool he was fishing. As I continued my charade, out of the corner of my eye I could see the chap closely watching me as if trying to determine whether I was really a fellow fisherman or a game warden. Kneeling at the edge of the pool just thirty or so yards below my suspect, I began to rig up my fishing outfit, all the while ignoring the lad. Finally satisfied that I was a member of the fishing fraternity, he went back to his fishing as if I didn't exist. It was very apparent that he was snagging, and with a vengeance, I might add. He would hurl a weighted hook clear across the pool, let it settle a few feet down, then jerk the rod violently. Then he would let the hook settle again and repeat the jerking motion until the snagging gear was at his feet. Then the casting and retrieving would begin all over.

Getting together my gear, a two-ounce spoon affair, I began to cast in the large slow-moving pool below where he was fishing. This gave me the opportunity to observe his snagging casts and memorize his method of operation for later testimony. Fishing like a normal fisherman and not getting any bites, I started moving slowly toward his position without getting in his way. The object of my attention had completely forgotten me as any kind of threat and continued to fish to his heart's content. I kept moving slowly upriver until the two of us were on the same long, quiet section of the fishing hole. Kneeling down on the sandbar a few feet away from my snagger, I prepared my rig for what appeared to be an afternoon's fishing for salmon by changing my terminal gear, this time to a bright red spoon. My snagger continued to be deeply engrossed in his illegal activity, which allowed me time to examine my prey as well as his illegal gear (in California, violators were charged both for the act of snagging and for the use of illegal fishing or snagging gear). While I was still pretending to be fussing with my equipment, my snagger made a long cast into the river, giving me the opportunity to step over to him, reach out and grab the fishing rod and reel from his surprised hands, and at the same inform him that I was a Fish and Game warden.

This move gave me the evidence I needed to show in court the snagging gear he had used and to identify it as his; it also kept him from throwing the entire fishing outfit into the river, as most snaggers were wont to do in an attempt to beat the "use of illegal gear" charges. However, such attempts rarely worked because when testimony of the officer and the accused conflicted, the word of the officer almost always carried the day. Then the suspect was usually charged with Section 5652 of the Fish and Game Code for littering, which would cost an additional $100.

The man absolutely froze. I reeled in his line with the snagging gear still attached and laid his rig down on the sandbar. Taking out my badge, I formally identified myself and told the very quiet and unmoving chap, "Let's walk back to your pickup."

Once at his pickup and out of sight of other fishermen on that section of the river, I asked for his driver's license because I needed that information to issue him a citation. He quickly produced his driver's license and fishing license, all the while remaining very quiet. His silence was a little odd but not all that unusual, so I commenced to write him a Fish and Game citation for snagging and use and aid of illegal fishing gear. In those days snagging was a major fishing offense and drew a $250 fine and revocation of fishing rights for a year.

Use of snagging gear was also up there, with a $250 fine, revocation of fishing rights for a year, and confiscation of the illegal fishing gear. Even at the value of today's dollars, that was a tough penalty.

I looked at my suspect's vehicle to get the license-plate number for the citation and noticed that he was driving a brand-new Ford three-quarter-ton pickup. When I asked for his occupation, as required on the citation, he responded, "Mill superintendent at the Arcata Redwood Lumber Company."

Now, those guys made about $2,000 per month, or about $1,400 more than I did as a game warden. Big money, to say the least. Finishing the citation, I noticed that the man still hadn't said much. He was unusually quiet. You could tell by his body language, lack of eye contact, downcast looks, and very soft voice that he was really ashamed of what he had done.

Unable to leave well enough alone, as some game wardens will do, especially rookies, I asked him, "Why were you out there snagging the poor damn salmon? It is all that poor fish can do to get past everyone to get to his spawning ground, and then at the last moment have to run through a set of snag hooks. You make enough money to go out and buy any fish you want. You care to share with me why you went out on that river and joined the ranks of the rest of the damned outlaw snaggers?"

He turned and looked at me with eyes that just oozed hurt. He tried to speak several times, and nothing came out. Finally, when he was able to speak with an emotion-filled voice, his response caught me somewhat flatfooted. He said, "Mister, I was just trying to catch a salmon for my sick wife."

I said, "Hogwash. Go down and buy her one at Lazio's in Eureka and leave the damn salmon in the river alone."

The man gave me a look that was not of this earth. It was soft, hurt, ashamed, yet defiant in its defense of his cause. His eyes literally reached for my heart. As I said, it was a look not of this world but one I've seen and come to recognize many times since in my line of work.

He opened up and said, "You don't understand. I just brought my wife home from the hospital. She is dying of cancer. She hasn't been able to eat much at all, and the doctors don't give her much time. She has cancer of the stomach, and I've just had to sit and watch my best friend and childhood sweetheart slowly dying in front of me. Do you know what that's like?

"I just spent every dime I had in paying for every treatment the doctors could think of to make her well. I was unsuccessful, and now I'm so broke it isn't even funny. I don't have any more money to my name, not a single dime." He continued, "By God, today she felt like she could eat, and she was really hungry for a salmon dinner. I was not going to deny her that. I know it's only several more weeks and she will be gone, and I just had to get her that salmon."

Trying to step back emotionally from his words, I lamely said, "Getting the fish illegally isn't going to cut it. Sign the citation here; this is just a promise to appear and not an admission of guilt." Without any further discussion he signed the citation, took his copy, folded it into his shirt pocket, and quietly walked away. My eyes followed him to his pickup and watched him drive off with the river dust remaining as evidence of the moment I had just experienced. Finally shaking the conversation off my shoulders, I put away my gear and placed my citation book back in the glove box of the undercover truck. Wiping the sweat from my brow, I took one more look at the river and the fishermen. Satisfied that all was well, I stepped into the pickup and started it up.

A few moments later I pulled back up on the highway and continued my search for those along the river breaking the law. Driving down the road now was not as it had been earlier. I just couldn't get that look he had given me out of my heart and soul. The intensity and reality of those words kept winging through my head until it began to bother the hell out of me. A driving force in me kept saying, "Open up, look, try to understand." I did understand, I told myself. The man broke the law and would now have to pay the price. If he wanted a fish, he could have gotten one from the Salvation Army or some church group, I thought. Somehow, though, nothing seemed to provide the answer I was seeking.

Without thinking, I picked up the radio mike hidden under the seat of the undercover truck and called the Eureka Fish and Game office. I knew Nancy, our regular dispatcher, would get to the bottom of this and fast. Her husband worked at the hospital as the administrator, and he would have the answer I was looking for. I asked Nancy to call the hospital in Eureka and ascertain whether this fellow's wife had actually been there. Giving her the name of the chap who had received the citation, I figured the rest would be easy. Resetting the mike, I noticed that the driving force in me had lessened a bit, but it was still a force to be reckoned with. Shortly afterward, my captain called me on the radio and asked if I was near a land line. I told him there was a telephone in the next town, and he said, "When you get there, call me."

Moments later I had the captain on the telephone. He told me that the fellow's wife had indeed been in the hospital and had just recently been released with less than thirty days to live. Stomach cancer, Captain Gray said. Thanking the captain, I slowly hung up the phone as the words *stomach cancer* spun around in my mind.

Slowly getting back into the patrol truck, I sat for a while as the wings of the driving force flew around inside me again. I *had* done my job, and very professionally, I might add. Somehow that didn't seem so important now. In addition, as if I needed more added to my quandary, the citation had been issued in a judicial district presided over by one of the world's toughest judges. The judge was a fifty-eight-year-old grandma type, but what a tiger. She was very supportive of all her officers, and I couldn't have asked for better judicial backup in a very tough area and time where your fists were often used as much as your citation book. She was at her toughest when lied to or if an offender was a salmon snagger or used illegal snagging gear. Plain and simply, she hammered anyone who fell into those categories. Also, she had a policy designed to protect the unfortunates who came before her bench: she would not discuss any case with the law enforcement officer before the cited person had pleaded in open court and had his or her complete say. Then, and only then, would she talk to the officer about the matter. She flatly refused to listen to us on any matter before court, and I saw many an officer ripped to pieces by this woman when they crossed that self-imposed line of judgment.

I clearly remembered our first meeting when I had moved into the area to help with the enforcement of the Fish and Game laws— wow! At this introductory encounter she told me, among other things, "Don't ever try to talk to me about any pending matter you might have coming before me. If you do, I will rip your ass clear off. Is that clear, Officer Grosz?"

This directive, even coming from a fifty-eight-year-old woman no bigger than a pint of piss, was clearly understandable, especially when I considered the determination in her voice.

Knowing that I needed to talk to her about *this* matter, I made an appointment and visited her in her chambers. I said, "Your honor, I need to talk to you about a recently issued citation. I clearly remember what you told me during our first meeting, but this situation is so unique I just know you would want me to discuss it with you prior to any legal action." I thought that if I put it to her that way I would be home free and clear.

She stopped me quickly by saying, "Terry, you know my policy. I do not want to discuss it."

"Judge, I have to talk to you about this one." There was no way I could let her brush me aside like that. I thought, You have to try harder, Terry. I noticed that she was examining me closely. I wasn't sure if it was for a damn good rear-end chewing or a casket, but she was really looking me over with those gunfighter eyes of hers.

She said, "All right, talk to me, but if I feel you are out of line I will slap your ass in the county jail for six days for contempt of court with all the other boneheads you sent there, do you understand, Mr. Grosz?"

I said, "Yes, ma'am, I do."

"Commence," she said, and the blue-steel eyes told me I had better do it right. So I told my story about the fellow, the snagging, and the sick wife. Now came the hard part, or the "six days in jail" part.

I said, "Judge, I wasn't able to confirm the man's story about the sick wife until just recently, and would you, well, please be lenient in this matter."

Those steel-blue eyes turned cobalt blue and she said, "You are out of line to ask me that, and I resent what you just did! If you weren't like a son to me I would blast your ass into the county jail so fast that, even as large as you are, the jailers wouldn't see you go by! These goddamned people know better, and he will just have to pay the price."

I responded, "Yes, ma'am," realizing that to go any further was sheer folly. I left the judge to her thoughts and walked out the door of her chambers into the cold sunlight. Damn, what a hard woman she could be, I thought.

Feeling even worse, I went to Hoopa and bought a fresh salmon from the grocery store. It was a nice big chinook, and I had the merchant wrap it well. Opening up the citation book, I retrieved the man's address and drove to his house. The man saw me drive up and walked off the porch and over to my truck. "Yes, sir," he said, and then his voice trailed off. I had lifted the big salmon in its identifiable package out the window and into his arms. Tears came to his eyes as I said, "Enjoy, see you," and drove off. At least I saw to it that the man had a fish for his wife's dinner. Damn dust in my eyes, it is making them water. I guess I will have to vacuum the floor in this truck, I thought.

A week later, with a lot of trepidation, I appeared in court with my snagger. The judge's usual practice was to open the investigative file, read it, and then ask the defendant to step forward and enter his or her plea. My fellow, carrying the weight of the world on his shoulders, stepped forward and with downcast eyes full of shame pleaded guilty. Her courtroom practice also was to ask the arresting officer if he or she had anything to offer. I stood up, with the full ass-chewing she had given me earlier still fresh in my mind, and had started to provide support for my snagger when, to my surprise, the judge abruptly waved me back to my seat. I stood my ground and was starting once more to speak when a look at my judge's eyes told me that to do so would put me in harm's way.

I slowly sat down. Without further ado, she fined my chap $500 for each of his two offenses, gave him a year in the county jail, forfeited all his fishing gear, and revoked his fishing license for three years. I was sick. This poor guy had just had the world collapse around his ears. He had tried the best way he knew how to show love for his wife and for that was being reamed in a court of law. That was more than I was going to put up with, I said to myself. I stood up again, determined to have my say in court and to hell with "six days in the county jail." This time the judge put her finger to her lips in a gesture for me to remain silent. Standing there and sensing a surprise move, I did. She then suspended the $1,000 fine, suspended the jail sentence, suspended the revocation of fishing rights, and returned his fishing gear. Instead she put my lad on one year's probation for his offenses.

She then told him that if he ever appeared before her court again she would throw him into the county jail for one year. She finished by telling him to get his fishing gear and get out of her court, which he did in all due haste. Then, with a look and tone in her voice that told me to pay attention, she said, "Officer Grosz, will you meet me in chambers when court is over?" I nodded and sat through the rest of her courtroom activities, waiting for the proceedings to end so I might see what she wanted.

When she entered her chambers she took off her robe, sat down, looked at me, and then motioned for me to sit down. We sat there for a few seconds, and then she commenced to chew my ass clear off in language that would have made any sailor proud. All I could say was, "Yes, ma'am," to each of her charges. Looking back on this event, I think it had to be quite a sight. A 105-pound female (albeit a judge) chewing the hind end clear off a six-foot-four-inch, 320-pound game warden. All I could do was hang my head because I knew I had crossed her lines of judicial procedure and ethics, and this was her way of getting her point across. She plain and simply wanted no part of anything regarding any incident in question until the day of court. She felt so strongly about the fair-and-objective principle that she in no way wanted to compromise her objective decision and treatment of all in her charge and really meant what she said about prior knowledge of a case.

When she finished, which seemed to me to take forever, she said, "Now, come here."

I got up out of my chair and walked around the desk to her chair.

She said, "Bend down."

I said, "What?"

She repeated, "Bend down," and I did. She then gave me a kiss on the cheek and said, "Don't ever bring me a case like that one without letting me know the circumstances in advance. I appreciate what you did very much." With that, she rose and left the room, leaving one very large and confused game warden to himself and his thoughts. I was surprised, to say the least, at what had occurred that morning. I also came to the realization that I could walk her line, but I had better walk it very carefully.

A lesson that I learned at that moment is that everyone is a human being, no matter what they may have done. Treat them like human beings and you will find that your life, when you get near the end of that gift, will be a little brighter for your efforts.

I bet that fellow never snagged another salmon as long as he lived. Thirteen days later his wife died, but not before she had had several good salmon dinners courtesy of a young officer who had learned something on the Klamath River that day.

9

A Case of Crabs

IT WAS THE FIFTH DAY of Dungeness crab season off the north coast of California. I was standing on the bow of the *Rainbow,* a thirty-five-foot Fish and Game patrol boat, as it knifed its way north from Eureka to a section of Dungeness crabbing grounds off the Pacific coast. The *Rainbow* passed many fishing boats as it sped through the waves, plowing through the troughs and surfboarding down the backs of the crests. It was a typical stunning north coast day of brilliant blue sky, warm sun, and fairly smooth water with just high swells. The usual fog bank lay thirty or so miles to the west, and I gave thanks to God because I wasn't seasick yet. At the helm was Lieutenant Ken Brown, a close friend, excellent boat driver, and California state Fish and Game warden of twenty-plus years. I was his boarding officer (when I wasn't too seasick), a rookie game warden with just about one year of experience. At the time I loved sea duty and relished my interaction with the commercial fishing fleet, especially the work associated with boarding fishing vessels while at sea to make sure they were complying with state Fish and Game regulations. There was always an element of danger that added to the excitement when boarding at sea like pirates of old, especially if the person boarding fell between the vessels into the open sea during the transfer.

When we planned a boarding operation, Ken would approach the commercial fishing vessel from amidships and form a T with the two boats. Standing in the bow holding a short nylon rope attached to a stanchion for support, I would wait until the decks of both boats, pitching up and down, were level and then would jump from the *Rainbow* to the fishing vessel to be checked. Once aboard, I would check to make sure all of the fishermen (including the cook) had valid commercial fishing licenses, that their fishing gear (depending on the species pursued) was legal, and that their catch was legal and within the limits established by the Fish and Game Commission. It was a great duty in spite of the danger and, for the most part, obstinate fishing boat skippers and crews. Reboarding the *Rainbow* was a repeat of the initial boarding process except that I had a smaller deck to land on. However, the foredeck of the *Rainbow* had been sanded when painted, and when one's feet hit that deck they "stuck," so reboarding, though somewhat of a challenge, was not too bad unless the action was taking place on a high, rolling sea. Then things got a little dicey, to say the least.

Forgetting my job for a moment as we sped along at about twenty-five knots, I stood on the *Rainbow*'s bow and drank in the sights and smells as well as the forward motion of our boat meeting each swell. The pungent smell of saltwater, occasionally mixed with faint diesel fumes as we crossed the numerous wakes of fishing vessels, kept me in the world of reality. Standing on the plunging bow of a speeding vessel while it navigates through twenty-foot rollers is an experience one does not soon forget. The bow on which I was standing would drop into the water until the sea was just inches from my feet. Then the *Rainbow* would spring back up, crest a wave, surf for fifty to sixty feet down the back of the wave, and repeat the process time after time. It was easy to find yourself transported back in time by the wind on your face, the warmth of the sun at your back, and the water all around.

Ken's voice brought me back to reality with the words, "Let's board that one." Ken was pointing to the *Ella D,* out of San Francisco, off our port beam (left side). The *Ella D* had a reputation for being a little greedy and prone to push the limits of the law. Ken and I had cited the whole crew several times before for commercial fishing violations, and the boat was always a good bet.

Ken drove the *Rainbow* alongside where the skipper could see us and then hailed the *Ella D* with the outside speaker. He informed the skipper that we wished to board the boat and asked him to please come to. You would never have guessed that Ken's instructions had been heard. The *Ella D*'s skipper kept looking straight ahead and just ignored the Fish and Game patrol boat cruising alongside. Ken looked at me and then, with a determined expression, brought the *Rainbow* right up next to the speeding commercial fishing vessel, probably fifteen to twenty feet off, and again hailed the *Ella D.* This time the *Ella D,* in response to Ken's closing action, made a ninety-degree turn to port, forcing us to quickly adjust and pursue again from a new angle. That maneuver pissed Ken off, and he flew the *Rainbow* (a much faster boat) right alongside the *Ella D* and turned on our siren. The skipper knew that the next move on our part was to cite him for failure to allow us to board the boat for an inspection. To prohibit an inspection would automatically cost him his commercial fishing license, so he slowed down to a quick stop, which again mandated that we make a quick adjustment.

By now Ken was steaming! "Tiny," he said, "if that bastard has anything wrong, *anything,* you issue him a citation."

I nodded as I got set to do my job. This was the fun part. One misstep and I was in the drink, with the possibility of being crushed between the two pitching boats. With that incentive, I always jumped hard onto the other vessel just in case. Jumping back onto the smaller *Rainbow,* as I said earlier, was also a challenge but not quite as dangerous.

The timing of my jump was critical, but Ken was a great boat man and I had a lot of confidence in his boat-handling abilities. He maneuvered the *Rainbow* in at the standard T boarding angle, bringing it to within a few feet of the pitching vessel to be boarded. When the decks swung more or less even, I jumped onto the *Ella D* as Ken quickly backed the *Rainbow* away to avoid a collision. Ken would wait just a few feet away from the commercial fishing vessel, which was now allowed to proceed toward its original destination, watching me as I ran the routine Fish and Game checks.

Verner, the *Ella D's* skipper, was pissed, to say the least. Being six-foot-four and "touching bottom" at about 320 pounds, I was not too concerned. He was always in a bad temper, so I just kept a close eye on him and his activities and we usually got along just fine. Today was different. Verner grabbed a fish pew (an instrument like a pitchfork with one tine, used to rapidly sort fish after they have been dragged up from the depths by a drag net and dumped on deck) and waved it in my face. Wrong thing to do. Possession of a fish pew on a drag boat was a violation of state law because the user, in order to use the pew properly, had to spear each unwanted fish in the catch and toss it overboard. That meant the speared fish would die, thereby wasting a bottom-fish resource. Nonetheless, commercial fishermen often just "pewed" the unwanted or illegal fish overboard instead of sorting them by hand because it was the fastest way to sort out a catch.

I walked over to Verner and said, "Verner, hand me the pew and your fishing license."

He said, "The hell I will," and overboard the pew went.

I said, "That move will make no difference other than to change it from one ticket for possession of an illegal device on a drag boat to two charges. The second charge will now be for not exhibiting a fishing device upon demand, and that will run you another $250!"

Verner exploded and after many choice words about the Fish and Game department stormed back to the wheelhouse. That was fine with me—now I would have time to check the rest of the crew for compliance with state law, and I did. The only violations I discovered were those associated with Verner, which I addressed with two citations. Upon receiving the tickets, Verner quickly crumpled them in his large, raw hands and threw them overboard. No matter, I had the originals, and he would show up for court or I would come looking for him at a later date.

Ken brought the *Rainbow* alongside after seeing my hand signal, and my exit from Verner's vessel was made without further incident. Ken waved to Verner as we passed the *Ella D* and received the "high one" for his efforts. Standing beside Ken in the wheelhouse, I said, "I don't think that chap will ever change. He hates any kind of authority, and I think you and I are going to remain a target of hatred as long as he is fishing in these waters."

Ken looked over to me with a smile and said, "Yes, and you will give him reason to hate us even more with every ticket we will

write him in the future." We both laughed as the *Rainbow* continued its journey into the world of the commercial fisherman.

I noticed the fog bank was beginning to move landward as Ken
and I continued to work the commercial fishing fleet through four
more boat inspections. The lads had done right well, and no one
suffered any citations. However, my well-being was another matter.
Having boarded several ships, all the while breathing diesel fumes
and looking down at fishing licenses with collateral loss of horizon,
I was fast becoming seasick. Damn, there is no worse feeling in the
world than that affliction. Being a boarding officer for the Fish and
Game department and being seasick was doubly not good. Try
jumping from ship to ship at sea with the rubber legs brought on
by that impairment. Additionally, I had to put up with a lot of crap
from the fishermen when I puked over the side or on their boats.
Jesus, I used to get tired of being offered a greasy sandwich by a
fishing boat crew member just after puking. They always thought it
was funny. I wonder if they would have thought it was funny that I
was burning the images of their faces into my memory for later citations, with no mercy shown because of the joke.

Moving north through portions of the crab fleet, Ken looked intently at the various members of the commercial fishing fleet as if
looking for the one his gut feeling told him was wrong. The fog had
moved in, and it was now misting very heavily. Ken and I put on
our rain gear and continued boarding vessels as the day progressed.
The fleet was doing very well, and the catch of the day for the fishermen appeared to be better than average.

Several of the skippers whose boats we boarded gave Ken and me
Dungeness crabs freshly cooked in sea water. Normally the crabs
would have been a treat, but to a lad with borderline seasickness
they were pure poison. But I never turned down food in my life,
and there was nothing finer than the sweet meat of a freshly caught
Dungeness crab. I partook of the feast and, needless to say, paid the
price some thirty minutes later. Boy, did I ever get sick. I failed to
enjoy Ken's graveyard humor as he maneuvered the *Rainbow*
downwind so I could safely puke out of the wind and told me,
"Hey, it's illegal to chum for crabs."

That damn knothead, making fun of me like that. Of course, maybe I was the knothead for eating the fresh-caught crab in the first place. For the rest of the afternoon I didn't care if I lived or died. All I wanted to do was get home and off that damn boat. We had a job to do, so seasick or not, we did it. Being as sick as I was, I had to be extra careful when I jumped from ship to ship. As I said earlier, I jumped hard to make sure I arrived in the middle of the deck of the ship to be inspected. Being sick with a bad case of rubber legs made the leap that much more difficult, so I put even more effort into my launches to make sure I didn't miss.

In between boardings, trying to take my mind off the uneasy feeling in my guts, I scanned all our instruments, checking the operation of the ship. My eyes stopped on our new CB set, or part of one. Ken had requested a CB for the *Rainbow* earlier in the year so we could listen to the fishermen on their CBs while at sea. In typical state-operation fashion, we got the receiver but no transmitting equipment. So we used to listen to the fishermen talk as we patrolled the commercial fishing lanes and many times made cases we didn't even know existed because once they saw us, they couldn't keep their mouths shut. Since they didn't know we had a CB, they would yak about the "fish cops" and who should hide the illegal gear or catches. In due course, trying not to make it too obvious so as not to give away our CB secret, Ken and I would grab them. It was great fun, and made the California state coffers much richer than the cost of CB transmitting equipment, I might add.

Heading back to Eureka before I puked up my gizzard again, Ken ran across the *Garibaldi* out of San Pablo Bay, near San Francisco. It was staffed by an all-Italian crew, and Ken and I had caught it many times with illegal catches aboard. Ken looked at me with eyes that asked, "Do you have one more jump in you?" Without responding, I walked to the bow, grabbed my support rope, and said, "Let's get on with it before I die." Ken turned the *Rainbow* toward the *Garibaldi*. I noticed through the light rain now falling that this jump would be a little more difficult than usual. My legs were really rubbery, and I felt crappy. In addition, the seas were now running with steep thirty-foot swells and the *Garibaldi* had a higher deck railing than most. That meant I would have to wait for exactly the right moment to launch myself, or I would hit the side of the other boat and go into the drink between the two vessels. As Ken moved closer, the danger of the high, dangerous swells became readily apparent. Both boats were pitching and yawing, and I began to have second thoughts about boarding. Then a hurried conversation between the skipper and one of the *Garibaldi*'s deckmates caught my eye, making me forget my seasickness. They had worried looks on their faces and kept looking at us to see whether I could successfully board their vessel.

I looked back at Ken, and he had seen the same concern exhibited by the crew. I could see that Ken was going to try to catch the next small swell and run me right up to the other vessel, so I made ready. My preparations consisted of a short prayer and a gathering of all my strength to make the leap. The boats closed, and as the bow of the *Rainbow* went up and the side of the *Garibaldi* dropped into the wave trough, I jumped. Over the *Garibaldi*'s rail I went to the deck beyond, landing off balance on my boot heels. I hit so hard I started sliding down the pitching, wet deck of the *Garibaldi* toward the wheelhouse. Picking up speed on my heels as the *Garibaldi* dove into the wave trough, I was unable to get the full soles of my boots down on the deck to break my slide. The combination of the rain-soaked deck, steeply pitching boat, nothing but boot heels for traction, and a 320-pound seasick weight on top meant one hell of a cannonball in the making.

Down the deck I slid, throwing my arms around, trying to regain my balance and scattering crew members every which way but loose until I came to the hatch railing amidships. Hitting the railing at the speed I was going did nothing to slow me down. Instead it flipped me headfirst through the open hatch and over flat on my back into about a ton of live Dungeness crabs. *Crunch* went the crabs, and my heavy body came to a violent rest. I lay there for a moment getting my bearings and my wind back. Then through my foggy mind came the realization that those crabs not underneath me were getting revenge for the crabs who couldn't help themselves to a piece of my carcass. I had dozens of crabs grabbing me by the ears, arms, hind end, cheeks, lips, legs, and anywhere else they could attach their pinchers, showing their displeasure at my dropping in unannounced. I was glad I had not landed face first in these grabbing sons of bitches! Up out of the crab bin I came with a roar. I must have had fifty crabs hanging on to me, and goddamn, did it ever hurt! I tried to remove them as quickly as I could, but the damn things were not to be denied. They just hung on and let me know I didn't belong in their crab box. Realizing I couldn't get them loose by gently prying their pinchers apart, I began breaking off their legs instead.

Looking up, I saw the Italian crew members looking down at the game warden who had disappeared in a flash into the hold of their ship. When they saw that I was breaking off the crab legs to get them off my soft parts, they went berserk. Breaking off the crab pinchers would ruin their chances of selling them. No one wants to buy a crab without the pinchers attached, and the Italians speedily let me know that they wanted me to stop what I was doing, right now. I thought, Tell it to someone who doesn't have a jillion of these little bastards hanging all over him, as I continued ripping off those who remained to ruin my day. Then my seasickness hit me again, and I began to broadcast-puke into the boxes holding the crabs. The Italian crew went ballistic now, as did the crabs on the receiving end of my lunch donation. God, what a hell of a wreck that moment was. A puking game warden, pitching vessel, diesel fumes, rotting smells, crabs hung all over me like a Neptune Christmas tree, and I falling into the crab boxes with my hands and arms as I tried to remain standing every time the ship rolled into the next wave. Of course, I was rewarded with more crab ornaments on my arms and hands each time they went into the boxes to steady me.

After about three minutes of this mess, I was able to grab a bulkhead and stand upright. Jesus, was I a mess. Welts everywhere, and I do mean everywhere. Sore all over inside due to my seasickness, with more on the way and a pitching vessel I would have one hell of a time getting off of without breaking my damn neck. Damn, there sure were a lot of places I would rather have been at the moment!

Then I saw it. In a corner of the hold were four big crab boxes full of female crabs (prohibited) and short crabs (less than the required width). There were at least several hundred pounds of these prohibited critters, way over the 2 percent error rate the Fish and Game department allowed any commercial fishing vessel! I moved my welted body over to the suspect boxes and confirmed my observation. In addition, I discovered two more boxes with more of the same hidden under a tarp. Ken's intuition about these lads had been right on the money.

Forgetting my sickness and welts, I scurried topside and with hand signals let Ken know we had a keeper. Ken pulled alongside, and I hollered the information about the illegal crab cache. He just grinned and gave me the high five. I think I would have happily settled for some Pepto-Bismol. Meeting with the skipper of the boat, I told him what I had discovered and asked him how the illegal crabs had gotten there. He just shrugged his shoulders in resignation and continued to look at me like a trapped rat. I then told him we were seizing his catch and he would have to follow us back to the docks in Eureka. I also told him that if he or any of his crew tried to destroy the evidence, that act would lead to jail for all his lads as well as additional charges. He had been through it before and understood that after going to Eureka we could offload his catch, and he could then settle up with the state for his greed. Also, at the docks Ken and I could weigh and photograph the illegal catch and then return it to Humboldt Bay, thereby allowing the crabs to live. As a formality, I explained the law about the females and short crabs so we wouldn't have any trouble in court later on, and he acknowledged the information with a nod. Before I left, I turned and again reminded him about the consequences of the destruction of evidence, including the potential loss of his boat. The look in his eyes told me we would not have a problem in that arena if losing his boat was the order of the day. Flagging Ken alongside, I jumped back to the *Rainbow* with less trouble than I had figured and then walked around the deck and reported my find to Ken. He was as elated as I was.

Then he looked at my face and arms and said, "What the hell happened to you?"

Ignoring him, I said to God, if He was listening that day, "Let me live long enough to eat every Dungeness crab that lives on this planet!"

Ken, knowing my penchant for seasickness, just grinned and mumbled, "Please Lord, let it be on someone else's ship." Damn him. He had the ability to make me laugh even if I felt like dying, and I did.

Ken slid the *Rainbow* in behind the *Garibaldi* for our trip to the harbor in Eureka. By trailing astern of the suspected boat, if they had a change of heart and tried to throw the evidence crabs over the side we would be in an excellent position to observe and photograph every move they made.

Standing back by Ken at the wheel, I was glad we were running for home. He kept the *Rainbow* out of the wake and diesel fumes of the *Garibaldi,* and as long as we were moving I remained less seasick. I was pleased with my effort for the day and began to puff up a bit, as we Germans are wont to do after good efforts. Then I was brought back to earth by a CB transmission from the *Garibaldi* to an Italian friend of the skipper back at the docks in Eureka. I heard the skipper say, "Hey, Lauri, do you have your ears on?"

There was a pause, and the message was repeated. Ken and I were both all ears. Knowing the fishermen did not know we had a CB on board, we thought they might give out some good information on the air that we could put to good enforcement use later on.

"This is Lauri, Tony, what's up?"

"Hey, Lauri," the *Garibaldi* skipper responded, "are you going home the same way tonight?"

There was a moment of silence, as if Lauri were trying to figure out what that request meant, and then she responded, "Yeah."

The skipper continued, "You know, Lauri, the way home by the zoo?"

Again a pause from Lauri and then a somewhat questioning answer: "Yeah, Tony, are you all right?"

There was a measured pause and then the skipper continued, "Yeah, what I need you to do is stop by the zoo and get me a gorilla!"

There was a long pause. Ken and I gave each other questioning looks. Lauri said, "Tony, *are* you sure you're all right?"

Tony responded, "Yeah, but I need a big, ugly gorilla. Fish and Game put a gorilla on my boat today that tore the hell out of everything from above the deck to all my crab boxes below, and if they can have one, I want one too!"

Ken started laughing and finally was laughing so hard that he had to let go of the wheel and double over with mirth. I didn't think it was *that* funny. But obviously it was, because I could hear laughter on Lauri's end of the CB as well. Gorilla! It was OK to be big enough to eat hay, and I had been called that before by the fishermen as I made my rounds, but a gorilla—brother. I had to admire the lad in the *Garibaldi,* though; he had a sense of humor. He would need it once he got hit with several tickets for gross take of a restricted species, I smiled to myself. I guess there was some compensation for him, though, because he would receive those tickets from Fish and Game's only active-duty *gorilla.*

Needless to say, after that incident the Fish and Game squad changed my nickname from Tiny to Migilla.

10

My Friend Tom

IN THE EARLY FALL OF 1967 I moved to Colusa County from Humboldt County and rented a home; it was more like a chicken coop than a house, but my bride and I made do. As a game warden, I was responsible for enforcement of the state Fish and Game laws in the northern half of Colusa County, a chunk of real estate approximately 1,100 square miles in size. My half of this county was capped on the west by high, rugged mountains, bordered by the Sacramento River on the east, and quilted on the valley floor by every form of cropland known to inhabit rich soils, especially rice, the staple grain of many nations. The high mountains were unique in their own right, but the magic of this district lay in the valley floor, which was the ancestral home of millions of migrating waterfowl.

The main Fish and Game office was located in Sacramento, and hundreds of warden stations dotted the state on an as-needed basis. This was a good arrangement because the local officer could relate to his people and wildlife problems and not be bothered too often by the big wheels from the main office. Periodically, someone from the main office would call with a problem or assignment, but generally they left the field officers alone to do what we did best.

One of the main-office duties was to check the deer-tag receipts sent in by all successful deer hunters, not only to ascertain the kill data but to check compliance with the tagging laws. Tags that were plainly in violation of the law, such as those used in the wrong hunting district or questionable regarding who really shot the deer were sent to the field warden in the county where the violation originated for investigation and adjudication.

In those days, though not today because of the huge human population and reduced resources, California had a system of A and B tags for deer hunters. A hunter could kill two deer, but one had to be killed in the coastal area (A tag) and one had to be killed in the inland area (B tag). Once an animal was killed, it had to be labeled with the appropriate tag before it was transported, and the hunter had fifteen days to send the receipt portion of the tag indicating a kill and other information in to the Fish and Game headquarters. Most hunters were responsible about returning their tag receipts, and I rarely had a problem with this report system in my district.

One day I received a packet of information in the mail from Sacramento that included several deer-tag receipts and questions about their validity. Looking back on that day, I remember that there was one A tag that had been attached to a deer taken in a B district. It wasn't a big deal, really, but in those days the Fish and Game officials in Sacramento wanted us to issue citations to individuals who didn't take the time to read the regulations before they tagged their deer. Following instructions, I called a Mr. Tom Okimoto, who lived in the Sacramento River Valley town of Yuba City and who unfortunately had used his A tag in the B district of Colusa County, and asked him to come over to my house when he got off work at Terhel Farms so we could square away this problem.

Mr. Okimoto arrived shortly thereafter, concerned about why he had been called on the carpet by the local game warden. What a man I was about to have a once-in-a-lifetime opportunity to meet! He was a Japanese fellow about five-foot-eight who weighed about three hundred pounds. He had a quick smile, an easy laugh, and a look in his eyes that bespoke wisdom earned from many years of hard work, liberally salted with the marks of the prejudice that went with being Asian in a white European America. I asked Mr. Okimoto if he had recently killed a deer in Colusa County. His reply was priceless, for no other reason than the honesty and innocence with which it was presented to me. "Mr. Grosz," he said, "I was running a bean harvester on the east side and jumped this buck up out of the beans, and since I saw him several days earlier, I had thrown my rifle in the harvester, and when he got up this time I shot him."

The words flowed like water in response to my question, regardless of the fact that he had confessed to another Fish and Game violation, namely, taking a game animal from a moving vehicle. I stood in amazement, looking at this man who was a real piece of Americana: honest, hardworking, more than likely poor as a church mouse, yet exuding the energy of a good human being taking in the world as it stood. Looking at this picture of a man as hardworking and honest as the day was long, I thought Sacramento could go to hell on this one. I wasn't going to issue Mr. Okimoto a citation for an improperly tagged deer, much less for shooting one from a motor vehicle. For some strange reason, unknown to me at that time, I took an instant liking to this man. He was a work of art and a piece of history, and I wanted that in my life as well.

I said, "Mr. Okimoto, you did violate the Fish and Game laws, but it is a minor violation." As soon as I said, "minor violation," I could see the concern clouding his face.

"Am I going to jail?" came his concerned reply.

"No, nothing like that," I responded. "I propose you bring me your set of deer antlers and the other deer tag." As I spoke, I could see his dark eyes hanging on every word I uttered. Continuing, I said, "If you do that, I will put the correct deer tag on your antlers, destroy the old tag, and not issue you a citation for the violation." I could see in an instant by the look on his face that he considered my proposal to be fair. He would be out one deer tag, I told him, but he said he didn't have the money to go into another part of the state to hunt anyway, so the two worlds called it even and sealed the deal with a firm handshake. Tom went home and came back an hour or so later with the antlers and unused portion of his deer tag, and the deal was squared with the state of California.

That little bit of generosity, common sense, or God's guiding hand (children, fools, and game wardens, remember) was to grant me a remarkable friend for as long as he lived. Tom combined a little bit of the old and a whole lot of the new and represented the very best in what he did, not in a manner for the whole world to see but in a manner of quiet excellence. He loved people and valued their friendship. He loved to fish—no, he lived for fishing and was happiest when a fifty-pound striper was on his fishing line or in his boat. But he really excelled at working with his plants and the land. God may have been a fisherman, but His charge Tom was a man of the soil. There wasn't anything Tom couldn't grow, and better than anyone else I chanced to meet throughout my years in the Sacramento Valley. After our deer-tag episode it wasn't uncommon for me to come home and find a bucket of the world's best peaches, plums, vegetables, or honey on my doorstep in the garage. For the longest time I couldn't figure out where those wonderful items were coming from. It was all the more surprising for me, a game warden in a town that hated game wardens with a passion, to receive gifts of this quality and volume.

One day while I was at the marina gasing up my patrol boat for a trip down the Sacramento River to check fishermen, Tom approached and asked, "Did you enjoy the last batch of peaches?"

I said, "Yes; do you know who is bringing them to my house?" Tom got a little twinkle in his eye and told me they had come from his garden in Yuba City. From that moment on Tom was my special friend, and to this day my eyes still get misty when I remember that he is dead.

As I grew to love and understand my new friend, he opened up to me, and what a revelation. During World War II Tom had been detained in an internment camp at Tule Lake, California, for being an Asian American in the "right" place at the "wrong" time. America has inflicted no greater an injustice on its people than the stain of this action imposed on a people who had done nothing to warrant being treated as aliens and enemies. As an amateur historian, I can find no explanation to justify what happened to that segment of our American people.

When the United States ran out of Anglo men for the war effort, the government began to recruit among the Japanese Americans in the internment camps. My friend Tom told me he volunteered just to get out of that camp, even though his parents strongly objected, and he fought for his country in Italy during that great war. After we had spent a lot of time together over the next few years, he opened up further and told me he had been severely injured charging several German machine guns on the Gustav Line after a friend of his had been hit and in the process earned several Silver Stars for bravery. Needless to say, Tom was screwed up physically after the war, especially his back, where, according to him, machine-gun bullets had done their work well.

As our friendship grew, Tom became a regular visitor to our home. He would arrive with his trademark bucket of fruit or vegetables and ask for me. If I was home, he would come into the house to visit. If I was not there but due shortly, he would wait outside for me, even after being invited in. I guess his old Japanese politeness died hard. He would wait outside, many times in 100-degree heat, with a glass of iced tea and a smile on his face, knowing full well he would bring a smile to mine as soon as he had shared whatever information he had. Tom may have been old-country Japanese, but he had a love for America and her resources like I haven't seen in many people in my fifty-plus years. He also had a mind like a bear trap for the details of serious illegal activity concerning the area's wildlife. I haven't seen the likes of his exactness of detail, I might add, since we parted at the "Great Divide" years ago. He was remarkable in that his intelligence would be punctuated with names, locations, and even the exact times that these illegal events were to unfold. I was forever amazed by the specificity of Tom's data, whether the illegal activity were in Glenn, Butte, Colusa, or Yuba County, especially regarding the exact times of occurrence. After following up on Tom's information on several occasions and always finding it correct, I listened intently whenever he chose to share his findings with me. Even today I can remember many events that followed Tom's descriptions to the letter. For instance, Tom would tell me to be at a particular ranch or spot in the outback, and the fellows would kill the ducks at five-fifteen P.M. I would be on the spot, and the lads would blow the ducks up at, say, five-seventeen P.M.!

Tom and his information were not of this world, and I damn sure liked hearing from that old man. With the facts I learned from him, I caused a lot of lads immense pain, not to mention financial loss, for their foolish deeds. Then, when I met Tom again later, I would

relate the story of the latest apprehension, and he would just grin.
I think my efforts to slow down the bad guys brought Tom a lot of
joy. Over the years we grew to love each other like father and son:
we were two men from two different cultures but very close in our
life's mission when it came to America's heritage.

Tom's back kept bothering him, and I noticed that it became
harder and harder for him to get in and out of his vehicle or lift
items of any weight. Finally it got to the point that the years were
accomplishing what the German machine guns hadn't been able to
do. One day, after watching hopelessly as my friend fought his back
pain, I suggested he see a doctor. Tom said, "Terry, I would like to,
but I just don't have the money right now."

The very next day my friend Tom and I went to Yuba City and
visited a back specialist to see if modern medicine could undo what
the machine guns and time had done and were doing. The doctor
examined Tom and advised him that an operation was in order if he
were to continue any kind of ambulatory life. His back was going
to have to be fused if he wished to continue doing the things he
loved. Tom was really concerned about this turn of events and
scared to death to go under the knife on the operating table.

I paid the doctor and said to Tom, "Let's get a second opinion."

A little later I took some time off and went with Tom to San
Francisco to get a second opinion. It paralleled the first opinion: either undergo surgery and be able to live some semblance of his former life or continue at his present rate until crippled. Even as a close
friend, I couldn't help Tom make that decision. He had to weigh the
odds and then challenge them if he wanted to continue his lifestyle.
He knew that his age and weight were against him. Stacked on the
other side of the balance were his gardening, his work in the fields
as an equipment operator, and his love of fishing.

Tom thought about the operation over the next two weeks and
finally came out to my home to talk with me about it. I noticed he
could barely get out of his car. I greeted him warmly, trying not to
show my concern over his rapidly deteriorating condition.

Tom said, "Terry, what should I do? I could barely get out of bed
this morning."

"Tom, that has to be your decision. You know yourself better then I do."

Tom looked me in the eye and said, "Terry, if I ever want to fish again, I have to be operated on, and that is what I'm going to do."

I thought for a second that I saw something in his eyes, a flash of times past, perhaps, but maybe not. "Tom, if you don't have enough money, count on me for what you need," I told him.

He answered, "No, my brother from Los Angeles loaned me the money. I'll be all right." There was that look again. I don't know how to describe it, but it wasn't of this world. I remember wishing at the time that I knew what it meant. Tom left for San Francisco the next day to undergo several days of tests followed by the surgery.

During that time I had been assigned to work trout fishermen in Sierra County in the high Sierras of California. When I came back a week later, I was stunned and grieved to learn that Tom had died on the operating table. An artery had ruptured, and before the doctors could get it under control Tom had had a stroke and perished moments later. Now I understood the look I had seen before he left my home that last day we were together.

It almost goes without saying that this man enters my thoughts several times a year, God rest his soul. God, what a hell of a man.

I remember going to Tom's funeral in Colusa County, the historical home of his parents, that snowy spring day. I walked into the small church where funeral services were to be held, and there sat just two other people to see Tom off. His wife and friend of many years, whom Tom had purchased in the old country as a photograph bride, according to common practice, for $93, and his old Anglo fishing partner. It was kind of a sad close to a life that had been so vigorous and fair, but I guess God has his ways. This was one of those ways you just don't question.

Tom's memory is forever burned into my soul. I will never forget that man. I will continue to remember him many times a year until that look crosses my own eyes. Someday I know God will need a good game warden, and maybe He will take me the same way He took Tom. Maybe Tom will be up in whatever that place is, growing vegetables for me and telling me when and where the bad guys will be killing pheasants or ducks. Maybe I will be just as good a game warden up there as I was down here—who knows? I don't know, but one thing I hope for is that I'm as good a man down here as Tom was.

Come to think of it, there were four people in that little church on that cold, snowy day so long ago if one counted "the fisherman."

11

State Line Road

STANDING OUTSIDE IN THE morning's coolness, I stretched my
tired legs and shoulders, stiff from sitting all night in the front seat of
my patrol vehicle watching for poachers illegally night-hunting
deer. Turning, I looked eastward at the coming dawn. The sky was
still black but starting to show a streak of reds and pinks splashed
along the horizon. The air was heavy with the perfume of big sage
and the latent smell of dust from the random but determined travels of deer hunters along the surrounding dusty roads the day before.

It was September, and I was still in the process of stretching my
wings in my chosen profession of state conservation officer as it led
me down its many paths toward what were to be the ultimate travels and traditions of my life. I was young, a bit of a dreamer, with an
intense interest in the history of the land and its peoples as well as
the wild things it nurtured. I had been married only a few years to
one of the world's finest women, and thirty-five years later still am.
She is such a sweetheart: realizing what emotions ran deep within
her man, she always let me run like the wind. I had my health then
and the world as my stage, a combination that allowed me to be on
deck this promising morning, stiff but in fine fettle. I thanked the
good Lord above for another day and, after letting my eyes roam the
darkness in front of me one more time for anything out of place,
reached through an open window into the front seat of my patrol
vehicle and took a piece of cold fried deer meat (game-warden fare)
from a plastic sack.

Letting the spicy taste and texture of the meat slide over my
tongue, I quietly chewed as I let my ears and eyes work the land
silently lying under God's cloak of night. I had parked the evening
before on a long, sloping knoll covered with big sage, interspersed

with sparse patches of western juniper and ponderosa pine. The soil was dry after many months without rain, its powdery texture typical of the dry transition conifer forests of northern California. Before me lay the great state of Nevada, extending as far as I would be able to see once the dark of night changed to day. Lying before me, though unseen at that moment, was a primitive rocky dirt road that acted as an informal boundary marker between the states of California and Nevada in Sierra County. It had been a wagon road in the early glory days of the past, a conduit for freight from the markets and supply houses in Reno to the hungry California gold fields along the eastern spine of the Sierras in Sierra, Alpine, and Plumas Counties during the 1850s. Now it was utilized only during deer-hunting season to gain access to some of the finest remote deer-hunting areas remaining in those two states. I thought how sad it was that the hunters gave the old wagon road no thought, viewing it only as an access road with no understanding of its roots in early Nevada and California history. Shaking the clouds of history along with my lack of sleep from my head, I again turned my eyes to the empty black void to the southeast soon to be represented by hundreds of thousands of acres of sagebrush and the American hunter.

That season's deer hunters were why I was there, and had been all night. Every group of people, from priests to police, has representatives of the good, the bad, and the ugly. Those human predators from the bad and ugly sides represented what I called the "dark side" and if not checked would continue along their selfish paths of resource destruction until there was nothing left for those yet to come. This area I now had under surveillance along the California-Nevada boundary had a bad reputation for hunters killing too many deer, and the wrong sex at that, because of its geographic isolation and the absence of officers in this neck of the woods. Well, not if I had anything to say about it, I mused. Today would be different, I thought, feeling good about my timing and current location. Yeah, before the day's end it would really be different!

I did not mind the loneliness, the cold, the lack of sleep, or the odd food and weather. In fact, I enjoyed the kinds of challenges the profession offered. That was what it was all about: I against the world of people out there illegally taking what was not theirs. I now know that for the most part only God, my fellow officers, and I cared whether I was out there or not. For the most part the American people, including the politicians elected to look out for their interests, are a greedy, self-centered, shortsighted lot who don't give a damn whether our natural resources last. As long as an action doesn't interfere directly with their lives, they historically couldn't care less. Look at what has happened to our great coniferous forests, the vast herds of bison, the clouds of passenger pigeons, the hordes of salmon, the pods of whales, and the clean air and water. I rest my case.

The wildlife I see out there today is nothing less than a tribute to those who came before me, carrying the same heavy shield of responsibility I wore so proudly that fine day so long ago. I'm glad in many ways that I was one of the fraternity blessed by God to carry such a responsibility. I now know I will leave this world with two thoughts crossing my dimming mind and eyes as the light and life flow from my body: first and foremost, I will know that I was blessed with the world's best wife and friend (whom I will love forever); and second, I will wish the best of luck to those who also serve, for they will certainly need it.

◦⟲◦

The cold that comes just before the dawn brought me again back to the moment at hand, which included the sensation of a cold piece of greasy deer meat still uneaten and resting in my hand. Taking another bite, I again surveyed my arena for the day, now being quickly illuminated by God's "Walt Disney-like paintbrush" in the skies to the east. Far below me to the northeast on the Nevada side of the border, I could see several sets of headlights moving slowly up the mountain on the old wagon road, now called State Line Road. It was that all right—a road that ambled along the boundary between Nevada and California in that remote part of the world—and not much more except to a single game warden on his patient stakeout. Little did I know that before the sun was to set, it would be a road and a day of many adventures.

I was a California Department of Fish and Game conservation officer assigned to the town and area surrounding Colusa, California. That station was located in the Sacramento Valley, many miles west of my current location in Sierra County, the district of Gil Berg, a friend and fellow game warden from my squad in Region 2. In those days we used to "flood the zone," that is, take wardens from their home districts if things weren't too busy and run them into another warden's area to help when that fellow was swamped with hunting or fishing traffic. When the warden receiving the help had some slack time, he would return the favor and come into another officer's district to assist during that lad's period of heavy work. That way we could really cover the ground and keep things hot for those breaking the law. Since those breaking the laws of humankind and nature were heading for a place reported to be hotter than all get-out, this provided us with an opportunity to give them a warmup, so to speak, of things to come.

Daylight rapidly began to replace the night, and I could now see the land before me as the sun's rays peeked over the horizon and quickly picked their way along the ridgetops and trees laid out below my lonely place of vigilance. This was always my favorite time of the day. The air was its cleanest, the smells their most piquant, and the songs of the birds that had made it through the night let those fortunate enough to be in their neighborhood really know when life was the greatest. The human soul is always glad to make it through another night, and mine was no different. Stretching to remove the last vestiges of stiffness earned by quietly sitting in a pickup seat all night, I let my eyes and senses roam my chosen domain for the day. Below me, stretching for miles, lay a land that was truly unique: sage interspersed with juniper and pine and the many varied heartbeats of the world of wildlife.

Snowbrush and buckbrush thickets dotted the landscape, all blanketed with rocky isolation. Truly an animal's, especially a deer's, paradise. Cover, water, and feed in abundance—what more could a critter ask for? The absence of humankind would probably be high on their lists, I suppose, if I were to receive an answer to that question. An azure sky replaced the blackness of the night, peppered with a few brilliant white clouds, and a light breeze from the north-west carrying the pungent smell of sage completed my morning awakening. It looked like it was going to be another hot day, but that was all right. My dad, Otis Barnes, had shown me numerous springs in this area in the days of my youth, and I would make use of them when thirst beckoned, as discoverers of the land and wildlife had done through the years before my time.

I was there that fine day because deer season was open on the Nevada side of the border and closed on the California side. Because of the remoteness of the area I now watched and its histori-cal deer-hunting excellence, a major problem prevailed. The Nevada hunters would hunt along their side of the border, but if a deer were spotted on the California side, *zip* went the bullet across state lines into the critter, and the resultant carcass would then be hustled over the border and tagged as a Nevada deer.

State Line Road, the old wagon trail of days gone by, was indi-rectly the culprit. Since it allowed hunting access into outstanding deer habitat, the human flood was on, and because of the remote-ness of the area the prevailing thought was the laws of the land be damned, just like the Old West. If you were the meanest son of a bitch in the valley, you took the law into your own hands, and that was that. However, in my day and age, that attitude didn't cut it. The law was there, and if those lads had taken the time to look over to the California side, they might have noticed the long arm of the law cleverly concealed on a hillside overlooking one hundred square miles of God's country. I certainly wasn't a John Wayne type, but a look into my eyes would have told them not to go where they shouldn't. I would bet that same look had been there since the start of the time when conservation officers dedicated themselves to the animals and to those humans yet to come.

Below me and to the northwest, a small doe stepped from her sagebrush hiding place and hesitantly stepped across State Line Road from Nevada into California. I watched her through my binoculars as she continued nervously across the open area sur-rounding the road and then slipped out of sight into a large buck-brush thicket. I continued to watch the area whence she came, and sure enough, my binoculars spotted a nice four-point buck (western count, meaning the deer had four points per antler) partially concealed by a juniper, watching where the doe had gone. Soon the buck also moved from his place of cover and trotted across the road of life onto California soil. Without stopping, he hustled his tail end into the same bushy thicket the doe had entered earlier. Soon the two of them fed into the view of my binoculars on the opposite side of the thicket. I watched them play, check their surroundings, test the air several times, and then go back to feeding.

A magpie landed on a juniper limb not three feet from where I stood leaning my elbows on the hood of the patrol rig and intently watched this bearlike thing, with special interest focused on my hand. I watched him from the corner of my eye without moving as he looked me over for any sign of danger. Seeing none, he flipped down to the hood of my truck and looked at me eye to eye. I could feel a smile start as we looked each other over. He couldn't have picked a safer spot to light and survey his world, right next to the world's largest game warden and all. Satisfied that I was no threat, he hopped onto my right arm, took the remaining piece of deer steak from between my fingers, and then glided off to another juniper tree for his breakfast. I could only grin. Hell, I weighed over three hundred pounds, and I didn't need that piece of meat anyway. This profession really had its moments, and those of you reading these lines who have been there know exactly what I mean. This was one of them, what I would call a "magpie moment"!

My two deer had moved during the magpie encounter, and it took me a few moments to relocate them. The buck had his head up and was looking back toward the Nevada border. Without giving it much thought, I continued to examine his movements and feeding habits with the keen interest of a biologist educated in wildlife management and with the advantage of an unseen intruder. Suddenly, in the surreal view of the binoculars, the upper part of the deer's neck spurted blood, meat, and sinew, and for a second he trembled, started to lower his head as if it had become a great weight, and then quickly disappeared from my sight. *Boom* came the sound of a rifle as I spun on my elbows, trying to locate the shooter who had just shattered the peace of my morning. A second *boom* helped me echo-locate a lad I hadn't even suspected was in my vicinity. He was standing on the Nevada side of the border, shooting across the hood of his Jeep, which had silently arrived and parked on State Line Road several hundred yards away.

What the hell—why two shots? There was only one buck in view on the California side of the border, and the hunter had dropped him with one shot right through the neck. Sweeping my binoculars back to the spot where the buck and doe had been feeding peacefully, I saw that the doe was also down and struggling on the ground as a great patch of red spread over a spot on her side behind her shoulder. She was dying, that was clear, and that son of a gun would pay for it, I thought. Doe season was not open in either state at that time! What I had just observed was illegal as hell. Well, that fellow shooting across the hood of the Jeep had come to the right place if he wanted a real old-fashioned "hoorah." He would get more than enough one-on-one attention before that day was over; you could bet your sweet ass on that!

What I got paid for took over, and I continued to watch my shooter, holding my binoculars with my right hand as my left hand hurriedly dug into the pocket of my vest for a notebook. Laying the notebook on the hood of my concealed truck, I recorded the time of the shots, the number of shots, the California location of the deer, and the description of my lone Nevada hunter gathered through the binoculars. The shooter, oblivious to the surprise the day would hold for him, looked nervously around to see whether anyone had seen him shoot the deer on the California side of the border. Satisfied that all was clear, he carefully laid his rifle down in the seat of his pickup and sprinted for the area where he had seen the buck drop at the first shot. I followed him in my binoculars from my position on the high ground, all the while recording his efforts for court should the occasion later arise.

The lad ran to the buck, quickly checked it out to make sure it was dead, and then, grabbing his prey by the antlers, commenced to drag the carcass as fast as he could go toward the Nevada line and safety—or so he thought. Once across State Line Road, he dragged the buck to the off side of his pickup, where no one driving by would see it. I was really interested in what he planned to do next with the doe, since killing her was illegal in both states. I didn't have long to wait. He quickly surveyed his surroundings again, then sprinted back across State Line Road to the doe's body. Checking to make sure she was dead, the lad grabbed her by the back legs and commenced to drag her at a dead run toward the Nevada side of the line. Crossing State Line Road, he continued his run into a thick stand of brush on the far side of his pickup, hiding the doe among the cover of that handy buckbrush thicket. Once she was safely out of sight, he returned to the buck lying not far from his pickup, hauled it a few feet away, and began to gut the animal as if nothing out of the ordinary had happened.

Once the deer had been gutted, he washed his hands, using a water container hanging from the back of his truck, and then tagged the animal so it would appear to be in compliance with Nevada law. He then loaded the carcass into the back of his pickup, covered it with a tarp, and looked around to see if anyone else were in the area. Again finding the area apparently deserted, to his satisfaction, he returned to the buckbrush thicket holding the carcass of the illegal doe. Now I really crawled into the binoculars, so to speak, to watch and record his every move. Dragging the doe to the opposite side of the thicket so no one who drove by on the road could observe what he was doing, he began to gut and skin the animal.

Boom, boom, boom, boom, went several rifles farther north along State Line Road, about a mile from the lad I was currently watching with the illegal buck and doe. Quickly swinging my binoculars from my lad to the area of the shots, I spotted two men running from a red-and-white pickup on the Nevada side across State Line Road and onto the California side. They disappeared behind a small grove of pine trees and after a few minutes came back into sight, one carrying two rifles and the other dragging what appeared to be a small forked-horn buck (two-point western count). They ran to the Nevada side of the road, dropped the little buck off by their pickup, and then ran back across the road into California. They ran behind the same small grove of trees, were absent for a few minutes, and then appeared dragging another deer, this one appearing to be a spike buck (a buck with unbranched antlers), an illegal kill in both states!

Damn! I had gone from a pleasant morning in the backcountry into a swirling mess involving four illegal deer and three hunters, all separated by about one mile as the crow flies. How the hell was I going to handle this mess and catch all of them?

About that time the two lads with their two illegal bucks began to drag their ill-gotten gains behind a large stand of buckbrush near their vehicle. I supposed they were going to gut the deer and find some way to hide the illegal spike for transport back to their homes. Switching my binoculars back to my first illegal hunter, I observed him stuffing something behind the back seat of his pickup. He looked all around for any sign of danger to him and his illegal operation and, seeing none, began to again wash off his knife, meat saw, and hands.

Well, it was now or never; it was apparent that he was done and about to leave. I had to make my move if I were going to apprehend this chap before he headed back into Nevada. Realizing I had a good thing in my cover for the patrol rig, I decided to go it on foot. Grabbing my citation book and binoculars, off I went down toward my first violator. Keeping trees and bushy thickets between me and my culprit, I got to within about two hundred feet of his position. Now I had to cross State Line Road, and the area between me and my quarry was pretty open. Luck was with me, though, and he didn't spot me as I sped (or lumbered) across the road as fast as my size would allow (I was not all *that* slow: I could still run an eleven-second flat hundred in those days). Once on the other side and again concealed by some bushy areas and a few trees, I again moved toward my unsuspecting quarry. Moments later I had sneaked to within twenty feet of my man before he realized I was upon him.

When I announced, "Good morning, state Fish and Game warden, how are you doing?" he about jumped through his skin. Whirling around, he focused on me with an intense gaze and answered, "Fine, how are you?"

I nodded and said, "I don't have a lot of time, so let's cut to the chase and get down to business. I observed you illegally kill two deer, both in California."

The lad just froze and then, trying to gain the high ground, started to argue.

"Look," I said, "I don't have time to argue with you; I will do that in a court of law if need be. Right now I have to move down the road and apprehend two others for violation of the same laws, and I just don't have time to mess around with you! Give me your driver's license, car keys, and hunting rifle, please."

He hesitated until I added a very strong "Now!" which made him spring into action. Grabbing the gear I had requested, I told him to wait right there and I would be back after I had dealt with the other two chaps. My man just nodded, numbed by the fact that his day had just turned to something brown and ugly, as evidenced by this humongous game warden who was there one moment and the next was jog-trotting down the dusty road and out of sight with his car keys, driver's license, and rifle. Passing the rear of this man's pickup, I memorized his Nevada license-plate number without breaking my stride.

Down State Line Road I lumbered toward the area where I had last seen my two other chaps and their red-and-white pickup. Rounding a turn at the top of a hill, I observed the two lads still in the process of gutting the deer behind their "safe" brush pile. As Winston Churchill once said, "They built a fortress but forgot to put a roof on it." From my high ground I could clearly see the lads as they hurried through their little chore of cleaning the two illegal deer.

Moving behind a tree for cover, I surveyed the ground before me and laid out a ground-attack plan that should not fail because of the lie of the land. Moving down the hill with a small ravine as cover, I was able to move to within one hundred yards of the two lads. Climbing out of my ravine, I continued to use cover, half crawling, half running in a stooped-over position until I was within thirty to forty yards of them. Briefly resting for a moment to quiet my pounding heart and regain my breath, I checked out my final run.

There were several juniper trees halfway to the lads that I could use for cover, and a blanket of squaw carpet (a low-growing ivylike plant) would afford some quiet in the final area I would walk over.

Off I went, with my eyes never leaving my targets for an instant because at this range and with the degree of my element of surprise, I knew it was the kind of situation in which bad things could happen—like my getting shot by surprised people doing bad things. When I was about fifteen feet from the lads, one of them looked up briefly and then returned his eyes to what he and his partner were doing. Then all of a sudden it dawned on him that a large fellow dressed in green and carrying a badge was bearing down on them while they were gutting an illegal deer!

"Run!" he yelled as he bolted from his kneeling position. With that, he sprinted for the pickup parked thirty yards away. The other fellow jumped up and, not knowing what the hell was going on, turned and ran straight into me. One hand on his shoulder pretty well took the steam out of his run for the roses. The poor lad, between being scared and the confrontation that had just taken place with a giant bear of a man, arranged for his backbone to completely disappear and wilted in my hands. The other fellow continued his run to the pickup only to realize that I had his buddy and the owner of the pickup—the one with the keys, that is. He slowed to a walk and just stood his ground by the truck, waiting for his share of the execution, which soon arrived.

"Morning, fellows," I said. "How is the deer hunting?"

Neither said anything. They just looked at me as if I were a ghost from the next world.

"Well, let me fill you in on how the hunting has been," I said. I went on and explained what I had observed and, pointing to the dead spike and forked-horn, asked if any of what I had described was untrue. The lads just looked at each other and gave in.

"You have us," one said, and the other asked, "What happens now?"

I filled them in on the standard procedure: seizure of the two deer, seizure of both rifles since they were Nevada residents (taking the guns would assure their appearance in court in California, since

California would not extradite them for a wildlife misdemeanor once they got back into Nevada), and citations issued to both of them for violations of California laws. Both lads settled down from the original scare, and I issued citations for taking deer illegally in California during the closed season and for possession of an illegal deer, to wit, one spike buck. I seized both rifles and deer and marked them with the appropriate evidence tags. Leaving the two deer in the shade of a tree to avoid spoilage, I bade the lads farewell after advising them not to try to take the evidence and to be sure to appear to pay their fines for their morning's activity or their rifles would be forfeited and a warrant issued for their arrest. Taking the two rifles and the rifle seized from my earlier violator, I started back up the hill to my first illegal shooter. About twenty minutes later I came upon him quietly resting under the shade of a pine tree and smoking a cigar. Laying down the three rifles, I fished out his driver's license, took out my citation book, and laid it down on the hood of his Jeep pickup.

The lad got up, sauntered over to the truck, and casually asked, "Do you have any professional courtesy?"

"What?"

"You know," he said, "any professional courtesy for a fellow law enforcement officer?"

Looking at the lad, I answered, "That may be a little rough, with the two illegal deer and all."

My voice was pretty damn hard as I tried to convey my idea that a good officer would not put another officer in such a predicament or have the gall to ask for special consideration in these circumstances. The edge in my voice, punctuated by a night of little or no sleep, was enough warning for the lad to stuff that approach for the duration. I told him what I had observed that morning and asked if he had anything to add.

He said, "Do what you have to do, but you may get a surprise once you write out these tickets."

Looking him dead in the eye, I said, "That's what I get paid for," and let it go at that. I knew I was just moments away from ripping the ass off this arrogant, out-of-line officer, so I bit my tongue. It turned out that he was a deputy sheriff in a county in Nevada adjacent to Sierra County in California. Apparently he felt that he had a few connections in Sierraville, where this case would be heard, but I didn't care. He had committed a flagrant violation of California law, and as far as I was concerned he was going to have to pay the piper.

Putting an evidence tag on the four-point buck I had observed feeding earlier and another on his rifle, I asked, "Where is the doe?"

"What doe?" he asked.

"Look," I said, "if you want to play that game, I will find it myself and then book you into the nearest bastille I can find, so let's quit with the cute behavior."

He said, "Well, I guess you'll just have to find it."

I looked around the brush pile where he had gutted the animal and around the vehicle and could not find the deer. There were no tracks leading away from the truck, so I knew he hadn't moved the deer far. Then I remembered that I had seen him put something in the seat area of his truck. Looking inside the cab, I saw just the usual hunting gear at first. I pulled the seat back forward, but all I could see in the storage area was a sleeping bag. Then it dawned on me that a bloody sleeping bag was out of the ordinary! Pulling the sleeping bag from behind the seat and opening it, I discovered the missing deer. This lad was fast with the knife and bone saw, I thought. The deer had been cut up into six chunks, placed in the sleeping bag, and hidden behind the pickup seat.

When I looked over at the deputy, he just shrugged and would not let his useless eyes meet the fire in mine. I tagged the deer parts as evidence, collected his rifle and the other deer, and, not wanting to ruin the rest of my day by booking this law man gone bad, bade him farewell. He quietly got into his pickup and as a last word indicated I had not seen the last of him before he drove off down State Line Road in a cloud of dust. The thought that maybe I should have booked the arrogant son of a bitch ran through my mind as I turned away. I had a feeling he was right, but I had a lot of evidence to take care of and had to get cracking, so I pushed the thought out of my mind.

Carrying the three rifles, I walked back to my truck parked on the hillside, laid them on the passenger seat of my pickup, and took a long pull from my canteen. After drinking my fill, I paused and surveyed my hideout. The deputy would probably tell everyone he passed going down the road that I was up on the mountain, so I probably would not make any more money from the lads coming from that direction. But that still left the other half of this huge area for me to rattle around in, and that was more than enough work for anyone, even someone my size.

Driving back down to the spots where the lads had parked their vehicles, I loaded the four deer into my truck and covered them with a tarp so they would not be filled with road dust as I drove the back roads in my remote neck of the woods. I planned that every time I stopped to set up a lookout for other wildlife violators, I would park in the shade and unwrap the tarp to allow the carcasses to cool to avoid spoilage. Looking over my area one more time for anything out of the ordinary, I started up my pickup and turned south down State Line Road for whatever adventure it might bring. The road was very rough, and since I was driving a 1964 Dodge 2x4 pickup, I took it easy. Good old Cal Fish and Game— no use giving the officers the equipment they needed, just the cheapest. Oh well, that was life, and I was enjoying my day in the backcountry. In fact, when a game warden is in the backcountry, there is no difference between him and a king. Damn, life was good—and just about to get better.

Rounding a steep downward curve on the road I was traveling, I almost ran head-on into a blue Ford pickup slowly coming up the road. Slapping on my brakes to avoid a collision, I noticed two lads standing up in the back of the Ford holding hunting rifles and looking earnestly over the terrain for evidence of deer. The driver looked normal except for a bad case of the "big eye" when he saw the patrol truck and its "law dog" driver. The Ford's front-seat passenger, not aware of the presence of the law, kept looking out his window for any sign of deer as well. Throwing my truck into park, I quickly stepped out just as the lads in the back realized a game warden was in easy grabbing distance. Not that they would want to grab one my size, mind you. Almost as if on cue, they both cranked open the bolts to their rifles, and each jacked out a live round of ammunition. One live cartridge flipped my way and, without missing a step, I caught it in my hand. The other lad's live round flipped forward, clanged off the hood of the Ford right in front of me, rolled off, and dropped at my feet. In California it was illegal to possess a loaded rifle in a motor vehicle on a way open to the public, and they were in California. Those two lads had sure as hell stepped into crap when they jacked those live rounds out in front of me, and, from their expressions, they knew they were now standing in it! The lad on the passenger side of the Ford, now realizing that the person in front of him was a game warden, bent over and tried to unload his rifle before I caught him with a live round in the chamber. Two quick steps brought me over to his side of the vehicle, and I was able to watch him unload a live cartridge as well.

Three up and three down, as far as I was concerned! A rifle lay on the seat between the driver and his passenger. Announcing who I was (as if it were needed, with me standing there in all my glory, uniform and all), I asked to examine his rifle. The passenger handed it out to me through his open window, and I found that it had a live round in the chamber as well. Four for four in the loaded-rifle-in-the-motor-vehicle category, I thought. No doubt about it, my day was getting better. I had seen seven lads so far on this patrol, and every one of them had violated the law. Damn, so much for the hunter ethic! I got three of the lads off on one side of the road and had the driver move his rig to the side so other vehicles coming along might pass. All the lads were from California, and none needed to be told that possession of a loaded firearm in a motor vehicle was illegal. It was just the opposite in Nevada. They could possess a loaded firearm in a motor vehicle in Nevada, that is. But if they stepped across the loaded-gun-in-a-motor-vehicle line into California, the Nevadans were zapped the same as their California counterparts.

I asked for and received everyone's driver's licenses and hunting licenses. All my California hunters had Nevada nonresident hunting licenses, so they were legal in the hunting department. However, they

all received citations for possession of loaded firearms in a motor vehicle on a way open to the public. They were a rather surly lot, and
I had the feeling they were outlaws incarnate, but since everything
else checked out I just issued their citations and let them go. I did not
seize their firearms as I routinely did with Nevadans because they
were all from California and I could pick them up on warrants if they
failed to show up for court or pay their fines. With a wave of the hand
and an admonition regarding the laws of the state, I watched them
disappear into the dust that was State Line Road.

It was getting hot as the sun reached its zenith, and I now became aware that my small breakfast (the one half eaten by the magpie) was causing the big guts to eat the little guts inside my rather
large carcass. I was not far from a little spring called Granite Spring
and decided to go there for lunch. Several miles down State Line
Road, I turned west onto another even rougher road. Dad had
brought me here when I was a boy after a fishing trip on a small
stream not far from here. The spring was nothing more than a
trickle of water coming out of a pure biotite granite bluff. The
water was icy cold, and if you drank too much at one sitting you
would get a headache like you get when you eat ice cream too fast.

I pulled up in a little grassy area next to the spring but somewhat
out of sight, and as I stepped from the patrol truck I spooked about
twenty chukar, a kind of partridge, from the weeds where they had
been drinking and resting. A smile crossed my dust-and-sweat-cov-
ered face. It was always nice to see wildlife in their environment
doing what they did best. After a long stretch, I took out my ice
chest, moved over to a small juniper alongside the spring's run-off
area, and sat down in the shade. Digging out my lunch of Donna's
fried chicken (eat your heart out, Colonel), some of her fine homemade bread with butter, and a piece of spicy homemade pumpkin
pie, I was set. Adding a cold cup of Granite Springs water, I had a
repast fit for a king and felt as if I were one for the moment. I sat
there quietly, eating my lunch and enjoying what God and Donna
had provided for me. As I savored my food, I let my mind wander
back to the times Dad and I had sat in this exact spot and he had
filled my head with the history, both Indian and Anglo, of the area

I now roamed. Moments like that are few and far between for most common folk, but not for a game warden. They occur daily if one is a part of the "thin green line" and is out every day in the elements one calls home. The air was full of the calls of hundreds of unseen chukar waiting for me to leave so they too could drink the cold, clear spring water. I saw a covey of sage grouse carefully skirting my truck as they marched to the spring overflow for a drink of life. Then two mourning doves whistled in and, after a careful look-see, also headed for the spring overflow not twenty feet from me. It doesn't get much better than that!

I sat there with my mouth full of good food, ears full of the sounds of nature, and heart full of gratitude for another day of life, but my special moment was soon to be trashed. The grating growl of a couple of dirt bikes (there were no ATVs in those days) broke the spell as I realized they were coming my way. As my world filled with the unmuffled growl, my training went into high gear. Two lads soon swung into view, moving down the road toward the spring. They wore hunting garb, and each bike had a rifle in a scabbard across the front. As they pulled around behind the spring and into view of my patrol rig, I saw a slight hesitation before they continued on to the main spring. Rising up from my disturbed meal, I walked over to the two lads as they dismounted to get a drink.

"Morning, lads. Doing any good?" I asked.

They said they hadn't seen anything that morning and were just getting a drink before leaving the area to head for another that might have a few more deer. Well, I couldn't figure why they hadn't seen any deer, with their noisy dirt bikes and all! I tell you, some of these lads are as dense as hardwood posts. As they drank from the spring, I sauntered over to their bikes and asked if I could examine their rifles.

"Why?" asked the heavy-set one.

"Because in California it is illegal to carry a loaded rifle in a motor vehicle on a way open to the public," I responded.

"Are we in California?" the other biker asked hesitantly.

"By about two miles," I answered. "May I check your rifles?" I asked again.

The men looked at each other and then nodded. Pulling the first gun out of its scabbard, I opened the bolt to find a live .264 round in the chamber. Holding the live round in my hand, I returned the unloaded rifle to the scabbard and reached for the other rifle. "It's loaded," blurted out the balding bike rider. I acknowledged his statement with my eyes and then removed the second rifle from its scabbard. Opening the bolt, I removed a live .243 round. Closing the bolt on a now empty chamber, I replaced that rifle in its scabbard.

Turning to the two men, I told them they had violated the laws of California (not to mention ruining a perfectly good lunch) by transporting live rounds in the chambers and were each going to receive a citation for the error of their ways. They began to complain about not knowing the laws of California and not knowing they were in California, but I brought them to an abrupt halt with a sweep of my hand.

"Lads," I said, "it is your responsibility as hunters to know the rules of the road in this sport. This law is for your own safety and good, and it is strictly enforced in this state. Besides, the road is clearly marked with large wooden signs when you are crossing into Nevada or California."

Blank looks followed that bit of information. I asked for and received their driver's licenses and sat down to issue them citations. As it turned out, both lads were majors from Stead Air Force Base (now closed), and after the initial complaints they were fairly cordial. Since both men were active military, I did not seize their rifles because their military connection made it a piece of cake to guarantee their appearance in any court of law. After they received their citations, the two bikes growled their way away from the spring and out of sight and sound. Sitting down under the tree again to finish my lunch, I noticed that all was quiet around the spring. The noise from the bikes had pretty much driven away the wildlife.

I hurriedly finished eating, put my ice chest back in the truck, and re-covered my four deer with the tarp to keep the road dust and flies off them. Crawling back into my beast of burden, I started the engine and headed back the way I had come. When I reached State Line Road, I drove across it onto another trail-like road instead of heading north or south. The little road I was now on led up over a small rock bluff toward an expansive rocky table that ran east to west for about five miles. I had heard a vehicle laboring its way up this road when I first sat down for lunch and thought it might be a good bet for catching someone out of line once I finished eating.

My patrol truck carefully crawled its way up the bluff and onto the rocky table, only to be met with nothing. There wasn't a vehicle in sight. Getting out of my rig and crawling up on top of the cab to increase my view, I swept the miles of landscape in front of me with my binoculars, looking for the vehicle I had heard earlier. Seeing or hearing nothing, I crawled down off the top of the cab into the bed of my truck. As I checked the tarp over my evidence deer, I was surprised by the sound of five shots from the area of Granite Springs. The shots weren't from rifles but shotguns! I continued to listen and was rewarded by three more dull thumps characteristic of the sound made by the discharge of a shotgun. Sure enough, they were coming from Granite Springs—two shotguns, I would say, based on the discharge intervals and thumping sounds. The chukar! Someone was shooting the chukar at Granite Springs! Damn, season was closed on chukar, and some son of a bitch had the audacity to shoot *my* birds at *my* spring area.

Well, I would put an end to that piece of horse crap! Jumping back into the cab, off I went down the steep bluff as fast as I could push the old truck without tearing out the transmission on the rocks. Once on the road to Granite Springs, I stopped to listen some more. Since there was only one way in or out, I now had control of the destiny of the lads shooting the chukar during the closed season, and that knowledge gave me a good feeling. I heard two more shots, only this time they were coming from the ridge that surrounded the spring area. It seemed the lads had taken off from the spring area where they had jumped the chukar as the birds came in to water and were now pursuing them across the adjacent hills.

Driving a little way down the Granite Springs road, I blocked the road with my vehicle at a constricted point and walked the hundred or so remaining yards to the spring to discover a Dodge 4x4 parked next to the grassy overflow area with both doors flung wide open.

It was apparent that the two occupants had leaped out hastily in order to kill as many of the unsuspecting chukar as they could before the birds fled to the less accessible hills and cover. I moved off to one side, sat down under a juniper, and waited for my quarry. I knew they had to return to their truck, so I was in no hurry. In about twenty minutes a lone lad returned empty-handed to the truck. He looked around and, not seeing anything out of the ordinary, left only to return a few moments later with his shotgun and four illegal chukar. He quickly threw these birds behind the front seat of the truck and then sat down to wait for his buddy. I wasn't more than twenty yards away, now lying behind the juniper tree and watching him, but the lad never saw me. Then I heard another person coming from behind me and slightly to one side. The nearby *crunch-crunch* of his footsteps told me not to move for fear of being seen. Soon I saw another lad arriving with six or seven chukar and a shotgun. He paused a few yards from the truck and spoke softly to his buddy.

"Is it all clear?" he asked.

"Yeah," replied his buddy, "there isn't a game warden within miles."

I just grinned. With the all clear, the second lad walked to the vehicle and also put his ill-gotten gains behind the truck seat. Then both lads put their shotguns into their scabbards and placed them in the front seat of the pickup. With that, they went to the spring to get a drink and wash the chukar blood off their hands. While their backs were turned, I crept down to their truck and leaned casually against the front fender as if I belonged. The lads were discussing the morning's hunt in excited voices as I stood there not thirty feet from them. Finishing their business at the spring, they headed back to their truck, still excitedly talking about their morning's exploits. When they were about ten feet away, they suddenly became aware of the rather large fellow leaning against their pickup and what agency he represented. Damn, you talk about two sets of eyes going from happy-excited to big as dinner plates—we had it here in a heartbeat!

"Morning, lads," I boomed. "How is the chukar hunting?"

Instant eyeball and body-language panic! Neither could talk for a few seconds, so I filled the hollow air space. "I'm sure glad there isn't a game warden within miles," I said.

Boy, did their day turn to that brown, smelly stuff! "How long have you been standing there?" asked the smallest of the two.

"Long enough to watch you two stuff about ten closed-season chukar behind the seat in your pickup," I responded.

They just looked at each other.

"Lads," I said, "why don't you just fish those birds out from behind the seat and hand me your shotguns."

Without a sound, the lads dug out the chukar from behind the seat of their pickup and lamely laid them down at my feet. Then, without a word, they handed me their shotguns. I found a live shotgun shell in each chamber, another violation of the law. Picking up the chukar and shotguns, I asked the lads to follow me to my patrol truck, where I issued them citations for the illegal possession of chukar and possession of a loaded firearm in a motor vehicle on a way open to the public. I could not write them up for taking game birds during the closed season because I had not actually seen them take any of the birds. But I had seen both lads in possession of closed-season chukar; hence the citation for possession. I seized eleven chukar, the live shotgun rounds, and both shotguns since they were Nevada residents. When the two lads left, they fairly had their tails tucked between their legs. Boy, this day was sure turning out to be a peach. Everyone I had crossed trails with so far had been issued a citation for screwing up. I had a truckload of illegal deer and now chukar and a front seat full of seized firearms. I began to wonder where this adventure would end. Little did I realize this whirl of opportunity would not end until dusk had settled in for the night that followed.

Pulling back out onto State Line Road, I noticed a vehicle up on the rocky bluff I had searched earlier, probably the one I was looking for just before I pinched my chukar hunters. It was now coming down the steep road in front of me and would soon pass very close to where I was parked. Quickly pulling my rig into a copse of trees, I got out and walked to a spot where I figured they would be too preoccupied with the rough road as they drove by to be looking for the long arm of the law. Hiding in a bushy thicket right next to the road, I waited. I didn't have to wait long. The laboring truck engine told me they were still coming my way, and they weren't far off either.

When I figured they were close enough to stop and control, I rose from my hiding place and stepped out into the road. They were about fifteen feet away when the driver noticed me standing there holding my hand up in a "stop" position. On went the brakes as he hollered something to his passenger, who was busily looking out the window on his side of the pickup for deer. The passenger looked out the front window at me and then bent over as people do when they are unloading a rifle in the cramped front seat area of a motor vehicle. *Bang* went his rifle, and flying rock particles stung my legs as the bullet slammed down through the floorboards of the pickup and into the road under the truck, throwing rock chips in my direction. The cab instantly filled with blue smoke, and both men bailed out of the truck holding their ears as the truck growled and ground to a stop. I noticed transmission fluid running out over the ground as the men continued to desperately rub their ears to get rid of the ringing from having a rifle go off in close quarters. I just stood there shaking my head as I rubbed my sore legs where the rock and metal fragments had struck me.

"Morning, lads," said the always happy game warden. "I hope that explosion wasn't a loaded rifle going off inside your motor vehicle."

Well, of course it was, but there is nothing like rubbing a little (or a lot) of salt into open wounds. Neither man answered. Neither could hear worth a damn, so I let them continue to dance around a bit as they tried to fix their poor ringing ears. After a few moments they settled down, and I guess the ringing got about as quiet as it would get. It was obvious that both men could have used an aspirin about then. I walked over to the pickup and removed both of their rifles from the front seat. The one from the passenger side smelled like it had just been fired and had an empty brass .270 cartridge in the chamber. I gave the passenger a questioning look, and he nodded and lowered his eyes. Checking the other rifle, a 7x61 Sharpe and Hart (a rather unusual caliber), I found it to be loaded as well. Removing the empty cartridge from the .270 and the live round from the Sharpe and Hart, I placed them in my pocket.

"Gentlemen," I said rather loudly to offset the ringing in their ears, "we have a violation of Fish and Game laws with the loaded guns in the motor vehicle and all."

They nodded in acknowledgment, and I continued, "I am going to issue you both a citation for a loaded gun in a motor vehicle, and I will need to see your hunting licenses and driver's licenses if you please."

While they dug those out, I looked in the back of the truck for any game and, finding none, checked out the cab area for game as well. Finding none, I knelt down and looked at the transmission. Yep, it was dead all right!. That rifle bullet had gone clear through and left a hole you could drive a truck through. The damage that 130-grain bullet had done was amazing!

Getting back on my feet, I took the licenses from the lads and asked them to accompany me to my vehicle. Once there, I issued citations for the loaded-gun violations and, since they were Nevada residents, seized their rifles, brass casing, and loaded Sharpe and Hart round. I then called a wrecker from Sierraville at their request. When all was said and done, the wrecker driver agreed to come get them in that remote part of the world for $250, which was a lot of money in those days! That expense plus a new transmission would certainly make this trip memorable for these lads, not to mention the icing on their cake in the form of a Fish and Game ticket for their loaded-gun violations. I guess the only consolation they got, if consolation is the word, was being written up by the world's largest game warden.

Leaving them there to await the arrival of the wrecker (with a promise that I would check back on them at nightfall in case he hadn't found them), I moved off to another long, sloping ridge that gave me a view of a zillion square miles below me and just sat there. The time spent awake the night before was now clashing with my youth and common sense, saying a little sleep was needed. I had been awake, more or less, for the past thirty-five hours, and it was telling. Moving into a small group of pines to camouflage the truck and shade my evidence, and with a view of all eternity below me, I let the heat of the day and sleep take over.

Some time later I heard the faraway sound of a vehicle being driven over a rough road. Opening my right eye, not wanting to lose the sleep that had taken hold of me, I quickly glanced at my domain below. Nothing. I let the long fingers of sleep again reach out for me, only to be disturbed again by the sound of a vehicle still moving somewhere below me. The hunter of men in me this time made me sit up and take note. It was amazing what this intoxicating feeling of hunting my fellow human could do for my physical being. I was not sleepy anymore, and for some reason known only to God and game wardens, I was now fully alert and on the trail.

Below me and about half a mile away a blue pickup slowly moved toward a small stand of trees where I remembered an old deer camp had once stood. Watching the truck through the binoculars as it climbed a small hill, I could look directly into the bed. There appeared to be a deer and another kind of animal in the back of the pickup. I thought there were three people in the cab. Damn, with just my 7x50 binoculars and the angle of the sun, I couldn't for the life of me make out what the mystery animal was. It sure as hell wasn't a deer, but what the hell was it? Both animals kept sliding around in the back of the pickup as it moved up and down and from side to side on the rough road. Finally the truck arrived at the old deer camp, and then I could see why they had gone there. The camp still had an old game pole, a pole or log tied horizontally high between two trees that allows the hunter to hang his game off the ground so he can gut or skin his kill more easily.

The pickup backed up to the game pole, and the lads emptied out of the truck and commenced to take the mystery animal out of the pickup and over to the game pole. They hurriedly tied a rope through its legs, hoisted it up on the cross pole, and began to skin it. Just the speed with which they worked on this animal told me something was wrong, not to mention the color of the critter. *Antelope!* The goddamned thing was an antelope! Another look with my binoculars confirmed my guess. It was an antelope all right!

My mindset had been on deer because that was why I was in this area, to work the deer hunters, and deer was the quarry of the day. It took a few moments to get my gears right. Damn, Terry, that's a sure sign of getting old, I told myself. Quickly pushing that thought out of my mind, I began to formulate a plan on how to approach the lads without losing them or the illegal animal in the process. The season was closed on these critters, and the antelope herd in California was closely guarded by state Fish and Game in order to allow it to expand from its current low numbers and limited area of habitation. Where in the hell did they get this critter? I wondered. Not in this area. They must have killed it somewhere on the flats below the mountain range I was now working. This was not antelope country.

I returned to the problem at hand: there was no easy way into that deer camp where the lads were industriously skinning their ill-gotten prey. They had chosen their ground well. I would have to cross easily a mile of open sagebrush on an extremely rough road just to get to the deer camp they presently occupied. In addition, another road led out the other side of the deer camp, off the ridge and onto State Line Road, with dozens of little feeder roads from there. If they got there, catching them would be very difficult, if not impossible. Patience was the name of the game, and I suppressed my overwhelming desire to roar forth like the Roman legions of old and just held the high ground.

Once finished with their task of skinning the antelope, the lads took what appeared to be two five-gallon cans from the bed of their pickup and, after cutting the antelope into pieces, stuffed the meat inside the cans. They placed what looked like several deer bags (cloth bags used to sack a freshly skinned animal carcass so it can cool while the dust and flies are kept off the meat) on top of the meat in the cans and carefully replaced the lids. With that, they placed the cans back in the bed of the pickup among the rest of their camping gear, hauled the antelope skin, hooves and all, about one hundred yards from the deer camp, and buried those remains under a large rock. Good, that would make it easy for me to find, I thought. The lads cleaned up their work area, washed their hands, and then dragged out the deer and commenced to prepare it for hanging on the same meat pole so they could skin it. Great, I now had my opening.

I waited and watched until they had this deer about one-third skinned. Then I left my hiding place on the hill and moved my patrol rig slowly down the rough and rocky road toward the deer camp. About halfway down, I stopped and looked over the scene. They had seen me and did not seem to be very concerned about my arrival. They just continued to skin their animal, and their lack of concern told me that more than likely the deer was legal. I continued on, arriving after the lads had finished skinning their deer and were sacking the meat in a deer bag. Pulling up to the camp slowly so I wouldn't raise any dust that could get on the deer meat and piss them off, I shut off the patrol-truck engine and stepped out of the cab.

"Afternoon, lads," I said as I walked over to the deer hanging on the meat pole. "Looks like someone had some luck."

"Yeah, Bob here, after some lousy shooting, finally got his deer," a bearded man answered.

I lifted the deer's head. It was a nice five-by-four-point buck and was properly tagged in accordance with Nevada law. Since I hadn't seen what state the deer had come from, there wasn't anything I could do but consider it a deer lawfully taken in Nevada. I checked all the lads' licenses, and all was in order. Since they all had Nevada hunting licenses, I informed them that they were in California and would not be back in Nevada until they crossed State Line Road, some four miles to the east. They thanked me and said they knew where they were and had no intention of violating California laws. It was great! They had a secret and were enjoying themselves tricking the stupid local game warden. I also had a secret, and it was just a matter of time before it came out!

Turning slowly and taking about twenty seconds to look my chaps over like a lion selecting a plains antelope, I said, "Why are you guys here?"

Every lad visibly changed his expression.

Without waiting for the lame answer I was expecting to follow, I said, "You guys are really off the beaten path, something people do when they have something to hide."

The silence was absolute. All I could hear was a grasshopper fiddling the last song before the winter of its life.

Finally one of the lads chirped, "We just thought we would go and see some country since we were here and all."

Looking him in the eye with a knowing expression, I said, "That doesn't make sense. Think about it, way out here in the middle of nowhere, over a very rough road and in blazing heat. It doesn't make sense to me."

The lads just stood there, huddled like shorebirds in a storm. I gave them my best steely-eyed look. Turning slowly back to the buck hanging on the meat pole, I slowly shifted my stare to the ground beneath the animal. I could see a few antelope hairs on the ground, mixed with deer blood and bits and pieces of their previous skinning and cleaning process. Kneeling so I was facing the three mute lads (wanting to keep an eye on them in case they tried anything), I reached down and picked up the antelope hairs, spent a measured amount of time examining them for effect, and then raised my eyes to theirs. I could see the cracks starting in their original fearless facade.

"Antelope hair," I said, "and fresh, I might add."

They were now watching me like cornered prey and wishing, I would bet, that they didn't have a secret like the one they held inside. I continued to look at the lads and said to myself, I'll bet you not a one of them could pass a turd right now if he had to. I arose holding the antelope hair and said, "Gentlemen, my dad taught me to track as good as any Indian that lived." I was lying, but how were they to know?

I continued with my tall tale, saying, "He also taught me to smell out game, and I am very good at that too. You can either lead me to this illegal antelope or I will find it myself. Your call."

I let the words sink in and watched for a reaction. Damn, this was fun, and full of that rush that comes from hunting your fellow man. I know I shouldn't enjoy it so much, but I did and do.

The bearded one, apparently the leader of this group, awoke from his fear and said, "Go ahead; we have nothing to hide. It's just like we said, we were looking the country over, but you can bet this is the last time we will if this is how the law treats us nonresidents."

I waved my hand in a huge gesture of showmanship to move

them off to one side. I walked back to the pool of blood and hair under the hanging buck, knelt down, and made a big show of smelling the ground. Boy, what a story they would have to tell their buddies and children about the game warden that was part Indian and part cat when this was all said and done. Rising into a crouch, I looked across the ground as if I were examining it for any sign. I didn't see anything, but I made sure they believed I had seen something bad. Moving slowly across the ground toward their pickup as if I were following a trail like the Indians of old, I headed directly for the bed area where they kept their camping equipment and ice chests. A quick glance told me I had their undivided and terror-stricken attention. I don't think there was a heartbeat among them at that moment.

I wiped an imaginary spot of blood off the side of their truck with my finger, smelled it, pretended to lick the blood off my finger, and said, "Yep, that's antelope." Turning back to the lads, I said, "Do you want to tell me about the antelope, or do you want me to continue?"

The bearded guy said, "Be our guest, we have nothing to hide." His voice sure betrayed him, though, and from the looks the other lads gave him, I think they thought so as well.

"OK," I said, "have it your way. I don't mind practicing my tracking skills. They haven't let me down in a dozen like situations, and I don't think they will now.

"Gentlemen," I went on lying, "I picked up fresh antelope hair under your deer, and I can tell the degree of freshness from its brittleness. I have a BS and an MS in wildlife management, and I learned during those programs that antelope hair remains brittle for up to forty-five minutes after the hide is removed from the body. So, I know an antelope was here sometime in the last forty-five minutes.

"Second, I smelled antelope blood mixed in the deer blood. It has a very pungent smell and can't be mistaken for deer blood, which in this country has a very strong sage smell." I hate to say it, but I lied again. I hope my mom doesn't read these stories, because if she does she will rinse my mouth out with soap.

"Then, gentlemen, I saw three sets of tracks leading to the side of the pickup. The footprints were sunken in the soil as if the owners were carrying something heavy. I was able to judge the depth of the footprints by the depth of those you are making now versus those by the truck." All the lads looked at their footprints as if they would be able to see something graphic. Hell, I only said that because I had read numerous times about Indians distinguishing loaded from unloaded animals or people by the depth of their tracks.

"Then I found that drop of blood on the side of the pickup that smelled and tasted like antelope blood. That tells me the antelope is in the bed of the pickup somewhere among your other camping gear. How am I doing, guys?" I asked.

There was utter silence.

"OK, let me continue."

I moved over to the bed of the pickup and looked at the two five-gallon metal tins. They were old lard tins, probably from some restaurant, cleaned out and converted to carrying containers used during hunting trips. Damn, there was blood on the rim of one of the lard containers! What a God-given break!

Looking over at the bearded one, I said, "Come here." He moved to my side, and I lied, "I can smell antelope blood in this area." Then, pointing to the lid of the lard can, I said, "Look at the bloody handprint on the top of the can."

The lad just froze and then, after looking and seeing, nodded acknowledgment. "I would bet you a ticket that can and probably the other one contains the remains of the antelope. Am I right?"

Of course I was right, I had seen the whole thing, but it was a lot of fun playing with my mice and showing them the unique powers of a game warden! Before he could get his feet under him I said, "I would like to look in that lard can, if I may."

The lad hesitated, then grabbed the can and took the lid off as if there were nothing in it but deer bags. I could tell it was his last act of hope and defiance. Quickly showing me the deer bags, he said, "See, nothing," and with that put the lid back on and placed the can back in the bed of the truck.

I reached over, picked up the lard can, and set it down between us. I said, "This sure is a very heavy can for just deer bags, and with the heavy smell of antelope and all, I think this is where I will find the meat."

I opened the lid, removed the deer bags that had been placed on top of the meat, and exposed the goods to six plate-sized eyes. The lads were dead, and they knew it. Their frozen look and bad cases of the big eye just confirmed that fact.

"Well, gentlemen, why don't you get the other can and let's put it into my truck instead of yours for safekeeping." I took the first can over to my truck, and one of the lads was not far behind me with the other. I asked for and received their driver's licenses, got out my citation book, and commenced to write all of them tickets for illegal possession of an antelope. Since none of them wanted to tell me where the critter came from or how it came into their possession, illegal possession was the safest way to go with a citation. I seized the rifles to assure the men's appearance in California court, seized the antelope and the lard buckets for safe carrying of the meat, and asked if they had any questions.

They all looked at each other, and finally the bearded one asked how I was able to smell out the meat. Giving him a dead serious look, I told him it was a secret Indian trick my dad had taught me and I was unable to share that information with them for obvious reasons.

He just shook his head and said, "We really thought we had it made on this one, and then some stinking half-Indian game warden had to come along. No offense, officer, but being caught in a situation like this is a once-in-a-lifetime situation."

I said, "No offense taken, and yes, it is a once-in-a-lifetime situation." It really was. I have yet to make a similar case during the rest of my career. With that, we parted ways. They were somewhat amazed at what a game warden could do, and I could just imagine the stories they told when they got back to where they came from. It wasn't every day one was apprehended by a game warden who had the hands of a surgeon to test the brittleness of hair, could track footprints across rocks, could smell antelope meat even when it was hidden in a can with a lid on it, and was built like a bear—and, after all my long hours in the saddle, probably smelled like one as well. For me it was just another opportunity to slide home a lesson, between the third and fourth ribs, as we would say in the profession, to those who chose to violate the wildlife laws. Somewhat skewed, but a lesson nonetheless.

I let my lads move off and out of sight before I retrieved the buried hide, head, and feet of the antelope. I figured if I needed an ace in the hole in court, the hide and other parts would provide the evidence needed. Besides, it would give me a questioning point, under threat of perjury, if this case ever went to trial and the lads lied about what had happened that day. Loading my new evidence into the truck, off I went to another part of my chosen patrol area to see what more I could run across in my efforts to ruin anyone else's day. I stopped along another portion of State Line Road about ten miles from my last contact, pulled off into a pine and brush thicket, got out of the truck, set up a lawn chair in front of my rig, and tiredly sat down. Damn, what a day this one had been. In a period of about twelve hours I had met sixteen people and written every one of them a ticket and had seized four deer, one antelope, eleven chukar, and eleven rifles and shotguns. No wonder my tail end was dragging.

Sitting there in the last heat of the day watching the sun move to the tops of the mountain range to the west was really relaxing. I let my mind wander over times and events past, but not so far that I couldn't bring it back at a moment's notice if something illegal occurred. The air was quiet, bird movement was nil, and hunting traffic appeared to be checked by the lad in the lawn chair. Dark followed dusk, and with it came thoughts of going home to my wife, Donna, and her fried chicken, mashed potatoes, gravy, and garden-fresh peas. Damn, I was starting to get hungry, especially after I realized how little I had eaten throughout the day of adventures along State Line Road. Pulling my tired frame up and out of the lawn chair, I became aware of how stiff my old carcass was. A smile started across my face as I loaded up. Reaching down to a switch on my dash, I set off the siren and let its sound splash across the ridges and valleys around me. I was instantly rewarded as the echoes diminished by the new sound of "song dogs" (coyotes, as the Indians named them) as they ran up and down their musical scales from every point of the compass around me. There truly is something to be said for the opening of a man's soul during moments like that. I had worked hard all day for the world of wildlife, and now, during the last vestiges of daylight, the world of wildlife was singing to me its song of life and praise.

Heading down the dusty main road toward Sierraville, I took the time to enjoy the beautiful red, gold, and gray sunset. I never tired of what God was able to splash across the skies for those of us who cared to notice, and tonight was no exception. I smiled and thanked Him for another good day. Using the available starlight and moonlight, I practiced my sneak technique with the patrol vehicle by running down the backcountry roads without any lights. It was always a challenge, but I always found it exciting to run along the edge, and tonight was no different. Several times I had to brake suddenly to avoid hitting a surprised deer or a porcupine ambling down the road, but all in all I found my skill in running the dirt roads without lights to be more than adequate. Rounding a high turn in the road, I was able to overlook a small grass-and-sagebrush meadow below. I stopped to enjoy the quiet of the moment my high-ground position offered only to be disturbed by a set of tail- and headlights moving slowly down the road below me. The way the driver was riding the brake, I wondered if he would have any left by the time he got to the bottom of the grade. Then the vehicle stopped. The backup lights came on, and the vehicle backed up the road and swung its headlights out across my little meadow. It stopped with its headlights illuminating the field, and my evening was destroyed by the quick double *boom-boom* of two rifles going off. From my position high above, I could see that the rifle flashes associated with those shots had come from the back of the vehicle below me. A pickup, I guessed, with two shooters in the back shooting over the headlights. Down the road I went without lights toward my shooters. I had to get closer.

Half a mile down the road, I was about a quarter-mile from the culprits, and the binoculars brought the drama unfolding in the meadow below into focus. The driver of the pickup, because of the area's remoteness and his belief that no one was left in the back-country, was spotlighting deer with his truck headlights. He had discovered something, probably deer, in the meadow and had lit the animals so the shooters in the back of the pickup could get a clean shot. Sweeping my binoculars over the inert pickup with both doors flung wide open, I spotted four lads hurriedly dragging what appeared to be two deer across the meadow. They threw the two carcasses into the back of the pickup, then two lads got into the back and the other two into the cab and the vehicle headed down the dirt road away from the meadow. Down the road I went in pursuit, still not using my lights. I slid around a few corners and almost went off the road a couple of times when I went from a moonlit stretch of the road into a part that lay in the shadow of trees, but God takes care of game wardens, fools, and little children, and tonight was no exception.

The lads who had just shot the two illegal deer were not in any hurry, and I found myself gaining on their vehicle. I could now smell their road dust and occasionally the exhaust from their vehicle as I drew closer. Finally I was able to see their headlights and brakelights ahead of me, and I slowed down accordingly, trying to figure out my plan of attack, four against one and all. My plan wasn't long in coming when the lads stopped at another meadow and headlighted a deer. Both gunmen shot again from the back of the pickup, killing the animal in an instant.

Rolling to a stop not thirty-five yards from their vehicle, I quickly turned off my motor and waited out of sight behind a slight turn in the road. All four lads again bailed out of their rig and headed out across the field, chattering as if they were on a picnic. I guess in a weird sort of way they were, but the ants were about to arrive. I sprang from my patrol vehicle, grabbing my five-cell flashlight as I went. I was armed with my .44 magnum pistol and shot expertly with it, so I was not really concerned about my ability to control the situation. It is amazing how immortal we feel when we are young.

I eased up to their pickup and, reaching across the front seat, removed the keys from the ignition. They had left the truck with the
lights on and the engine off, so no one noticed my little act. Then,
positioning myself behind the truck, I waited. Pretty soon here they
came, heads down to avoid the glare of the headlights they were
walking into, and then lo and behold, it dawned on me! These were
the same chaps I had written up on the mountain earlier in the day
for loaded guns in their vehicle! The California guys I had felt were
dirty but at that time couldn't do anything but write them up for
the loaded-gun violations.

Well, well, well, it was now time to pay the piper, and this piper
was the largest they would ever hear play the "jailhouse rock"! I
waited until they were about ten yards from their vehicle and then
said, "Game warden, lay those rifles down in front of you, *now!*" The
lads just froze, and for a moment I suspected a firefight might be on
the way, or at least a flight to avoid the long arm of the law. To avoid
either, I quickly shouted, "Bob, Dan, Allen, and Joseph [I remembered their names from the morning's tickets], do as I say and avoid
going to jail!" The sound of their names being called out went
through them like a knife. It was a physical thing; I could actually
see them change gears from what they were thinking before they
did what they were told.

"Now," I commanded again, and the two lads with the rifles laid
them down on the ground. I ordered them to step away from the
rifles and told them I had the vehicle keys, so they shouldn't think
about trying to drive off. With that information, they gave up the
ship, moved away from the rifles, and sat down in the area illuminated by the headlights. I removed the bolts from the two rifles that
remained in the cab of the truck, sticking them into my vest pocket.
I then moved into the field, carefully watching them all the while,
removed the bolts from the two rifles on the ground, and stuck
them into another pocket of my vest. Walking backward out of the
light beam of their truck so I could keep an eye on my lads, I instructed them to remain where they were and told them if they fled
the scene a warrant would be waiting for them by the time they arrived home. Continuing to walk backward, I reached my patrol rig,

grabbed the mike, turned on my ignition, and called the Sierraville county sheriff's office.

When the dispatcher responded, I described what I had, the location to the best of my ability, and the names of the lads still sitting in the meadow. I said I was going to issue the men citations for their illegal deer and that if I didn't call the sheriff's office back within the hour, they should expect the worst and remember the names I gave them. They dispatcher told me a deputy would head toward my location but I shouldn't expect him for a least an hour and a half. I acknowledged the message and returned to the task at hand.

First I collected all the rifles and bolts and locked them in my truck. Then, returning to their truck, I told the men of my radio call to the sheriff's office with their names, violation, and all and informed them that if I didn't show up at the trailhead shortly, the sheriff's office would be looking for them. I also mentioned that a deputy was now on the way and that if anything did happen, they would still have to get by him. As I delivered these words of wisdom, I could see any fight they might have had in them run out on the ground like a spilled Coke. I then called them over to the pickup one at a time and wrote them up for spotlighting, shooting from a motor vehicle, possession of a loaded firearm in a motor vehicle, illegal taking of a game animal with the use and aid of a light, and illegal possession of a game animal. Whatever fit the particular lad was what he was cited for.

Once I finished writing up each lad, I had him return to his spot in the field and then called another one over for his opportunity to meet me again. When I had finished, I dragged the two deer from the back of their truck and stacked them on the road. I then called the lads over to the truck one at a time and had them get in the vehicle. I gave the keys back to the driver and instructed him to hit the trail and expect to be stopped by the deputy somewhere along the road down near the trailhead. With that, four tight-lipped lads departed, trading their evening of merrymaking for an evening of self-examination.

Once I was sure they had left my part of the country, I loaded their three illegal deer into the bed of my pickup, including the one in the field that had just been killed, and headed down the mountain behind them. True to the dispatcher's word, the Sierraville County sheriff's office had a man at the bottom of the run who had stopped and was holding the four lads. Once I arrived, he let the lads go, and the two of us then gutted the three deer to avoid wasting them through spoilage. Thanking the deputy for his help, I finally hit a paved road and truly enjoyed its flatness without having to roll over bumps every two feet.

My ass was really dragging as I pulled up into Gil Berg's driveway and turned off the patrol truck's engine. Stepping out of the truck, I found that my day's adventure was far from over. Gil came bounding out of the house and said, "Terry, move your truck to the back of my house, fast!"

I said, "What?"

Gil repeated his statement, and the urgency in his voice told me to move it. After I moved the truck and stepped out of it one more time, Gil told that the local justice of the peace was going to issue an arrest warrant for me for contempt of court, or whatever charge he could dream up. It seemed that I had cited the judge's cousin during my day's sojourn in the backcountry. I was tired and not in the mood for this kind of bullshit. I had worked hard all day, and done a rather fine job, I might add, and to be met with this kind of petty politics made me see red.

"What the hell are you talking about?" I asked.

Gil said, "Did you write a deputy sheriff from Nevada today?"

"Damn right I did," I answered. "The bastard shot a deer in California with a Nevada hunting license and then shot a doe in California and hid her behind his truck seat in a sleeping bag."

Gil said, "Well, that was the judge's cousin, and he is pissed you didn't extend some professional courtesy to him."

I just laughed. "Gil," I said, "let that bastard go? What would you have done?"

"Probably booked the bastard, especially after he shot the doe," was Gil's reply. I had known it would be—Gill didn't let any knothead get away.

"Well, now what?" I asked.

Gil said he would talk to the judge, especially in light of the illegal doe, and see what he could work out. But he also cautioned me that because the judge was pissed, I could expect small or no fines for all the lads I had caught during the day. With that bit of information and without blowing my stack, I unloaded all my evidence and tickets for Gil to process in front of his mad judge and left for a night's rest in Downeyville, a small gold-mining town down the road and out of the way of a possible illegal arrest warrant issued by a judge who should have stayed home!

As I drove toward Downeyville, I got madder and madder at the turn of events. I had done my job and done it well. If that dingbat judge wanted a "hoorah," I knew just the son of a gun who would give it to him. I checked with Gil the next day, and he told me the judge was still mad and would probably throw all my cases out of court just to get even. That did it! A few minutes later I was on the phone to Dan, a newspaper reporter friend in one of the gold-mining towns in an adjacent county. He eagerly took down the facts and the next day called the judge for his side of the story before he printed it. He told the judge he was going to look into this "professional courtesy" thing, and if there was any truth to that part of my tale, it might not look too good for the judge, especially in print. Dan also told him that it wouldn't take long before other mountain-area newspapers followed up on the story, and soon the judge and Sierra County wouldn't look so good in the eyes of the public, especially the voters in his county. Well, surprise, surprise, my cases cleared the court docket with excellent fines and the court upheld the seizures of all the evidence, including the rifles. It seems that even the deputy paid a fine commensurate with his violation and shortly thereafter found himself looking for work.

That day so long ago on State Line Road will stay with me probably until the day I die. It seemed that everything I touched turned to gold for the state of California and mush for the violators.

I hate to see that kind of ethic practiced in the sport of hunting, but it happens, and that is part of reality. The problem is that with the drastic changes I have seen over the years, more and more of this kind of anticonservation attitude is manifesting itself through-

out our society. If you don't believe that, then just work a major
wildlife roadblock on an interstate out west and you will see for
yourself that what I say is true.

Speaking of reality, that judge lost the next election by a land-
slide. Some say the pen is mightier than the sword. I would say that
probably was the case in Sierra County that time so long ago.

12

Taking a Load of 4's

THAT NOVEMBER OF Novembers in 1967, I was working on the Garvin Boggs Ranch, just southwest of Terhel Farms, checking waterfowl hunters. This area comprised harvested rice fields bordered by private duck clubs and was within a few minutes' flying distance of the Butte Sink, ancestral loafing grounds for hundreds of thousands of migratory waterfowl. In short, it was a mecca for waterfowl and the activities they attracted. This particular area had a reputation for the illegal taking of over-limits of ducks, late shooting of night-feeding waterfowl, and commercial-market-hunting activities.

Moving slowly through the area on foot during daylight hours on a nonshoot day, as I was wont to do, I chanced to locate a tarp-covered seven-place duck picker carefully concealed in a deserted ranch outbuilding. A duck picker is a work of art in the duck-hunting community. At the time, such a picker consisted of a small round drum with numerous rubber fingerlike attachments at intervals along the outside of the drum. The drum was attached to a spindle, and a power source whirled the drum and fingers at high speed. All the duck picker had to do was slowly insert the duck into the whirling drum, and with a simple rotation of the bird's body, the rubber fingers attached to the outside of the drum would do the rest. In the hands of an experienced picker, the duck would be picked clean in a matter of minutes, the skin would remain unbroken, and the duck would be ready for the oven. A seven-place duck picker, or one that seven pickers could operate at the same time, could process a tremendous number of ducks for the commercial market in short order. Hence, my more than unusual interest in my newfound picker and my resolve to work the immediate area harder to preclude its ugly use.

Inside the deserted shed were seven six-foot-long cotton sacks full of feathers from those members of the world of waterfowl that had been unlucky. I imagined that the reason for bagging up all these feathers was to keep them from flying around outside and acting to alert the waterfowl-hunting law enforcement community. A one- or two-place duck picker was the norm, and such pickers were used by many of the duck clubs located in the area. But a seven-place duck picker to me indicated a device to further the ugly business of the commercial-market hunter. Leaving the shed as I had found it so as to avoid the possible movement of the picker to another spot, I went on with the rest of my patrol, keeping the image of that seven-place duck picker dancing in my head. People wouldn't have a picker like that unless they planned to use it. Unfortunately, in Colusa County such use usually meant the illegal processing of hundreds of ducks for the commercial market or a bunch of buyers' freezers. With that in mind, I decided to give that side of the valley a little more of my attention until my curiosity was satisfied and I was assured that the killing of ducks and geese was within the law. That simple curiosity got me as close to being killed as I want to be. But in the process I learned, and lived to fight another day.

Several nights later while on patrol at dusk watching the ducks boil out of the Butte Sink like bees, I noticed they had changed their feeding patterns and were now pouring into the harvested rice fields on the east side of the county, just south of the Terhel Farms area. Realizing that the market hunters were probably also watching the ducks and waiting for their destructive opportunities, I decided to switch from daytime to night work in that area.

One night soon after that, about ten P.M., I moved quietly and without lights into the area where I had earlier located the seven-place duck picker. I parked the patrol truck off the levee road and down in a dry ditch where it would be out of sight and covered it with my camouflage parachute. Crawling up out of the ditch and just sitting there beside the ditch road in the tall water grass, I listened to the night sounds while I examined the harvested rice fields in front of me through the "eyes" of my night-vision equipment. The night-vision equipment was of Vietnam vintage, but it was better than most people had, and with it I could easily see and identify objects up to four hundred yards away, so I was satisfied. Putting my equipment down, I cupped my hands around my ears to intensify the sounds of night and was able to pick out the location of a large mass of feeding ducks by the flowing-water sound they made with their bills as they fed about three-eighths of a mile from my place of concealment. Indexing a full-metal-jacket, 110-grain cartridge into my 30 M-1 carbine and checking to see that an extra fifteen-round magazine was strapped onto the rifle stock, I started moving toward the feeding mallards and pintail. Minutes into my travels, after again cupping my hands to my ears for echo-location of my feeding ducks, I estimated that there were probably between ten thousand and twenty thousand of them happily feeding in the rice left for them by the resident farmer's Hardy Harvesters (a popular brand of rice-harvesting machine in the Sacramento Valley at that time).

Moving across the harvested rice field, bathed in the soft glow of a quarter moon, I became acutely aware of the crunch of the rice stalks underfoot and the whir of whistling wings overhead heading for their feeding compatriots. The birds were sweeping back and forth across the skies, drawn to the sound of thousands of feeding waterfowl and the ancestral knowledge that high energy food in the form of rice kernels needed to sustain their migration lay just beneath them for the taking.

Catching the wind's direction, I altered my line of travel in order to move upwind of the feeding mass of waterfowl and looked for a rice check (rice checks were systems of dikes with inserted rice boxes that allowed the farmer to adjust the water level across an entire rice field) in which to conceal my rather large carcass. Finding that check about thirty-five yards from a small access road and a semidry ditch, I offloaded all my equipment and burrowed into the water grasses and rice left unharvested along the rice check. The smell of damp earth and the pungent odor of dead crawdads along the dike hit me as I nestled in, and I began to let my mind ramble as to why I was here. I had found that serious bunches of greedily feeding ducks always stayed turned into the wind, especially mallards and pintail. That way any foreign sound would quickly be borne to their ears, but more importantly, it meant survival. In the case of danger, the feeding waterfowl could much more easily rise into the wind than try to get airborne flying with it. Hence, I always tried to get upwind and stay upwind of masses of feeding waterfowl. That way I was at the business end of a stalk of commercial-market hunters if they decided to give it a try, and sixteen times during my career I had illegal night gunners crawl right by me on their way to large masses of ducks, leaving me behind their backs for easy pursuit when they shot the birds.

When I looked out across the dry rice field, a large collection of feeding and whirring-in-and-out waterfowl less than one hundred yards away was readily evident through my binoculars and night-vision scope. Watching thousands of swirling waterfowl feeding is not only a sight to see but music to the ears, especially to one who lives for the outdoors. Aside from the cold, watching the world of wildlife enact a drama that was eons old was truly food for the soul, but tonight it carried a dangerous twist. Lost in watching the feeding waterfowl, I did not see danger approaching until it was almost too late.

Laying my equipment down on my rice check, I took one more look to the front of my position before I began looking to the rear and sides for human intruders. What was that? There it was again! Directly before me, just yards away, was what appeared to be a large mound crawling toward the feeding and unaware ducks. Hardly daring to move against my rice-check cover, I slowly raised my binoculars and focused them on the lump only to discover that it was three human beings with shotguns crawling slowly toward the mass of ducks, using a rice check as cover. Instantly I knew what was about to happen. Those three lads, if their sneak was successful, were going to intercept the carpet of feeding ducks and blow them up, shooting all together into the mass as the ducks fed up to their hiding place behind the rice check. The three chaps continued easing toward the ducks, but now they had spread out until they were about five yards apart; then they hid behind a rice check immediately in front of me. As the birds continued to feed toward the newly set trap, I waited. It was a hopeless feeling. The men really had to shoot in order to violate any laws. So I just sat there waiting for the carnage to come.

The moments seemed like hours; then suddenly I heard a whistle from one of the chaps. This technique was common among commercial-market hunters. One minute the ducks would be happily feeding, making all the noise in the world, and the next they would hear a whistle and go instantly silent. Immediately, all the ducks would raise their heads to better locate the sound. When they did, the shooters would slam one shot of hot lead right into their raised faces, killing many with their first volley. Since the feeding waterfowl were densely packed together on the ground, actually touching each other, only the birds on the edges could leap into the air to flee. Each outside duck's departure freed a space for the next duck, and the process was quickly repeated. While this fly-away process was being repeated on the outside of the feeding thousands, the ducks in the middle of the flock would start walking away from the danger, awaiting their turn to fly. In short, what you had going on in front of the guns was a "sheet" of ducks lifting up from the ground and flying away. As the living sheet lifted, the gunners would punch a twelve-foot hole in the portion before them with each new shot. If the market hunters had chosen to take the plugs (a mechanical device limiting a shotgun to only three shots) from their shotguns, thereby increasing their shell capacity from five to seven or more, depending on the make of the gun, the resultant carnage could be terrific. Many times when I had located a shoot, or drag, that had occurred the evening before I would pick up anywhere from three hundred to five hundred crippled ducks—*after* the shooters had picked up several hundred dead birds and left! You can see why the state and federal officers worked the commercial-market hunters so hard in order to reduce this tremendous waste of the waterfowl resource.

The ducks raised their heads in alarm at the sound of the whistle, and the three men shot into the thousands of raised heads and necks. Birds that had been happily feeding moments before now rose in terror in their attempt to escape the sure death and sheets of flame in front of them. The roar of fleeing waterfowl covered the echoes of the shots and drowned out the small sounds of the hundreds of ducks flopping on the ground in their dance of death. As this carpet of ducks rose from the rice field and fled to the safety of the air, the three gunmen finished shooting, dropped to the ground in an attempt to conceal themselves from the eyes of any game warden who happened to be in the area, and began to look around to see if anyone was coming to investigate what they had just done.

I held my position as the sounds of the night returned to abject quiet. Except for the sound of a few ducks still calling or flying overhead to investigate the feeding area for merit, it was silent as a tomb. I had already selected the largest chap of the bunch because I thought he would be the slowest. I knew I couldn't catch all three, but I sure planned on putting a hurt on the largest one, in the form of a flying tackle if I were given the opportunity. My shooters waited about twenty minutes until things quieted down and they were comfortable that no one was around to chase them. Then, as if on command, they rose to their knees and looked all around the now deserted and quiet rice field. After another long look around in the pale moonlight, they stood up, laid their shotguns down, headed over the rice check that had hidden them, and quickly started picking up the hundreds of dead and dying ducks.

That was my cue. I slowly rose to my knees, checked my pistol and carbine, got into a half crouch, and began to slowly trot toward the largest of the three shooters. I hoped to get as close as I could before being seen, thereby saving my strength for the footrace across the rice field that was sure to follow. I hadn't taken more than two or three steps when something that felt like a board or a giant hand hit me in the back and sprawled me face down in the rice field, where I flopped around on the ground like a beached salmon. My entire backside, from my legs to the back of my head, hurt like there was no tomorrow. I reached back to grab the areas hurting the most, and my hands came away slick. At that point, I knew I had been shot. I rolled over and saw the three men I had trotted out to catch running like hell across the rice field. Taking the 30 carbine, which fortunately had stayed in my hands during this episode, I fired all thirty rounds from the magazine knee high at the fleeing lads, thinking they were responsible for my injuries. My mind was racing, trying to put this picture together, when all of a sudden I thought, Damnit, Terry, you are bleeding from the back. Your shooter is behind you, not in front!

I quickly did a combat roll to my left, forgetting the pain when my back hit the ground, acutely aware of the danger from behind, and in the same motion rejected my empty thirty-shot magazine and speed-loaded the fifteen-shot magazine that had been fastened to my rifle stock. As I faced the direction that had been behind me, it became apparent that the first thirty shots from the carbine had ruined my night vision. I stayed low and pushed my eyes to the limit, trying to adapt to the night once again, as I continued combat rolling to make it harder for any second volley coming my way to connect with my already bleeding carcass. In the interim, my night vision slowly returned. It seemed like hours, but soon I could see the land before me in detail. After studied examination of this field of fire, I was satisfied that the danger was gone. There was nothing behind me but a road and a ditch, and there sure as hell was no one there. I turned back in the direction I had last seen the three chaps running, but they were nowhere to be seen. I figured I had killed them with the thirty rounds from the carbine as they tried to escape.

By now I was really hurting like a son of a bitch, not to mention getting stiffer than a poker. Using my carbine like a cane, I pushed myself up and started to shuffle back to my patrol vehicle and help. As I inched along, between being pissed off for getting ambushed and hurting I was very thankful that I was still alive. But boy, was I one mad son of a bitch! Being a poor game warden had probably saved more of my hide than I cared to admit. Not having a lot of money in those days, I had to wear a lot of cheap clothes in layers in lieu of using the light down clothing that was available for the well-to-do outdoor set. That night I had on long underwear (top and bottom), jeans, a heavy wool shirt, and a heavy canvas hunting jacket. Fortunately for me, where the shot hit it cut out chunks of the canvas cloth, formed balls of cloth, and, owing to the increased surface area of the projectiles, penetrated the skin only about three-eighths of an inch in most instances. Back at the truck, I slowly took off my clothes and removed the cloth-covered lead pellets with my fingers as best I could. When I added up the lead extraction at the truck and later, 189 size 4 lead pellets were pulled from my magnificent carcass. Nine pellets remain to this day, and I carry them as a reminder of my mortality and that night long ago in the rice fields.

I got into my patrol rig and headed to the Colusa County sheriff's office to report the shooting of one rather large state officer. When I arrived, I crawled out of my truck and walked slowly toward the back door, only to meet Sheriff Alva E. Leverett, or, as we affectionately called him, "Pappy," coming out.

He took one look at me and said, "Tiny, what the hell happened to you?" Through clenched teeth I told him some bastard had shot me with a shotgun out at the Boggs place. Pappy grabbed me and spun me around back toward my car, then, changing his mind, shepherded me over to his own patrol vehicle. When he grabbed me, I goddamned near swung at him because I hurt so badly. As Pappy opened the door to his patrol car he said, "We can't let word of this get out. If the commercial-market hunters know you have been slowed down, they damn sure will take advantage of that fact, not to mention you. Now, get in." What he said made sense through my pain-fogged mind, and I did what I was told.

We proceeded to his house, whereupon Pappy stripped me down to nothing and had me stand there while he pulled the remaining balls of shot from the places I hadn't been able to reach earlier at my pickup. Thank God his wife was not home to witness that event.

Pappy told me, "Son, you were full of number 4 shot. Whoever took a shot at you really didn't want you there and made his point, I would guess."

Then out came the iodine, and boy, did that hurt. I told Pappy,

"Why the hell don't you use whiskey or gunpowder like they do in the movies? It sure as hell couldn't hurt any more!"

He just laughed and said, "Just you wait until I get to your ass; you will regret those harsh remarks." He wasn't wrong either. When he was finished he took an old flannel sheet, tore it into six-inch strips, and commenced to wrap me up like a mummy. I looked like crap, but it sure stopped the leaking.

By now I was starting to thaw out from the chill acquired while lying in the rice field earlier in the evening, and with each minute the pain was increasing. In addition, I got a good look at my backside in the hall mirror and discovered I was the ugliest combination of blue, purple, yellow, and brown I had ever seen. To top it all off, the pain was really starting in like there was no tomorrow. Four long, deep pulls from Pappy's bottle of Wild Turkey whiskey started to take away the hurt, but now there was another problem.

Pappy took another look at my backside "shotgun Picasso" and said, "You can't let that little gal of yours see this, Tiny. If you do it will worry her sick."

That thought had also crossed my mind. Since the beginning of our married life I had always slept nude because nightclothes made the bed too warm for me to get a good night's sleep. To go to bed now with some sort of covering like pajamas would alert Donna in a second. Pappy was right: I had a problem.

Pappy continued, "How are you going to get around this one?"

"Well," I said, "she teaches school, so what I'll do is just work all night, and when she goes off to teach I'll go home and sleep. I'll just continue this pattern for as long as it takes to heal up."

Pappy thought for a few minutes and then said, "That might work." He continued, "We need to keep this incident to ourselves and see if we can smoke out who pulled the trigger." Again, what Pappy said through my pain- and whiskey-filled brain seemed to make sense. I quickly agreed.

"Also," he added, "I'll come out each day after Donna has gone to school and change your bandages. That way you won't get an infection and won't be leaking all over her bed sheets, which will give you away as well." Damn, I thought, good old Pappy. Always thinking of the angles. Waiting for the whiskey to work its magic, I filled Pappy in on the whole episode. He listened intently and said, "I think I know who the shooter was, but I won't say for fear I'm wrong, because you might kill him before I could slow you down." He had that right, I thought.

Seeing that the whiskey was finally kicking in, Pappy asked, "Are you up to some walking back out there in the rice field?"

"Sure."

"Let's go back to the field and see if you hit any of the bastards who shot the ducks. It'll be daylight by the time we get there." I noticed he wasn't too worried about me. I think he knew it was nearly impossible to kill anyone my size, so being county sheriff and all, he was now worrying about those who cast the votes—or possibly it was those who had been in front of me and the 30 M-1 carbine and maybe now couldn't vote. Anyway, we went back to the sheriff's office, got into my truck, and ventured back to my recent field of battle.

In the rice field, I took Pappy to the spot where I had hidden before the shooting. Then I showed him where I had risen to my feet and started to run after the largest of the shooters. I didn't have to point out where I had hit the soft ground rather abruptly after being shot, and then a pile of 30 carbine shells marked the spot whence I had fired at the fleeing lads I suspected of killing for the commercial market.

From there we walked to the spot where the market hunters had lain in wait for the ducks and traced their footprints from their place of hiding to where they had started to pick up the dead and dying ducks. We walked through the bodies of about five hundred ducks, following the footprints of the market hunters as they walked, then ran, then really began stretching it out before they hit the ground and started crawling like turtles as I commenced firing the carbine. The crawl marks led us to a dry irrigation ditch, where the lads, now able to stand, had run like the wind toward a white ranch house and away from the field of fire. Damn, for all that smoke and fire, I hadn't hit a single chap. You can bet, though, that it was a long time before these chaps tried something like that again.

Back we went to my original place of concealment, and then we backtracked in the direction from which the shots that had taken their toll on my back and legs had come. There was another dry ditch behind my position in the field where one could plainly see the tracks of a "drop-off," or a person positioned to protect the backs of the market hunters. He had walked down the ditch and stationed himself behind his friends in the field, totally unaware of me in between him and his partners. Lying in the ditch were three freshly fired Winchester Mark 5 number 4 shot casings. I really had taken a hell of a load of 4's. The tracks in the ditch also ran back toward the white ranch house. However, once they left the ditch we were unable to determine where they had come from or gone to. Pappy and I picked up the dead ducks and the three Winchester Model 12 shotguns dropped by the hunters when I had started shooting and left the field. Pappy took the guns and after one year sold them, using the money for Christmas gifts for the poor kids in the county. I picked up the ducks, 543 of them, had them picked and cleaned, and gave them to the old and poor of the county.

I went home, took about three thousand aspirin, and tried to get some sleep. I commenced my little charade with my wife and kept it up for the next thirty or so days until I healed. Pappy worked his magic, and here I am today, none the worse for wear except a little ego that was blown away that night. Donna, sharp lady that she is, was a little suspicious at first, but my white lies, told with urgency, sold her on the work needed at night in the rice fields. As a result, I skated through her sharp, blue-eyed gaze, and she was none the wiser. It was kind of neat that I was able to keep this episode in my life from her for the next five years, so she wouldn't worry. In fact, I kept this episode from just about everyone for many years.

Sometime during January, just after the Christmas holidays, I met a fellow named John Griggs on a street corner in Colusa. He had a reputation for being a hothead and confirmed it again that day. As he approached me, he got a big grin on his face and said, "I understand you got your ass dusted last winter out at the Boggs place."

I said, "John, only three people knew about that: the sheriff of the county, me, and the son of a bitch who pulled the trigger. As far as

I'm concerned, you're the bastard who pulled the trigger." The shock in his eyes confirmed that I had the right man. I continued, "Now, I want you to listen, and listen very carefully. I am going to kill you. When you pulled the trigger, you jeopardized my family over a few ducks, and I'm going to kill you for that. You don't ever shoot anyone over a few ducks, but I'm here to tell you that when you didn't think and strayed over that line, you slipped a noose over your neck just as sure as there is a God. It's OK to screw with me, that's what I get paid for, but when you screwed with my family, and that's what you did when you pulled the trigger, you stepped over the line."

All the color drained from his face and he squeaked, "You can't threaten me like that! You can't say you're going to kill me! I'll have your job for that; I will report you for this."

I said, "Go ahead. You have a long criminal record of fighting law enforcement officers every time you are stopped for vehicle violations or drinking while driving in this county. When I kill you, I will just tell the court you came at me with a weapon and I had to kill you. It's that simple. If you want to run and tell someone I threatened you, go ahead. No one will believe you. It's just your word against mine, and your reputation is pretty bad with law enforcement in this county compared to mine."

John knew I had him, and he just stood there, stunned at the direction I had taken and his own knowledge regarding this incident. I went on, "If I catch you in the field hunting, I will kill you. Just remember, with your rotten police record, I'll just tell the investigating officers that you went wild when I went to check you and I had to defend myself. Then, bingo, we are even." I am sure that by that point in our conservation, my eyes had turned gunfighter blue, and that moment had not been lost on John. He couldn't even speak. His lips just mouthed words that didn't come. The look in his eyes told it all. He had come to gloat and instead found a wall of intensity he couldn't overcome or lie through. I have seen that same look in the eyes of dying men or those who didn't care if they lived or died. It is a unique look, but one you recognize when the time comes. I turned and walked away before I really lost control and killed him right there on Main Street with my bare hands.

It was kind of funny that over the next few years, every time I met John in the field, even if he was with his friends, he would always break down his shotgun or rifle, depending on what he was hunting, and give the parts to his buddies. He then kept his hands in plain view and responded to my every question as if not wanting to anger me.

As a result of this little "hoorah," the illegal duck hunting and commercial-market hunting on that side of the valley ceased entirely for the rest of that winter season. I didn't hear another rattle of shots by market hunters that season anywhere on that side of the valley. I guess the word got out that they had "dumped" the game warden but had not killed him or injured him badly enough to keep him out of their hair, so they decided instead to stay out of mine.

I guess that's the price one pays for not doing it right the first time, regardless of what side of the fence you are on. By the way, I later learned that John had moved away from Colusa to become a guide and outfitter in Wyoming.

I wondered if John knew that he was now living and working in my new federal law enforcement district. In the fall of 1989 he found out. ...

13

The Gold Dust Twins

IN THE SPRING OF 1966 I successfully competed for one of twenty-five California state Fish and Game warden positions among 1,300 other applicants. Having passed the written test, oral examination, and physical, twenty-three of the successful twenty-five were soon shipped off to a basic law enforcement academy in the foothills near San Bernardino in southern California (the remaining two didn't have to go because they had already met state training requirements). What a hole! I don't remember how the rest of the chaps felt, but I had traded Humboldt County in northwestern California, with its 140 inches of rainfall per year (temperate rain forest), for San Bernardino County, a lower Sonoran Desert clime with no rainfall per year. It was hot, smoggy, and loaded with a jillion people, and the instructors treated the twenty-three Fish and Game recruits as if we were the lowest level of life in the entire law enforcement community. Basically, they didn't recognize wildlife law enforcement as "real" law enforcement. Today's FBI statistics annually show that officers practicing wildlife law enforcement in all its realms suffer a nine times higher injury and death rate than all other types of law enforcement. I guess that is "real" enough.

It soon became apparent that we game-warden types had better band together in order to survive the prejudice of the penal code law enforcement officers and instructors. This we did, with a few mishaps that were more or less squared away by Captain Hal Mefford, our Fish and Game "house mother" and a damn good man. In the end we supplied six of the top ten academics, we swept the shooting trophies, I was nominated the class president, the top athlete came from the Fish and Game lads, and one of our officers killed all of the pet cats that belonged to the prisoners who maintained the academy grounds and cooked all of the trainees' meals during the week. Cat lovers should be aware that cats are among the most efficient predators on the face of the planet. The area around the academy, the only green spot for miles, was a lure to every cottontail rabbit in the country. The prisoners' cats would constantly drag in these cottontails, leaving them to rot on the campus sidewalks, until one of our officers, let's just call him Mike, took to killing the cats with his pistol on the weekends while the prisoners were back in lockup. The rest of us would have helped Mike kill the cats, but we couldn't hit them. Fortunately, Mike could, and when we departed there wasn't a cat left to kill the cottontails.

The practice of using prisoners to do the grunt work at the academy ended shortly after we finished the program. It seemed that they had even had one of the prisoners doing all the ammunition loading until he intentionally stuck a lead bullet in the powder-drop tube on the automatic loader for about five hundred loading sequences. Then he removed the bullet and let the machine continue loading cartridges. This lad mixed the fully loaded cartridges in with those lacking powder and then left the country. Officers on the pistol ranges were surprised the next week in the speed-shooting sequences with "squib" cartridges followed by fully loaded rounds, and the subsequent explosion when the loaded round found the barrel of the gun obstructed by the squib round. Needless to say, prison details at the academy ended shortly thereafter. Let's hope the cats did as well.

The San Bernardino County Sheriff's Academy was utilized by many law enforcement entities, and we game wardens found ourselves representing one of thirteen different agencies in our particular class. There were eighty officers in this class, twenty-three of whom were game wardens. Being the largest single voting contingent, we ruled the waves, so to speak. My being selected class president was an honor, I thought, until I rapidly found out that I had to answer to all the complaints (mostly justified) lodged against us game-warden types by the others, which was a pain in the last part over the fence. The problem stemmed from a clash between "us" and "them." Every one of the game-warden recruits was college trained, many with master's degrees. With a few exceptions we were older than most of the others in our class, highly confident in our abilities (though in some the confidence was misplaced), and aggressive to a man. This attitude, I am sure, was seen by the rest of the class as arrogance, and their reaction caused a lot of tiffs. We game-warden types lumped together in that class went on to become lifelong friends and supporters of each other throughout the years we were professionally and personally associated. Death took many early, but that did not deter those of us who survived from sustaining our academy relationships.

One of the friendships I made at the academy was with Bob Hawks. Bob was a short little son of a gun (of course, most everyone is shorter than I am) of California Indian descent. He was an excellent pistol shot, always let you know where you stood in terms that were easy to understand, and was totally dedicated to catching those breaking the law. Our friendship grew throughout our time at the academy, and we kept in touch as best as we could after we left and were assigned to different duty stations scattered throughout the state. One day along about 1968, I received a phone call from my Fish and Game captain, Jim Leamon. Jim told me that the newly selected game warden for Yuba City was none other than Bob Hawks, and he asked whether I know Bob. "Hell, yes," I said. "We were the best of friends in the academy."

Jim said, "Good, how about showing him around, especially the east-side boundary area between your two districts, when he arrives?"

I answered, "Sure, that would be no problem. I can use the help, especially on some of the night-fishing camps along that eastern boundary."

Jim told me that Bob would be arriving in the next couple of weeks and advised me to set some time aside to give him a hand, especially on the administrative side of the work required by his district policy. I told the captain I would be happy to help and complimented him for making such an excellent selection.

I spent the next several weeks working night fishermen and deer spotlighters, altogether forgetting the arrival of my friend in Yuba City because of this extensive but exciting work load. Patrolling the east side of my district early one morning, I was surprised to hear Bob calling me on the radio.

I responded, "Bob, what is your location?"

He gave me a 10-20 (location) about ten miles away, near a great little restaurant I knew, so I told him to meet me there. Our reunion was, as expected, noisy and full of name-calling on both sides. Bob and Lynn (his wife) had just arrived at their new home in Yuba City, and Bob told me that Captain Leamon had directed him to work with me for two weeks to learn the ropes, so to speak. I was really pleased to have Bob in our patrol squad and couldn't wait to get going, so I said, "How about starting tonight after I get a few hours' sleep?"

Bob answered, "Sure, what time and where do you want me to meet you?"

I gave him directions to my home in Colusa and we parted company, two very happy warriors who were soon going to make history in the Sacramento Valley Fish and Game squad.

ᕗ

That evening Bob arrived at my home and had a chance to meet my wife, Donna. They hit it off immediately. Bob and Donna were a lot alike, very quick, sharp-witted, and personable. I had to give Donna the edge, though, when it came to one-upmanship. She was lightning quick with her wit, and when she was in top form, few could stay with her. As I said, an instant friendship developed between those two, which further cemented the friendship between Bob and me. Since I was now ready to go, off we two warriors went into the night to see what life had to offer.

Slowly moving through some of my valley areas, basically farmland, Bob and I, like any friends who were something of a pair of knotheads, got to challenging each other to lofty pinnacles of endeavor regarding who we would catch that night and what type of case it would be. I challenged Bob to pick a case, *any case,* and my district would produce it. A little bit of bragging was normal in

Colusa County, especially if I was on one end of the "wind." In fact, a whole lot of bragging would occur before the night was over, and, fortunately or unfortunately, depending on which side you were on (legal or illegal), God was listening. Now, when God listens in on these kind of conversations, which He really shouldn't do, a little bit of the devil gets into His mess kit. The next thing you know, God has gone and done it! Regarding the aforementioned challenge, good old God got to mucking around big time, and Bob and I paid the price!

Bob, always up for a challenge in which he could shame the German, or "Nazi," as he called me, thought long and hard and then said, "How about a set-line case?"

Damn, he picked a hard one right off the bat, I thought. Maybe I had been too hasty in my mouthing off. However, a good German can't back down in the presence of his friend the "Digger Indian," as I called him, so I said, "Sure. and how many hooks?"

Bob said, "What?"

"It's not hard to make a set-line case in Colusa County. How many hooks?" I repeated.

He thought for a second and said, "How about eighty?"

Goddamn, I about flipped. I had only made six set-line cases in Colusa County since my arrival a year earlier, and none had had more than twenty hooks. They were few and far between and a bear to make. Maybe this time I *had* gone too far in the "wind" department. But seeing Bob's eagerness to trap me, I said, "No problem. Butte Creek, here we come."

A set line was nothing more than a very heavy monofilament line, eighty- to one-hundred-pound test, stretched from bank to bank on a small slow-moving river or stream with shorter, lighter monofilament lines tied at intervals along the main line with hooks and bait at their ends. These secondary lines trailed off on the downstream side of the main line, which was usually anchored to tree roots on the streambank or some other object that would hold up under the weight of the line and any fish that it might catch. Set lines were very effective at removing large numbers of fish all at once and were outlawed in most western states. In Colusa County, the minimum bail in those days was $100 for the set-line offense plus $10 per hook on that set line. In 1968 that added up to very big money in short order if one were apprehended running set lines of any magnitude.

It was dark now, and Bob and I prowled Butte Creek like Genghis Khan did the steppes of Mongolia. We discovered several people with minor fishing violations, but no set lines were to be found. Bob, obviously enjoying my friendly-competition-caused discomfort, was really giving me a razzing. I was trapped by my big mouth and knew it, but damned if I would give in to that stump of a person! We had a hamburger riding on our little challenge, and I *never* lost a hamburger bet.

About two A.M. I noticed the wake of a boat moving up the creek ahead of our patrol vehicle as we ran without lights along the east-side levee of Butte Creek. Bob spotted it about the same time I did and put his binoculars on the boat running at the head of the wake. Just like clockwork, the boat moved to a stand of willows on the east bank of Butte Creek. The two lads, not aware of our presence, shut off their boat motor and used shielded flashlights to pick up the sub-merged main line of a set line and to pull themselves slowly hand over hand along the set line, across Butte Creek to the west side, checking and rebaiting the hooks and removing the fish. They re-moved eleven catfish as they went, knocking them on the heads and throwing them into a gunnysack in the bottom of their boat.

Bob and I couldn't believe our eyes! That was the mother of all set lines. No two ways about it, that monster had to be at least one hundred feet in length with at least eighty hooks. Once finished, the lads started up their outboard and proceeded upstream to their fishing camp, where they removed their fish from the gunnysacks in the boat and placed them in ice chests for safekeeping. Damn, talk about too good to be true. Bob and I forgot about our little bet as we swung into the behavior commonly associated with game war-dens starting to hunt their own kind, that is, humans in the "screw-up" mode.

"Bob," I said, "they came from downstream; that means they must have more set lines down there."

The lads' activity had not been lost on Bob, and he said, "We better get this rig out of here where they can't see it so we can start following them on foot as they move up and down Butte Creek."

I hurriedly agreed and moved the patrol truck off the levee and into a thick stand of cottonwood trees. Over the truck went my camouflage parachute, and we were set for any action that was to follow. Moving back to the levee on foot, Bob and I positioned ourselves directly across from and out of sight of the fishing camp and patiently sat there amid the jillions of biting mosquitoes. One hour later, the lads got back into their boat and slowly headed down Butte Creek, all the while watching out for the local game warden yet not seeing us patiently jogging along the levee in the dark thirty or so yards behind them. Sure as hell, the lads went about 150 yards downstream to another bunch of willows growing along the east bank of Butte Creek, retrieved a submerged set line with a bow hook, and commenced to move along the line to the west bank, all the while removing fish and debris and rebaiting the hooks. Finishing that chore, they floated downstream a short distance, started up the motor, and moved carefully up the center of the stream, where the set line would be sunk to its deepest point, to avoid cutting the line with their propeller. Bob and I jogged back upstream after the lads to their second set line, the one we had originally spotted them working on, and again watched them repeat their earlier actions, checking and rebaiting the fish hooks. Once finished, the fishermen again floated downstream a short distance, started up their outboard motor, and then moved upstream over the center of the set line and back to their fishing camp to wait through the next line-checking interval.

Moving back down the levee to the lower set line, I stripped naked and entered the water below the line. Swimming upstream in the dark, I carefully felt for the submerged set line. Locating it, I followed it across Butte Creek, checking the hooks until I found one with a catfish on it. Hanging on with one hand against the stream's languid flow, I took the fish in the other hand and with my teeth nipped off the very tip of its dorsal fin. That way I had a marked fish for the bad guys to sack up for evidence, if needed, to more than establish that these lads were really the ones guilty of running the set line—and it didn't hurt the fish in any way. Carefully releasing the fish with the hook still in its mouth, I let the line settle back down into the water to the depth of my arm and then quickly let go so I would not be caught by the hooks on either side. Floating downstream until I was free of the line, I swam to shore and grabbed Bob's hand for assistance in getting up the steep, muddy bank. Fighting off the mosquitoes attracted to my carcass, I hurriedly dressed. Bob and I then sat patiently by this set line and waited.

About forty-five minutes later, here came our lads. As one of them reached for the set line tied to a willow limb on the bank next to where we were hiding, Bob, who had hidden his tiny body in the willows, reached out and grabbed the bow of the boat. At the same time I turned on my flashlight and told them, "State Fish and Game wardens. Hold it right there!" The two lads froze, not having dreamed there was a game warden in miles, as I moved down the bank and grabbed the stern of their boat.

After we identified ourselves and showed them our badges, Bob had one of the lads get out and stand by me. Bob then got into the boat, and he and the remaining lad cut the set line attached to the willow on our side and drifted across Butte Creek, rolling up the rest of the set line. Cutting it free from the west-bank willow bush, they returned to our side of the stream. Bob handed me the rolled-up set line, and then he and his "partner" moved upstream to the other set line and repeated the retrieval process.

Counting the hooks as Bob took the two lads' driver's licenses, I came up with a total of 167 hooks! This, plus the thirty-five fish over the limit they had back at camp, amounted to $850 total per person in fines (we couldn't go higher than $500 per offense, hence the $850 total for both offenses). Both lads were apprised that failure to appear would send the system after them, and from their scared behavior it was apparent that they would gladly take care of their fines (as they did). Bob and I squared away our evidence, including the fin-clipped catfish (which turned out to be unnecessary), and headed for home with visions of $1,700 in fines dancing in our heads. Without a doubt, this was the largest set-line case made in Colusa County up to that time. Man, was I tickled, not to mention relieved at winning the monster-case bet with my partner.

"What time tomorrow?" was Bob's question as he removed his gear from my truck to load into his for the trip to Yuba City and home.

I said, "How about the same time?"

"OK," he answered. "What could top this, eh?"

"I don't know," I said. "But take your best shot—*any case;* it will be a piece of cake."

God damn it, I did it again.

Bob said, "See you," as he sped off into the night. Damn, he had that "trap the German" look in his eyes again, I thought.

I stood there in the darkness of the morning and said to myself, "Terry, there is no way to top this."

God just laughed.

∽

The next evening Bob and I loaded our gear, some cold water, and sandwich-making materials as we prepared for the evening's patrol. "How about double or nothing?" he said.

Damn, I was hoping he would have forgotten my bragging remark as he sped off into the night the evening before. No such luck; he was too quick for that. "Whatever," I said in a somewhat lame voice.

"OK," Bob said. "How about a frogger with at least one hundred frogs over the limit?" The limit on bullfrogs in California at that time was twenty-five per person.

Damn, that meant the offending lad would have to have at least 125 frogs. Not wanting to back down at that point, I growled, "OK, you made the call, now be prepared to buy two of the most expensive hamburgers ever."

Bob just laughed, and off we went into the night to work the north end of the 2047 Canal area, my best bullfrog habitat. Starting at the 2047 Canal as it left the Colusa National Wildlife Refuge, Bob and I headed north along the canal levee road with all our lights turned off. Sneaking along the canal like that made it easy to see lights along the fishing areas, which would alert us to the presence of fishermen or froggers. But we drove almost the entire length of the canal without seeing any fishing or frogging activity whatsoever.

Starting to get worried about my big-mouthed bet, I turned onto a small dirt road leading along the north end of Delevan National Wildlife Refuge, hoping someone was frogging along the 2047 Canal on the east side of the refuge boundary. Bob and I hadn't gone one hundred feet east when I spotted a dim light on the refuge, a closed zone, obviously someone illegally fishing or frogging. We stopped the patrol truck, quietly closed the doors, and walked the one hundred yards or so to the source of light. Approaching the small canal whence the light was emanating, we were surprised to see a small canoe being paddled by one chap with another man lying in front, leaning over the bow, *frogging by hand*. (Froggers usually use a long pole with a frog gig on one end to spear the frogs.) There were several gunnysacks full of something alive in the middle of the canoe, and the fellow in the bow held another partially filled sack between his legs. About that time, Bob and I spotted the lad in the bow grabbing a frog that was illuminated by his headlamp and putting it into the gunnysack between his legs. That was enough for us, so on went our flashlights, which almost caused the two chaps illegally frogging on the refuge to jump clear out of their small canoe.

"Evening," I said, "how is the frogging?"

The lad in the stern said, "Fine," in a somewhat weak voice, probably realizing their hind ends were in worse shape than the frogs they had in the gunnysacks. Bob and I got them out of the canoe and up onto the bank. A check of their driver's licenses revealed that they were from the San Francisco Bay area, and police officers from the San Francisco Police Department to boot! I informed them that they were frogging within the boundaries of a national wildlife refuge, a violation of federal and state laws. They didn't say anything, and when I asked for their fishing licenses, neither of them could produce one. I casually informed them that that was another violation. Again, no response.

I told Bob to see what was in the gunnysacks, and after a moment he said, "Frogs, Terry, hundreds of them."

Keeping a careful eye on my two very nervous cops, I told Bob to count them out into the canal (so they would live) and give me the score. About thirty-five minutes later Bob said, "Two hundred forty-seven frogs, Terry," and a quick glance into the canal confirmed that just about every frog in the neighborhood was out there bobbing in the water.

"Lads" I said, "you are looking at a $25 fine for no license, a $50 fine for fishing on a refuge, and a $25 fine for *every* frog in those sacks."

The two cops just gasped, and the short one said, "What about some professional courtesy here?"

Jesus, I was not prepared for what followed and almost jumped into the canal when it happened. Bob came out of that canal as if shot from a cannon!

"Goddamn you guys, you give all us officers a bad name. What do you mean some professional courtesy? You guys left that at the gate when you illegally entered the refuge, and if I was in my district I would throw your asses into jail so fast your heads would swim like those frogs out there in the canal."

Damn, my little buddy, true to form, made it rather plain to the two offenders that to pursue that "professional courtesy" line would not do! They clammed up, and Bob and I wrote them citations for their violations, which came to $575 each for the error of their ways. We escorted the lads off the refuge and watched their vehicle's tail lights disappear to the south on the 4-Mile Road.

I said, "Bob, we just did it again. Can you believe it? I hate to say it, but this is getting unreal."

Bob just looked at me and said, "That's the trouble with you Germans. Your race has lost so many wars it is affecting your brains, what little is left."

We both laughed, but something was sticking in the back of my mind, and I just couldn't put my finger on it. We continued to work most of the rest of the evening but were unable to top our earlier case, so I headed for home. As Bob was leaving, he looked at me with a twinkle in his eye and said, "Want to make it triple or nothing on the hamburger bet?"

Not wanting to push my luck any more than I had already, I answered, "No, let's just let it rest and enjoy ourselves tomorrow."

Bob said, "OK." But the tone in his voice was that of a hunter whose appetite was now whetted and who wanted more—much more. He left for home, and I gladly crawled into bed and quickly fell asleep.

~

About dusk Bob turned into my driveway and bounded out of his car and up the steps into my house with a hearty, "Hi, Donna. The old man tell you about our luck?"

Donna nodded, and Bob continued, "Just you wait and see what we are going to do tonight." Donna just grinned. She knew we were having the time of our lives at the expense of the bad guys, and she wasn't going to slow down the fun.

I was afraid of that. That damn little poop had another unreachable limit for the evening's events, and I sure didn't want to be let in on the secret. Oh well, I started this mess, I might as well see what he has up his sleeve, I thought. "What's up for tonight, Bob?" I asked.

"How about we catch six deer spotlighters?" Damn him, he knew the state average of spotlighters caught by a Fish and Game officer was *six per year,* not six in one night! He expected to catch that many in one evening? Brother!

I told Bob, "Be serious."

He said, "I am! If we can make the largest set-line and over-limit of frog cases in the state, what is to stop us?"

"Come on," I said, "let's go." I was half caught up in this race for the roses!

With that, out the door we went en route to the mountains in the western part of my district. If we were going to make a spotlighting case against deer hunters, that was where we would have to be.

Turning off the Leesville Road onto the Ladoga Road, I shut off all my lights and sat there for a few minutes to let our eyes adjust to the dark. The evening was hot, and both Bob and I had our windows down to let in any air we could (there was no air conditioning in state patrol vehicles in those days). *Boom* went the sound of a heavy rifle somewhere down the road we were sitting on!

"That shot sounded like it was no more than a mile or so down our road," I yelled to Bob as I started up the truck. Racing down the Ladoga Road without lights, we hadn't gone a mile when here came another vehicle hell-for-leather right at us. On went my headlights and red light, but the speeding vehicle was by us before I could blink. I always liked a good chase; a quick power turn of my vehicle and the race was on. We overhauled the speeding vehicle in about two miles and finally pulled it over after the occupants had managed to unload their rifles (it was illegal in California to have a loaded firearm in a motor vehicle on a way open to the public).

Bob sprang out of my still sliding vehicle and was on the lads in the stopped car in a flash. Putting my truck in park, I approached the car on the driver's side, and Bob and I got the four black male occupants out and made them stand at the rear of their vehicle in the glare of the headlights from my truck. Once we had them safely under control, we checked their vehicle. There were two spotlights on the floor and two 30-06 rifles with live ammunition and spent casings on the floor. Walking back to our four lads, I asked what they had been hunting, and they all looked at each other, but no one said anything.

I asked my question again, and the driver said, "We weren't hunting deer, we was only shooting jackrabbits."

Bob and I looked at each other and grinned. Who said anything about shooting deer? we both thought. Looking back at the driver, I repeated, "You were *only* shooting jackrabbits?"

The driver said, "You bet, that was all we was shooting at."

I said, "How many did you guys shoot?"

The driver said, "Oh, eight or ten, but we was not shooting the deer; we know that's illegal."

I said, "All of you who were shooting at the jackrabbits and not deer, raise your hands."

All four of the lads raised their hands. Brother, what dummies. Taking jackrabbits with the use and aid of a light was also illegal in

California. With that, I walked back to the trunk of their car. There was a snotlike substance and blood all over the rear bumper.

I said, "I see you have some blood on the rear bumper. Are your rabbits here in the trunk?" Without waiting for a response, I continued, "That's a great idea, keeping the rabbits and taking them home for dog food. You guys are to be commended for not wasting the meat. Is that where you're keeping the rabbits?"

"Yes," said several of the lads at the same time.

I walked back to the driver and said, "Why did you guys run when you saw the red light?"

"We was scared," was the reply.

Looking him right in the eye, I said, "I would like to look in the trunk of your car, if you don't mind."

"Sure, go ahead, if you can."

I said, "May I have the keys to the trunk, please?"

The driver answered, "That's what I was talking about. We lost them back there when we picked up those rabbits."

I said, "Let me see the keys you have in your hand," which he did. Sure enough, they didn't fit. I walked back to my patrol truck, dug into my toolbox, and walked back to the car with a crowbar. I said, "Lads, spotlighting any game animal in the state of California is a violation of the Fish and Game laws." Letting that sink in, I continued, "Since the 'rabbits' are in the trunk of the car, I would like to see them. If you are unable to provide the keys, I will have no option but to break into the trunk with this crowbar."

They just looked at me, and taking that as a "no," I stuck the end of the crowbar into the trunk lid where it joined the trunk frame and said, "Last time." No response. I started to pry up the trunk lid, and the driver said, "Wait; here are the keys."

Digging into his pants pocket, he produced a set of keys that fitted the trunk lock. With a turn of the key, the trunk opened, and upon lifting the lid, four dead-as-a-hammer does appeared as baggage. Looking at the men, I said, "Lads, these are the biggest rabbits I ever saw."

The lads had nothing to say as Bob and I placed them under arrest for illegal possession of a protected big-game animal, handcuffed them, and, after sitting them down in the road in front of our patrol truck, called the Colusa County sheriff's office for transport assistance. Carter Bowman, the Stonyford deputy, arrived about forty minutes later and transported our lads down to the jail in Colusa. Bob drove their vehicle, and I followed in my truck down to the state fire station a few miles away, where we left the car for safekeeping. Taking the deer, we hotfooted it after Carter and our load of deerslayers (two fewer than Bob had said we would catch that night). We booked the lads and gave their deer to two needy families. (I had made an arrangement with the county attorney that instead of throwing a whole game animal, guts, hide, and all, into a walk-in freezer, I could take just a small part of the animal—such as a foot or tail—and photographs to preserve as evidence and then immediately give the rest of the animal to such families for their own use. As a small-town game warden, I knew just about everyone in the area. If I seized a big animal, it went to a *big* family, and so on. The family signed a receipt for my records and then got some damn fine eating in the way of frogs, deer, elk, salmon, striped bass, and so forth.)

As we got back into my patrol vehicle, I looked over at Bob and said, "It's too late to go back into the western part of my county. Let's go over and work the warm-water fishermen along our mutual eastern border."

Bob said, "Damn, we almost made our six apprehensions." He paused and then said, "You're right, it's too late to go back into the mountains. Let's go over to the Hammond Ranch area and see if we can make any fish cases along Butte Creek in my part of the district."

I turned the patrol vehicle to the east, and away we moved from the Colusa County jail to our next adventure, which wasn't long in coming.

❧

Zip went the pencil-thin blue beam of a spotlight across the lima-bean field, followed almost instantaneously by the report of a heavy rifle. Bob and I, having our lunch at four A.M. on the edge of Butte Creek on the Hammond Ranch, damn near dropped our teeth in disbelief. We had been quietly sitting alongside the creek and had just spread out our lunch-making materials on the hood of the truck. We had no sooner started making sandwiches than a farmer's pickup entered the area and began checking some irrigation pumps on the north end of the lima-bean field where we were sitting. Once we were aware of what the men were doing, we continued with our lunch preparations, not paying any more attention to the pickup as it made its way around the field. That is, until the spotlight zipped out across the field, latched on to the eyes of a deer, and was followed by a Remington 7mm magnum 154-grain bullet! Needless to say, sandwich-making materials flew off the hood of my patrol truck as Bob and I slid around a corner of the bean field and along a dusty road in hot pursuit. Moments later we had in our clutches one old GMC pickup, two Mexican laborers, one still cooling four-point buck (very fat, I might add), a spotlight, a 7mm Remington rifle, and *our quota of six spotlighters!* Off to jail these lads went as Bob and I performed our ritual booking dance.

Leaving my house, Bob said, "Same time, different place, quadruple the hamburger bet?"

"Bob," I said, "we're running in the twilight zone; let's not push our luck."

To make these kinds of cases on call night after night is unnatural.

He said, "I know, but let's push our luck and see what happens."

"OK," I responded. "What the hell, we are on a roll." I was also a hunter of humans, and our luck over the last few evenings was not lost on me either.

"See you," Bob said as he drove off into the morning.

"See you," I returned, wondering what the hell was in store for us next.

❧

Responding to my ringing phone as I came out of a deep sleep, I was surprised to hear my captain's voice on the other end. "Terry," the voice said, "what the hell is going on over there?"

I said, "I don't know, Jim, but that little Hawks and I are knocking them dead."

He said, "You sure are. I just talked to Bob this morning to see how you two were doing, and I can't believe it. You guys are facing a potential collection of $6,000 in fines for three nights' work. At that rate I will have to call you two the Gold Dust Twins if you keep it up! Do you guys realize you have collected more in fine money in three evenings than the rest of the squad collected all of last month?"

"No," I said. "We have had a run of good luck it would appear."

"Luck, hell," Jim shot back. "What you guys are doing is unnatural."

I quietly agreed as the captain advised us to keep it up and then hung up. *Unnatural* certainly was the word, I thought as I lay back down to get some more sleep.

∾

"Hi, Donna," Bob said as he came into my house to get me for the night's patrol. This evening I was excited to see what we could do once turned loose in the rice fields of Colusa County. Not wasting any time, the two of us left with hardly a backward glance. My patient, long-suffering wife just watched us go with those intense blue eyes of hers, knowing she had married a kid at heart and would suffer forever for that mistake. God, how I loved her for letting me run. Climbing into the patrol truck, I turned to Bob and said, "What is our target tonight, chief?"

He looked at me as if he hadn't really thought about a specific target and then said, "A big duck case."

"Bob," I said, "duck season doesn't even start until almost two months from now."

"I know," he said with a twinkle in his eyes, "but you are dealing with the Gold Dust Twins here, and right now we are burning daylight."

Brother. Off we went to patrol the areas nearest Delevan National Wildlife Refuge, the only area in my district that had lots of ducks that early in the season.

As the sun began to set in the west, Bob and I had managed only to pinch a ditch tender for shooting American coots with a pellet gun and letting them lie where they fell. They were a form of waterfowl, but certainly not the big duck case Bob had ordered. Turning east just north of Gunner's Field, John Chenny's duck club, I headed toward a no-name duck club located along the 2047 Canal that was owned by a drywall contractor from San Francisco. I had been able to pinch members of that club for a myriad of wildlife violations in the past and figured it was as good a place to look for violations as any. I wasn't disappointed.

Driving by the clubhouse, Bob and I smelled burning feathers! There was one car parked at the clubhouse, which wasn't unusual even for this time of the year. Members would come up for a weekend of drinking and just general messing around, hunting season or not. Bob and I spotted the source of burning feathers, two smoking fifty-gallon barrels out behind the duck club, but kept driving down the levee so as not to alert the offending parties. Waiting until dark, we drove quietly back along the levee until we were about one hundred yards south of the clubhouse, parked the rig, and walked the rest of the way on foot.

The duck club appeared to be abandoned (there were no lights on inside), but the vehicle we had seen earlier was still there, and its motor was still warm to the touch. Thinking the lads might have gone to the bar in town in another vehicle, Bob and I began our search of the area, starting with the two fifty-gallon barrels. Inside the barrels were zillions of mallard and pintail feathers, including lots of pin feathers. Since this was September, most ducks would still be going through a moult and have pin feathers! That meant these feathers came from ducks recently taken, *before* the legal hunting season. A check of the weed field west of the clubhouse produced thirty-eight sets of guts recently removed from waterfowl of some sort. Further checking revealed fresh blood spots on the concrete step and porch leading into the back of the duck club proper. The front door was locked and no one responded to our knocking, so Bob and I just sat there with our evidence, quietly waiting for the culprits to return. Our wait ended just before midnight. Winding down the dirt road to the clubhouse came a set of headlights, accompanied by off-key singing that could be heard almost one hundred yards away. The vehicle slid to a stop next to the other parked vehicle, almost hitting it. Four noisy lads disembarked, one sprawling out flat on the ground to the cheers of the other three.

"Screw you guys," a voice said as the fallen man got himself up and staggered after his pals. "How about a duck dinner, uh, breakfast?" he roared after his comrades.

The lad opening the door shouted, "You got it," and headed for the kitchen. Bob and I raced to the nearest window and peeked in. Putting a half-empty bottle of whiskey down on the table, the lad went to the old refrigerator in the kitchen, removed a tray of freshly killed and cleaned duck bodies, and set it on the table. Bob and I just looked at each other and grinned. We were hot on the trail of another good case. Knocking on the front door, still able to see the tray of duck bodies through the glass in the door, I announced my presence to the lad who responded to the knocking.

He knew me and said, "Come on in, Terry." Then, realizing the ducks were in plain view, he added, "Oh, just a minute," and tried to throw a coat over the offending tray.

I said as I pushed my way in with Bob hot on my hind end, "Ralph, we need to look at your ducks, if you don't mind."

What could he say, and the deed was done. It seemed the lads hadn't been able to wait for the season to start and had shot the ducks the day before at a rice field where hundreds of the ducks had been feeding. Forty-four ducks later (we hadn't found all the sets of guts) Bob and I started writing the lads tickets for illegal possession of waterfowl during the closed season. We seized the ducks and their shotguns, advising the now fairly sober lads that they would be expected to appear in the Williams court two weeks hence and settle up with the judge or post bond ($500 each). If they decided to post bond, they could pick up their shotguns at my house once the court notified me it was OK to release them.

I told the lads, "The drunk-driving charges won't be filed, nor will charges for having an open container in a motor vehicle, if these wildlife charges are settled."

There were quiet murmurs thanking me, and with that Bob and I went gleefully out the door. Damn, we had done it again. We were really beginning to think we were the Gold Dust Twins.

We headed home after that. I took care of the evidence, and Bob headed for his home with a hearty, "See you tomorrow, same time."

I nodded and still could not believe our luck. We had written another $2,000 in tickets, over $8,000 total for several days' work. Damn, this was getting unreal.

∾

The next evening I met Bob in my driveway as he arrived. "Let's go," I said anxiously as we loaded his gear into my rig for another adventure. It didn't take much urging to get Bob into high gear either. "Where to this afternoon?" I asked.

"How about a large over-limit of dove?" Bob said. He kept looking me right in the eye, hardly wanting to break our run-of-luck spell, and I said, "The best place I have is over by Terrill Sartain's ranch, near where we made our deer case night before last."

Bob said, "Let's go," and we were off.

Arriving at Terrill's 66,000-acre deer ranch an hour later, we began to patrol the areas known to me for historical dove concentrations. We used the classic game-warden technique of driving through an area, looking and occasionally stopping to listen for shots. It was quiet and appeared deserted. I didn't expect to find many people out other than those from the ranch who would be hunting on private ground and behind locked gates. But many times people in that situation, thinking they are safe from prying eyes, will stray over the line of legality, and that was what I was banking on that day.

For a while our continued patrol on that beautiful ranch produced not a soul or sound. Stopping to get a cool drink and relieve ourselves, Bob and I silently enjoyed our thoughts. Then *boom, boom, boom* went the sound of a shotgun to the south of us. It was almost dark, so we quickly got back into the patrol truck and headed south. There were several roads leading in the general direction of the shooting, so I took the first one I came to, but it panned out as the wrong road. Retracing our route, I was starting to turn onto another choice when I smelled dust in the air.

"Bob," I said, "I think our suspect rig has gone out behind us on the main road."

Without waiting for a reply, I spun the patrol truck back onto the main dirt road leading off the ranch and sped in that direction. Soon I began to overtake a dust trail and moments later saw a pickup truck stop about one hundred yards in front of us. A shotgun came out the passenger side of the vehicle, and another *boom* followed. The door opened, and a fellow ran to the edge of the road, picked up a bird, and ran back to the pickup. As the lad started to get into the truck, he looked back and saw our patrol truck. He froze, and in short order we had pulled up behind them.

Well, well. Wally Oppum and Wes Dollar, two men of whom I had heard nothing good since I had arrived in the valley. Wes was a mortician from the Chico area, Wally was a farmhand for Terrill Sartain, and both had reputations as killing sons of bitches when it came to wildlife. Bob approached the pickup from the passenger side and I from the driver's side. In the bed of the pickup were numerous doves, and it was easy to see, even in the fading light, that we had a huge over-limit. Bob and I exchanged glances. We had done it again: called our shots and were right on! Even in the 100-degree heat I felt a sliver of cold slide down my back. Continuing with the business at hand, we got Wes and Wally out where we could see them and went through the usual game-warden drill checking licenses, checking plugs on their shotguns, and counting out the doves. The limit in those days was fifteen per day, and they had 118 doves in the back of their pickup. Neither of the lads had much love for me, so Bob and I quickly issued them citations for possessing over-limits of dove, seized the birds, and told them they could appear or post bond. Either way they were looking at a $500 bill each for their little error in counting.

They went their way, and Bob and I stood for several long moments in the dark before he said, "This is getting scary." Now, for Bob to say that meant it *was* getting scary. I don't think I had ever seen Bob scared of anything, but he was starting to show some nerves at this point in the game. "There is no way, night after night, we can make a call and have it happen," he said.

Thinking the same way, I shrugged and somewhat lamely offered up, "The Gold Dust Twins."

"Bullshit," said Bob. "You and I both know we're in the Twilight Zone on this one!"

Dodging the discussion, I said, "Let's go home," and with that Bob and I headed home, two grown men with their tails neatly tucked between their legs. Another $1,000 in tickets spun through my head as we journeyed home. God must really love little children, fools, and game wardens, I thought.

Bob arrived at my place about noon the next day, so I fixed him lunch. He told me he had been talking to the captain, and Jim just couldn't believe our phenomenal luck. In fact, Jim had apparently contacted Sacramento and told the "head shed" of his two tigers tearing up the Sacramento Valley. I just looked at Bob, and he looked at me. "Nice tuna sandwich," he said.

That afternoon found us up at Lake Ladoga checking fishermen. Neither of us had suggested a target case for that day. It seemed as if we hadn't thought of it. Heading through Stonyford and down the Leesville-to-Ladoga road, we passed through several old, deserted ranches. We were both lost in thought and just enjoying the hot air flowing through our open windows.

"You have tule elk in your district, don't you?" Bob asked.

"Yes, I do," I said. "Not very many, about sixty head I think, but yes."

"Damn, it would be nice to make an elk case, wouldn't it?" Bob said offhandedly.

We quickly looked at each other but said nothing. We didn't have to—our eyes said it all.

We hadn't gone more than a mile or so farther down the road when my Fish and Game radio came to life with, "234, Colusa County."

Picking up the mike, I said, "This is 234; go ahead, Colusa."

"234, is there any violation if one kills an elephant in Colusa County?" continued the familiar dispatcher's voice.

Laughing, I said, "Colusa County, this is 234; there is no season or bag limit on elephant. They can take as many as they want."

Bob and I started really laughing but were brought up short by the continuing radio transmission: "234, correction, *elk,* not elephant."

I looked at Bob, and he just stared back at me. "Colusa," I continued, not laughing now, "elk are a totally protected species in California; there is no season or bag limit."

"234, what is your location?" continued the dispatcher.

"One mile from the California Division of Forestry station near Leesville," I responded.

"234, we just got a report that an individual just now killed a tule elk near Cache Creek. Can you respond?"

"We're on our way," I responded. "ETA twenty minutes."

I put the patrol truck into the "fly" mode, and off Bob and I went, roaring down dirt roads at speeds faster than a sane man would drive. There had never been a case in Colusa County of anyone illegally killing a tule elk. This would be a first, and I wanted in on the action. It dawned on me as I hurled down the Leesville Valley dirt roads that Bob was looking at me in a very funny way.

"I just mentioned it," he said. "I didn't even think about it, just mentioned it offhandedly about the elk case and all." His voice trailed off, and I think our thoughts were racing around in our heads just as fast as we were moving across that valley to get to the scene of the kill. This game we were playing was becoming not of this world and out of hand!

Arriving at the Cache Creek kill scene, Bob and I were greeted with a dead seven-point bull elk, poached in broad daylight right along State Highway 20. It seemed a tourist had been filming the feeding elk herd from the highway when a lad had come along, shot the herd bull with his brand-new .444 lever-action Marlin, and then commenced to gut his kill. All this had been captured on film, and all Bob and I had to do was go over to the shooter, conduct a short interview, issue him a citation, finish gutting the elk, and load the carcass. Heading for Colusa and a locker plant, Bob and I drove in silence for a long while. Both of us were hot, sweaty, covered with elk blood, and deeply lost in our thoughts, among which was a recently issued $1,000 citation, the very first for killing a tule elk in Colusa County.

Bob finally said, "I think I have the hang of how Jim wants me to work in the district. Maybe we don't need to work together anymore for a while."

I said, "You really do have it together, and there is not much more I can do to fill you in on how the district is run, so maybe you're right."

More silence followed, and then Bob said, "The Gold Dust Twins. There really is something to be said for a German tank driver and a Digger Indian game-warden team."

I said, "Bob, I know neither of us is superstitious, but let's just let this one lie, OK?"

After another pause Bob said, "Right; we aren't superstitious."

After that we didn't work together often on major projects, but when we did Bob and I always knocked the bad guys dead. This unusual chemistry even carried over to hunting together, or anything else we did. The two of us, the German and the Indian, were always extremely successful when running side by side. Damn, I just remembered that he never did pay up on those hamburger bets. Damn his scrawny hide.

I wonder what it would be like to make a case involving ...

14

A Rocket in the Car

ONE HOT JULY DAY IN 1968 found Warden Bob Hawks and me checking warm-water game-fish fishermen along the Butte Creek area of Colusa County. This area was frequented by African Americans for the catfish and carp fishing, which was some of the best in the state. Occasionally a salmon or two would go through this area, and the level of fishing excitement would go even higher when one had a thirty-five-pound king salmon flopping at one's feet. Because of the excellent fishing, over-limits and littering became a problem, and after numerous complaints from adjacent landowners and other fishermen, Bob and I decided to pay a little visit to the area to see if the long arm of the law could help in cleaning the area up.

Our method of operation was simple. We would wait until dark, walk along the east side of Butte Creek, which was all private and behind locked gates, and watch the fishing activity on the opposite side through our binoculars. When we detected a violation, we would sneak back across the creek under cover of darkness on one of the few private bridges, zap the offending souls, and issue citations for the error of their ways. It made for an ideal law enforcement situation but was hell on wheels for the bad guys. They never did figure out how the game wardens always had the goods on them and were able to make the cases they did.

One evening Bob and I slipped over to Butte Creek after noticing it was loaded on the west side with fishermen. Moving along on foot on the east side of the creek as we always did, we saw many fishing camps but none that elicited our enforcement interest. Then, after walking about a mile, we spotted a likely-looking camp. A few minutes' observation with the binoculars confirmed numerous violations. The fishing camp under observation contained seven automobiles and twenty-one fishermen. There were lanterns strung along their side of the creek that gave the camp a Christmas-like atmosphere. Ice chests, fish stringers, Coleman stoves, and fishing equipment abounded. When we counted the number of fishermen and the number of fishing poles, it became clear that we had numerous violations of state law on that issue alone (California allowed only one pole per person in those days).

Bob and I sat there in the dark with our binoculars, watching the lads fish and duly noting those who used more than one fishing pole in our notebooks for the ticket-writing that was to follow. Then out of the dark came a huge black woman, whom we hadn't noticed before, clad only in her white underpants. In and of itself, this was strange, to say the least. But a quick count of the men in camp, all twenty-one of them, made it even more unusual. This woman was a rather large specimen, three hundred–plus pounds, I would venture. She was prancing around the men like an unbroken spring colt and was rather loud of voice, as I recall. It quickly became plain that she had been brought along to provide pleasure to all the men, and she wasn't wasting much time.

Bob and I sat there and chuckled as we watched events unfold. The center for the main event was a '58 Chevy station wagon, parked in such a manner that its rear end was pointed toward the creek—and, of course, Bob's and my position about thirty yards away. The tailgate was down, and a mattress had been placed in the back of the car. This lady was servicing all the men, one at a time. She would finish with one chap and holler out, "All right, Shorty, it's your turn." With that hard-to-turn-down invitation, in would go another lad, and the process would start all over again.

Bob and I decided we would have some fun at these folks' expense. I left Bob at the streamside, went back to my patrol car, and picked up several SCRAM depredation rockets. These were nothing more than eight-to-ten-inch-long rockets, like the ones you see in Fourth of July fireworks, that we used for waterfowl-depredation herding work in the valley to keep the ducks, geese, and coots out of the rice. To launch the rocket you used a handheld launcher, hooked the rocket to a launch rod fastened to the middle of the flash pan, lit it, aimed it, and let it go. These little rockets were faster than greased lightning and traveled about a thousand feet after ignition, blowing up with one hell of a bang. Not only were they an excellent depredation device but they could possibly be used to scare the hell out of people fishing at night along Butte Creek—and that theory was about to be tested.

I walked back to Bob to find that our young lady was back in the Chevy with another chap. This was too good to be true. I placed the rocket on the launcher, aimed it high over their heads so it wouldn't hurt anyone when it went off, and told Bob to light it. As I stood behind the willows, Bob lit the fuse, and after a second of burn-down the rocket ignited. As the rocket roared off the launch rod, horror of horrors, it clattered through some willow branches directly in front of our position that we hadn't seen in the dark of the night. The branches deflected the damn thing downward so that instead of going up in the air over the target and exploding harmlessly, the rocket streaked across Butte Creek right into the back end of that '58 Chevy, roared over the two "lovers," and hammered into the windshield in a sea of sparks!

The rocket, with plenty of burn time left, continued to roar back and forth across the inside of the windshield like a trapped mosquito, only with a lot more punch. In abject terror, Bob and I watched that rocket just a rattlin' and a clangin' on that windshield, still going full bore! Needless to say, the rocket had scared the living hell out of our two lovebirds, who came bailing out of the car nude as jaybirds. The rocket skittered back and forth for several more seconds, then went to the explosive stage and detonated like a hand grenade right in the car. The whole car lit up like there was no tomorrow—and there wasn't for the windshield, which shattered into a million diamond-like pieces. Blue smoke poured out both ends of the car, and the crowd of fishermen was now coming to life. The whole riverbank was alive with running, scared people. They were whoopin' and hollerin' as if a bear were in camp. I guess I couldn't blame them, but goddamn, it was funny! One minute they were happily fishing and fornicating, and the next their whole damned world blew up! Just imagine, they were sitting there contentedly when all of a sudden this roaring monster with one eye came across the creek, slammed into the car, attacked the windshield, and then blew up the car, not to mention wrecked a happy "love" affair.

It was the goddamnedest "hoorah" you ever saw. We had people running everywhere, trying to start their cars and get the hell out of there without running over their friends. We had a fat woman trying to find her underpants and put them on at a dead run. No luck on that one! The other of the "lovers" was hopping around on one leg trying to put his pants on when a fleeing car hooked one pants leg and dragged this chap through a campfire, all spread-eagled, before letting him go. Now that fellow was really hopping about trying to get the hot coals out of his shorts before disaster set in, if you get my drift. Another driver took off forgetting there were several fishing rods tied upright to his bumper, and these were dragged through the rapidly exploding camp in fine style, one with a flopping carp still on the line. I could imagine that when that car stopped running down the highway, all that would be left of that fish was the lips. Another car, backing up to miss one fleeing out ahead of it, backed over a large ice chest, crunching it underneath the frame. When that car fled, the ice chest was still firmly clamped underneath it and "growling" about its plight as the car moved out of sight. By now Bob and I were rolling around on the ground just roaring with laughter as the "hoorah" on the other side of Butte Creek continued to unfold.

About then two of the men from the fishing camp moved to the creek's edge and started shooting across at the location where the one-eyed monster had come from. Branches snapped off overhead, bullets walked across the creek to where we were lying on the ground, and mud splattered all over us from what seemed a zillion near misses. No longer did we find the chaos going on across the creek all that funny! Bob and I were up and running in less than a flash and, like twins, dove into a partially filled ditch at the edge of the road on which we had been lying earlier, laughing our insides out. To say they had our undivided attention at that moment was an understatement. To say the ditch had our undivided attention also was an understatement. Boy, were we a delightful mess after

coming up out of the rotten soup we landed in. That ditch was partially full of nature's delight, a soup not normally not found in any
French kitchen. It was, I'm sure, Mother Nature's recipe reserved
for those special people who screw with other people's fishing
pleasure and lives. Crawdads, twenty-seven species of fish, snakes,
turtles, and other unidentifiable decomposers had all been dumped
into the ditch and then drawn down to about two inches of a
waterlike solution. Add 100-degree Colusa County heat for a week,
along with all the aforementioned dead critters, and you have what
I would call a game warden's stew—especially when you add two
fast-moving game wardens.

We were armed only with handguns, and we knew better than
to return fire with that piss-anty armament. So we took off running
down the half-filled ditch full of dead frogs and other things that
smelled in the night for our patrol vehicles as the noise of rifle fire
faded in our mud-covered ears. The fishermen were rapidly aban-
doning their camp under the covering fire of the two shooters, and
two very smelly game wardens were also fleeing their position in
the dark of the night. After a short run to our patrol rigs, I called
the Colusa County sheriff's office in an attempt to have some officers block the road and catch the lads with the guns. The dispatcher
agreed and scrambled several units in order to try to head off the
fleeing fishermen. Bob and I jumped in our patrol vehicles and
tried to cut off these folks as well.

As it turned out, everybody missed everybody. I don't know
where in the hell those chaps went, but they flat got away. After the
futile chase, Bob and I returned to their fishing camp, and what a
scene greeted our eyes. There were still thirteen fishing rods out,
baited and all. The Coleman lanterns were still all over the place,
happily glowing, and ice chests full of food abounded.

I turned to Bob, who had a dead crawdad in his holster. "There
are hundreds of dollars of gear here. I bet they will return for it, and
when they do, they are ours," I said through a set of smelly lips. Bob
agreed, and we staked out the area until late in the morning, but the
lads and their lady never returned. I wonder if the strong odor Bob
and I were emitting had something to do with it. Boy, did we smell,

and talk about sticky—brother! Bob and I gathered everything up and took it to the Colusa County sheriff's office in the hope that the lads would claim the equipment later. No such luck, so the next time the sheriff's office had a seized-equipment auction they sold all that gear and kept the money to use for Christmas gifts for needy kids in Colusa County.

Over the years I have often wondered what went through that chap's mind when the rocket hit the front windshield in their love nest. He must have thought that was the best woman he had ever had because about halfway through the experience the whole car blew up. I'll bet the next couple of times he had sex, he sure as hell looked over his shoulder to see if that screaming, one-eyed thing were coming at him again. Of course, then again, maybe he kind of hoped it would.

15

Now We Are Even

I MOVED FROM Humboldt County to Colusa County in the summer of 1967 and began living in the small, historic Sacramento River town of Colusa as the resident Fish and Game warden. I had been assigned the northern half of Colusa County, an area of approximately 1,100 square miles, which I discovered was a veritable natural resources treasure house. There were salmon, striped bass, sturgeon, and steelhead in the Sacramento River, which passed through part of my enforcement district. There were largemouth bass, two species of crappie, bullfrogs, crawfish by the bucket load, and catfish in the Sacramento Valley waterways, with trout in the high country. The valley floor was loaded with quail, pheasants, coots, snipe, and in the fall clouds of waterfowl that spoke of days long past. There were black bears, mountain lions, turkeys, tule elk, mule deer, and bandtailed pigeons in the mountainous western part of the county. Throw in the mule deer dwelling throughout the valley floor along with the muskrats, beavers, raccoons, and bobcats, and you had a westering man's delight. Looking back on it now, I think this had to be one of the best districts, if not the best, in which I've ever had the opportunity to go forth and practice my trade.

Unfortunately, when natural resources are so concentrated, varied, and well known, one tends to find members of the human race inclined to take more than their share. Colusa County, with its historical record of being a haven for waterfowl commercial-market hunters, started right off giving the resources and me fits.

While learning the geographic reaches and peculiarities of the wildlife in the county in 1967 and 1968, I also had time to discover the resident good, bad, and ugly personalities of the local people. One man within this outdoor arena was probably one of the most

efficient and dedicated poachers and killers I have ever known. Let's
just call him Harry.

Harry was an unusual individual. He was a combat veteran of
Korea and had picked up a steel plate in his head for his troubles.
As a result of the war and the steel he carried in his skull and
throughout his body, it was not unusual to find him in the state
mental institutions trying to get right. If my memory serves me
correctly, he had been in and out of mental institutions some fourteen or fifteen times before our paths first crossed. He was an excellent, dedicated poacher and a crack shot with either a rifle or a
shotgun. Harry was also into drugs in a big way, and that influence
often colored his personality and actions. He was not the kind of
person you wanted to cross. I always felt that if he said he was going
to kill you, you should say your prayers because he meant it. It was
that simple.

As the days and months of learning sped by, I ran across Harry
many times in the outback and began to learn his methods of operation, how he thought, his favorite haunts, wildlife likes, and many
of his dislikes. I could see conflict coming: on one hand the aggressive game warden working the enforcement district like there was
no tomorrow, and on the other the poacher killing all he could as
if the devil were riding his coattails. Now when I think back on
Harry's behavior, I believe the devil really was close at hand. Hunting Harry was hunting the most dangerous game, and I lived for the
opportunities he gave me for the hunt. Months passed with many
close capture calls by the game warden but no brass ring. My lack
of success just intensified my pursuit of the man, and I was getting
better.

One hot July afternoon I was working my way along Lett's Valley near the Art Andreotti Ranch. While slowly patrolling on the
Leesville-to-Ladoga road, I felt nature's call and stopped on an old
concrete bridge that crossed over a dry creekbed. Stepping out of
my patrol truck, I listened to the sounds around me while my eyes
swept the adjacent oak- and grass-covered foothills. The Leesville-
to-Ladoga county road I was standing on ran in and out of the
foothills through several small, dry alfalfa fields. The country was

mostly deserted now, and the ranches that dotted the area were all
but abandoned. The coolness from the shade of the tall oak trees felt
good, as did the fresh, hot air on my sweat-soaked shirt. Glancing
around one last time to make sure I was alone, I walked over to the
edge of the bridge to relieve myself. Starting to urinate over the
bridge rail into the dry creekbed below, I noticed, much to my surprise, the urine stream almost hitting an elbow sticking out from
under the bridge! The elbow hurriedly withdrew out of sight, and
I heard a faint scuffling below me that sounded like someone repo-
sitioning himself.

Quickly placing everything back where it belonged, and pissed
because that's exactly what was trickling down my leg, I hollered
for the owner of the elbow to come out from under the bridge.
Nothing happened. Again I called for the person or persons under
the bridge to come out. Again nothing. Tiring of this little game, I
reached into my shirt pocket and took out two cherry-bomb firecrackers. Dropping one over the edge of the bridge so the mystery
person could see the little engine of destruction, I hollered, "I have
one of these I plan on lighting and dropping over the side next unless you come out, and right now!" There was a moment's silence
while the person below thought over my proposition and the deaf-
ening act that would follow noncompliance. Then I heard a shuf-
fling as the elbow appeared with Harry attached! Surprised, I
quickly went into a cautious combat mode and ordered him up
onto the road.

Harry crawled up the bank and stood in front of me, fixing my
eyes with a stone-cold stare. I said, "Harry, what were you doing
under that bridge?"

He matter-of-factly said, "My wife threw me out of the car, and
while walking home I figured I'd rest in the cool under the bridge
before continuing on." Not believing that story for a moment, I
looked down at his hands and saw that they were covered with dried
blood! Harry noticed my glance toward his hands and slowly placed
them behind his back in such a manner as not to bring attention to
them or his movement. I thought, This killing son of a gun had his
wife drop him off to hunt on foot and arranged for her to pick him

up at a later time and place. How clever. No wonder it was so hard to catch him illegally killing deer. Looking at him the same way he was staring at me, I asked, "Harry, what is under the bridge?"

Knowing full well I was going to look no matter what he said, he replied, "A deer."

Keeping my eyes on Harry, I reached into the patrol truck, took the radio mike off the holder, and called the Colusa County sheriff's office. The dispatcher responded, and I informed him of my location, that I was with Harry, and that the two of us were going under the bridge by the Art Andreotti Ranch to recover an illegal deer Harry had shot. The dispatcher acknowledged the message, and I signed off and replaced the radio mike on its holder. After my action of reporting in, I could see the resignation well up in Harry's eyes. Whatever thought he might have had on his mind before that had certainly changed now.

Looking Harry directly in the eye, I said, "Let's go."

We started down the steep bank that led to the dry creekbed and the space under the bridge. Sure enough, there lay a field-dressed three-point buck in the cool sand under the bridge. I turned and looked at Harry, and he just shrugged. With hardly a word, I grabbed the antlers, Harry the hind legs, and we carried the deer up the bank, loading it into the bed of my pickup. I then told Harry to assume the position, searched him, handcuffed him, and placed him in my truck after informing him that he was under arrest for the illegal possession of a deer. After that I asked, "Harry, where is your rifle?"

Harry just looked at me, and a repetition of the question drew the same lack of response. Seatbelting Harry in so he couldn't escape (his hands were cuffed behind his back), I went back under the bridge to look for his gun. A quick glance up under the bridge rafters produced a bolt-action 30-06 rifle and a bloody hunting knife and sheath. With that discovery my case was completed, and I returned to my vehicle for our drive to the Colusa County jail. The trip to Colusa was uneventful except that we passed Harry's wife on the road in their vehicle, obviously looking for him. I could also tell from the background voices in the radio room every time I used the radio that my trip and prisoner were starting to create quite a stir at the sheriff's office.

The booking of my semifamous prisoner went without any problems as he called his equally semifamous attorney, Bert Thompson, for rather belated counsel. Bert's arrival at the lockup was the usual staged show. He huffed and puffed Fourth Amendment rights concerns until, having a gut full, I addressed the fact that I had found Harry on a public road, under a public bridge, rather than invading his curtilage. The subsequent trial went like clockwork. Harry was found guilty and sentenced to a surprising three months in the county jail. Normally the Colusa County judges did not levy jail time for most wildlife violations, so I was surprised, to say the least. I had already given the plump deer to a needy family in Colusa, one with seven kids, so no one had been hurt except Harry and the deer. I had caught the meanest son of a bitch in the valley, and as I stepped out of the courthouse that day into the hot Colusa sun, all was good. Then it hit me. Harry had a wife and three little kids. They didn't have any source of income but Harry and the money he made from poaching and odd jobs. Harry didn't believe in welfare and wouldn't take a dime of public assistance. I knew his wife, no matter how bad it got, would honor her husband's wishes and not take a nickel of public support in his absence. Damn. The day quickly went from smooth sailing to a rock in the road.

As I got into my patrol vehicle, I decided I had better check on the welfare of Harry's wife and kids. Arriving in front of Harry's crackerbox house, I saw Mary, Harry's wife, working in the yard. She had changed from the simple print dress she had worn in court to jeans and a work shirt and was now busy sweating over hard work in her garden. I got out of the truck and walked over to her. She looked up from her gardening, and a clouded look instantly flew across her face. It was pretty obvious that she was in no mood to talk to the son of a bitch that had just gotten her husband sentenced to three months in the county jail.

I said, "Good morning, Mary." The accelerated pace of her weed chopping told me that if I had been a weed, I would have been history. Refusing to be ignored, I said, "Mary, I didn't break the law;

Harry did. I did my job, nothing more, nothing less." The weed chopping continued at a furious pace. I said, "Mary, do those little kids have enough to eat?"

She whirled with the hoe in hand and then, thinking better of her actions, placed it on the ground. Then, with a look as intense as any Harry could have given me, she said, "What the hell do you care, you bastard? You just threw my husband into that damn county jail for three months!"

I asked again, "Mary, do those little kids have enough food?"

Looking me right in the eye, she said, "That's none of your god-damned business."

In those days, the law could go a little further than it can today, and I did. Opening the gate, I walked into her yard, gently grabbed her arm, and marched her up the front steps, through the front door, and into the house. Letting go of her arm, I walked into the small kitchen and opened the refrigerator door. Its sole occupants were a half quart of milk and half a cube of margarine. Examination of the cupboards produced a sugar bowl half full of sugar and a half-empty box of cereal. That was it, nothing else. Without another word I left the house, drove to my evidence lockers, and retrieved about twenty packages of processed elk steak, striped bass, and pork steak (from wild hogs illegally killed on Colusa National Wildlife Refuge). I then went to Chung Sun's Market (the best in a four-county area for quality foods) and purchased several sacks of groceries, enough staples for an adult and three little kids for a week's meals. There may also have been some gum and candy in those sacks, come to think of it.

Returning to Mary's, I walked up to the front door with my arms loaded with bags of food and knocked on the door. Mary opened the door and without waiting for an invitation, I walked in and headed for the kitchen. Mary never said a word, just followed me into the kitchen. I took out the meat and laid it on the counter and unloaded the contents of the grocery bags onto the table so she could see what I had brought. Mary just continued to stare holes into me, and the little kids said nothing. With those thanks, I returned to my patrol truck and went back to work.

Thus began a weekly trip to Mary's with food so she and her children wouldn't have to go hungry in Harry's absence. In order to pay for these weekly grocery runs, I would claim what I was allowed for per diem expenses and just not use all I had coming (skip meals, in other words). I used this extra money along with packaged meat from my evidence lockers to care for Harry's family. This went on for the three months that Harry resided in the Colusa County jail, and not once did Mary thank me, *not once*. I thought many times that she was an ungrateful female, what with me taking care of her kids and all.

Oh well, if that is the way she wants to be, so be it, I thought.

At the end of his three-month jail term, Harry was released. The word from my informants was that Harry planned to kill me the first minute I screwed up and gave him the opportunity. That didn't bother me much because I was immortal in those days and after having apprehended Harry was now the meanest bastard in the valley.

About a month later I was passing down the same road on the Art Andreotti Ranch—in fact, I stopped on the same bridge I'd found Harry under. Needing to relieve myself, I checked to make sure no one was coming down the road and started to urinate over the bridge rail. While tending to nature's call, I let my mind wander back and was again relishing my apprehension of Harry when all of a sudden the stillness of the moment and my gathering of memories were shattered by the telltale report of a rifle.

Quickly zipping up my pants, I whirled around and was trying to echo-locate the shot when a second shot pinpointed the source for me: a small ridge behind the scruffy alfalfa field next to the bridge. I knew that piece of property was totally closed to hunting by the landowner, and anyone shooting out there was trespassing, not to mention probably killing deer during the closed season. I ran across the road and opened a gate into the alfalfa field and a dirt road that eventually led to the ridge whence the shot had come. Getting back into the patrol truck, I hurried across the field, driving down the dirt road toward the ridge where I had located the last rifle shot.

As I drew closer, I shifted into low gear and began to drive slowly in order to keep my dust trail to a minimum while I drove to the top of the oak- and grass-covered ridge. Stopping the truck below the top of the ridge, I got out and quietly shut the door. I checked my .44 magnum pistol and slowly inched my way to the ridgetop so I could look over without being skylighted. Below me lay another of the numerous valleys that ran forever through those weathered hills, heavily covered with scrub oak and cheat grass. Far below me I heard voices, but they were too far away to make out what was being said. Good, they didn't have a clue I was even in the country. I listened for a while, and it was pretty easy to figure out that there were at least a couple of people down there and that they had an animal down. From the direction of their voices, I was able to pretty well pinpoint their location in a grove of oaks about seventy-five yards southwest.

Getting impatient, I began moving slowly toward their position, one stalking foot at a time through the dry cheat grass. The talking continued as I moved toward them. It's kind of hard for a six-foot-four, three-hundred-pounder to sneak, but I was doing OK, or so I thought. Getting within thirty-five yards of my culprits, I paused to echo-locate their voices again, all the while cussing the thick stands of oak trees and brush that were making this sneak necessary. The talking had ceased. All I was greeted with was the silence usually found in oak forests under a full midday sun. After waiting about thirty minutes, I again got impatient and started moving toward the location where I had last heard the suspects talking. Approaching a small clearing, I came across an animal's blood trail, which quickly led to a dead doe. She had been cleanly shot through the neck, gutted, and left in the shade of a large oak tree. Around her were many footprints in the soft dirt, one set of which led to a bloody hunting knife and two spent cartridges (probably saved for reloading).

The poachers couldn't have been too far away, and I started looking around the hills for them. I was in the opening of a small clearing with the dead deer, and I started getting a nervous feeling standing there, knowing the poachers were probably out there somewhere watching me. Moving quickly back into the cover of the timber, all the while cussing my stupidity for standing in a clearing like that, I reverted back to my survival training. Slowly circling the dead deer's location, I quickly came across the track of two individuals. They were walking backward toward a thick pile of brush, which I slowly moved toward. When I reached the brush pile I found that two people had recently stood there and more than likely watched me approach their hard-won gains. Their tracks led from the brush pile, all the while walking backward, into a deep, brush-covered ravine where pursuit would be futile. Making sure they weren't circling me, I slowly moved back to the dead deer. Picking up the bloody hunting knife, I recognized it as the one the court had returned to Harry after his last conviction. For a moment my body temperature was lower than that of the surrounding air. If Harry had been on the other end of this knife and the rifle that had killed the deer … my thoughts trailed away.

Picking up the dead deer, I carried her to the waiting patrol truck for transport to Colusa and the hands of a needy family. During the whole trip home, I was pissed. I had needlessly exposed myself to the poachers, I hadn't caught them, and though I was sure Harry had killed the deer, I couldn't prove it beyond a reasonable doubt. Goddamn it to hell, anyway! Still mad from the screw-up, I decided to work the rice fields on the east side of my district, thinking maybe this stupid game warden could catch some poor soul with an illegal pheasant. It turned out to be pretty quiet in the rice fields, so I headed to an area along the Sacramento River to check fishermen. About halfway into the area I wanted to work, I was interrupted by my state radio. The Colusa County sheriff's office was calling me, so I responded.

The dispatcher asked if I would return to the sheriff's office; I had a visitor who wanted to see me. I agreed and turned the nose of my truck toward the office. I arrived about fifteen minutes later and was acutely aware of the warmth of the building as I entered. When you are still alive, you notice things like that. I met Lieutenant Del Nannon on his way out, and he told me my visitor was in his office and to go ahead and use it since he was leaving for the day. Entering Del's office, I met Mary, Harry's wife, hurriedly leaving. She uttered in passing, "Now we are even."

I grabbed her elbow and said, "Whoa, whoa, what do you mean 'now we are even'?"

She answered, "Earlier today Harry had you in his rifle sights and was going to kill you. I grabbed the rifle and wouldn't let him do it. I told him you fed his kids for the three months he was in jail, and he wasn't going to shoot you down like a dog as long as I was there. Anyone who did what you didn't have to do for us is not going to be killed that way. Not while I'm alive anyway."

She repeated, "Now we are even," and briskly walked out the door without so much as a look back. I stood there watching her walk away while her words spun around in my head. A strange calmness settled over me, a feeling like none I'd ever known. I became acutely aware that I would die only when it was my time. The feeling that flooded through me at that moment was one of destiny and the realization that those final shots would be called by someone or something other than a rifle held by Harry.

It was the damnedest feeling I had ever had up to that point in my career, but one I've had at least a dozen times since. I had the opportunity to cross a unique person who hated me on the one hand but on the other had enough compassion to let me live because I had shown kindness and fed her children. Her husband was an accomplished rifle shot and could have ended it right there on that brush-covered hillside, but it had not happened that way. I learned from that lesson on the hillside that no matter what, you should always treat everyone you deal with the way you would want your own family treated. By following that lesson, I have been allowed to learn many more lessons over a thirty-plus-year career in law enforcement. There truly is a lesson in loving your fellow humans.

Harry died thirteen years later of brain cancer. I don't know where Mary and the kids are. I have retired from the wildlife law enforcement profession and am still alive and learning while I await that final shot.

16

One Drop of Blood

DURING THE SUMMER AND FALL of 1968 in the Stonyford area of Colusa County, California, I had constant problems with the illegal spotlighting of deer. The killings would come so fast and furious that it seemed there wouldn't be any deer left if I didn't get my hind end in gear and catch the culprits.

I would be on patrol in the backcountry, a perfect deer habitat of brush and oak trees dotted with lush alfalfa fields and stock tanks, late at night or early in the morning before daylight, when all of a sudden there would be a warm gut pile looking me in the eye from its place in the middle of the road. It was obvious that these lads were pretty comfortable under cover of darkness doing what they did best. I found a kind of clue in the killing pattern on different days of the week: my rash of killings seemed to always occur on Wednesdays, Thursdays, or Fridays. This frustrating activity went on day after day, and it seemed as if I would never catch the culprit. But I was young in those days and had a wife who realized very well the type of husband she had married. She let me run like a hound after those who needed chasing, and I did. Since my normal sixteen-hour day wasn't doing the trick, I just doubled my efforts. Ah, youth—you can use up your body like that when you're young, but look out when you turn forty. Being immortal, like most at that age, I poured the fuel of life into the fire that raged within me. All to no avail, I might add, for I didn't solve the deer-killing mystery in 1968. I gave it my best shot, but it wasn't good enough. In fact, I felt that the lads were playing with me because I should have caught them, considering my knowledge of the area and the hours I spent in their pursuit. But sometimes you eat the bear, and sometimes the bear eats you.

In the middle of the summer in 1969 the familiar killing pattern in my best deer areas emerged again, namely, predawn killings, Wednesday through Friday, with the trademark gut piles in the road. You would think it would take a lot of gall to gut an animal on the road proper, but the country was so deserted, especially during the late-night and early-morning hours, that it was pretty obvious the chances of being caught were zip.

This scenario of gut piles, fences broken down where deer had been dragged over them from the alfalfa fields, and spent cartridges on the road began to drive the demons in me. There just wasn't a darn clue. Even the spent cartridges in the road were no help, being 30-06 in caliber. Aside from the 30-30, the 30-06 was probably the next most popular caliber and was common to every gun store in the nation. I used every technique I had learned from my training and from other officers. I even used techniques I had learned as a poacher in my youth, but all to no avail. This person, or persons, was better than I, but I wasn't in the mood to give up. I had good German stock in me, not to mention my mother's work ethic, and sooner or later these chaps would fall prey to this determination.

One Saturday the editor of the newspaper in Colusa asked if he could ride with me and do an article for his readers on a day in the life of a game warden. Looking over this chap, I thought he left a lot to be desired. He was a short, dumpy lad with glasses as thick as my windshield. His hair was thinning badly all over his head, and in a good blow he would end up in the next county. However, my department always wanted us to be available to the public, and I guessed this counted. Deciding I didn't have a problem, I told him to be ready to go at three-thirty the next morning. He looked at me in disbelief but, realizing this might be his only chance, said, "OK." Noting the hesitant response, I told the lad that if he showed up late he would be left behind. I could tell from the look I received in return that he would be there. He could smell a story—and a story he *did* get.

The next morning at three-thirty sharp, I picked up the newsman (who had been waiting since three) at his office and the two of us headed up into the national forest not far from the Stonyford

area of Colusa County near the Glenn County line. Deer season
was in full swing, and the backwoods were full of lads trying to
match their hunting skills against the elusive deer. Hunters could
take only bucks with forked horns or better, and the killing of does
was strictly prohibited. Figuring that activity would give my newspaper man the best opportunity for a story, I headed into that
human morass. As was typical in California during those days, the
early deer season was hotter than the hubs of hell; the temperature
usually ran from the mid-90s to 100-plus, and it seemed as if every
knothead in the country was there, all falling over each other in
their quest to kill a deer. Violations were common, as were hunting
accidents, and the deer hunting in Colusa County always seemed to
me to be less than what I would call a quality hunt. Maybe that's
why we wardens called it "hunting" instead of "killing." But the
hunting fraternity loved the opportunity to get into the woods, and,
by virtue of their presence, there I was as well.

Arriving in the national forest in the Lett's Lake area, my Clark
Kent and I spent an uneventful morning watching and checking
deer hunters as they pursued their sport in 100-degree weather in
the rugged terrain of western Colusa County. The newsman, whom
I had told to stay out of the way when I was tangled up with a violator, performed flawlessly. He managed to get pictures of those I
checked, even those I issued citations to, without an ounce of trouble. He would remain on the very edge of any activity, taking notes
furiously, even sketching when he couldn't use the camera without
being obtrusive. In between activities, he would interview me or
ask questions about my procedures during the last car stop. All in
all, he wasn't the drag I had figured he would be, and I was beginning to like the lad.

As the sun and heat approached their zenith, I turned down an
old dirt road that took me and my Mark Twain slowly along Sullivan Ridge. I pulled into a grove of trees along the road, shut off the
patrol vehicle's motor, and just sat there and listened. "Why are we
stopping?" were the first words out of his mouth.

"To see what God throws our way," I replied. I could tell that answer didn't really hold water in his world, but I was confident that

sitting during this period of the day was the best use of my time. A few moments later I heard seventeen shots fired from what appeared to be two rifles in Sullivan Canyon. I continued to listen and was formulating a plan for investigating this interesting turn of events when three shots were fired just down the road from where we were sitting. Those three shots sounded as if they had been fired from the road (a violation), and possibly at wildlife that had been scared up out of Sullivan Canyon by the barrage of earlier shots. I started up my patrol vehicle and headed in the direction of the three shots, getting there in time to see two lads dragging an untagged forked-horn buck (two-point western count) across the road to their waiting pickup truck. After a few questions, two Fish and Game violations surfaced, much to the happiness of my newspaper friend.

Finishing with my latest violators, I heard another vehicle coming up the dusty mountain road, then stop just below our position and fire one shot. Bidding the lads just cited a quick good-bye, I jumped into the patrol rig, as did my newspaperman, and away we went toward the latest shooting. Swinging around a sharp turn in the road, I surprised two lads just returning from the brushy area alongside the road. Stopping in front of their vehicle, I noticed that both of the pickup doors were flung open, indicating a hasty exit.

"Morning, gentlemen," was my greeting. "Having any luck?" The taller one said they had just seen a three-point buck but had not been able to get to him before he disappeared into the forest. Quickly checking their fingers, hands, and pants legs for the telltale signs of blood and finding none, I asked to check their licenses and weapons. Several citations later (no hunting license for the tall one and use of full-metal-jacket ammunition for his partner), my passenger and I were off to look into the earlier episode of the seventeen shots. We started back down the long hogback on Sullivan Ridge, following an undulating road along the rim that moved through small thickets of trees and brush as it trickled its way down to the valley floor below. About a mile down that road, I noticed a cloud of dust, which signaled to me that a car was slowly moving out ahead of us. The instinct of a game warden rose up in me and told me a problem was in the offing. I looked over to the reporter and with a knowing twinkle in my eye told him we would catch these lads doing something wrong. He looked at me with eyes unaccustomed to the instincts of a man who made a living hunting humans and who talked about future events as if lawbreaking were an everyday occurrence. His look betrayed the uneasiness of a man not touched by the feeling that comes when hunting your own kind but riding next to someone who does. I could just see the question on his face: How do you know there will be a violation there?

I commenced my stalk of the car with its dust-cloud banner as it moved down the mountain road. When the car I was following dropped down in the valleys or depressions of the road, I made sure I was on the rises directly behind it. When it was on the rises, I dropped into the valleys, all the time gaining. Soon I moved right up into the driver's dust trail, and now, for all intents and purposes, he was mine as soon as I decided to pull the trigger. My instincts were very strong at this point, and I just grinned. The thought that something was wrong here, really wrong, kept swirling around in my head. When I focused on the driver, it was apparent that he had not yet seen me tailing him. That was good. I didn't want to pull him over until I had a safe wide spot in the road. That way some other hunter coming down the road would not run over both of us, and if the lad was in violation of the law, I would have room to work. Because this vehicle had just emerged from Sullivan Canyon, I would have the opportunity to question the occupants about the mass of shots I had heard earlier. If nothing else, maybe they could shed some light on what had happened back in the canyon, which might lead me to a violation. Still, my instincts told me this was the car, so my interest in these folks in front of me remained very high.

A wide spot appeared in the road ahead, so I turned on the red light and instantly saw the driver's face as he turned to see what was behind him. Then he turned to looked at his single passenger. The look bespoke a crotch just grabbed by a pit bull. Their vehicle pulled over, and I followed them as they ground to a stop. Waiting until the road dust from the stop had passed both vehicles, I continued to watch the occupants of the car. They had just frozen in their seats. As the dust subsided, I got out of my vehicle and walked up to their car, noticing that the rear bumper was not dusty and had a snotlike material smeared over it. The car also appeared to be very heavily loaded in the rear, and all the camping gear that would normally be carried in the trunk appeared to be piled in the rear seat.

The driver and passenger had not moved and were intently watching me in their mirrors as I approached. Looking into the back seat, I observed a .22-caliber bolt-action rifle on top of all the camping gear and, looking forward into the passenger compartment, I saw that the passenger had a rifle held between his legs. Standing slightly away from the vehicle, I leaned down and, speaking through the open driver's-side window, asked the passenger to hand me his rifle out the open window, butt first and keeping his hand off the trigger. Since it was illegal to have a loaded rifle in a motor vehicle on a way open to the public, that was always the first thing I did in order to gain control of the weapons. The lad handed me his 30-06 bolt-action rifle without a problem, and when I examined it, I found it to be unloaded and in compliance with state law. Laying that rifle on the hood of their car, I then asked the driver to hand me the .22 rifle in the back seat, which he did. I noticed as he struggled to reach the rifle over his shoulder and hand it to me that he also tried to unload it. I immediately told him to hold it right there and not to mess with that rifle any further. When he pulled his hands off the gun, as I instructed, I reached into the car and removed the rifle safely. As I had expected, I found that it had a live cartridge in the barrel in violation of the Fish and Game code. I told myself that my instincts had been right regarding a violation in this car, but they still weren't satiated: more was wrong. I laid that rifle alongside the one taken from the passenger and in so doing noticed a single drop of dried blood on the stock of the .22. I didn't say anything yet about the blood but got both lads out of the car and had them stand by the front of my patrol truck, giving me the opportunity to reach into the rear seat of their car and pull out the driver's hunting rifle for examination. It was a 30-06 bolt-action, totally empty, so I placed it on the hood along with the other two rifles. I stood there quietly looking through the two men, noticing the total lack of eye contact and the fact that their body language placed them in the nervous category of a dog crapping razor blades. Not seeing any evidence of a deer in the back seat but remembering the "snot" on the rear bumper (usually found when someone has dragged a freshly killed or gutted deer over the bumper and into the trunk) and keeping the drop of blood on the .22 rifle stock in mind, I figured a few questions were in order. Looking at the driver, I said, "I see you cut your ankle while hunting."

"What do you mean?"

"Well, if you were hunting back there in Sullivan Canyon, it's known for its rugged talus slopes and difficult hiking conditions. I noticed this drop of blood on your rifle and figured you had cut yourself while hunting deer in that area."

He quickly said, "Yes, you're right, I did cut my ankle back there while crossing a talus slope." Sometimes when you hunt humans, who are considered the most dangerous game, and you're close to the kill, the metaphorical smell of blood has to be one of your sharpest senses. That smell was now flooding my nostrils. I think another smell was flooding the nostrils of the lads being interviewed. ...

"The blood was on the stock of the .22-caliber rifle, gentlemen," I told them. "It is illegal to hunt big game in California with a bullet less than .24 caliber." Their silence was such that you could hear a slight breeze moving through the pine trees. They just looked at me as if there were no tomorrow, as did my newsman.

I said, "Let me see your ankle; I have a first aid kit and will patch it up for you."

He said, "No, that's OK, it's all right."

I said, with a whole lot more authority in my voice the second time, "Let me see that ankle, now!"

He lifted up his pants leg, and no blood was to be seen. I said, "All right, men, let's take a look in the trunk of the car, if you don't mind."

The driver didn't breathe for a moment, then walked the short distance from the front of my truck to the rear of his sedan, placed the key in the lock, and opened the trunk. Then he stepped back to let me move forward and look inside. In the trunk were jammed seven does with their heads and feet cut off. Packed around the deer were U.S. Forest Service handi-talkies, flares, pots, pans, kettles, and silverware stolen from the Forest Service fire cache at Lett's Lake.

Looking back at the two men, I said, "Lads, we seem to have a slight problem here. Care to tell me about it?"

The men said nothing for a few moments, and then the driver said, "Well, what you see is what you get. We have nothing more to say."

"Fine. Both of you are under arrest for the illegal possession of seven deer." I advised them of their rights, searched for any weapons on their persons, and handcuffed them. At that point I became aware of the forgotten newsman, who was hurriedly taking pictures and notes as events unfolded around him. He was beginning to get a look in his eyes that spoke of the memory of the hunt from generations ago. Good for him, he was alive, I thought. I placed both men in the back of my patrol truck, the newsman drove the defendants' seized vehicle, and down the mountain we went to the town of Stonyford and into the open arms of the resident deputy sheriff, Carter Bowman.

At Stonyford I transferred my prisoners to the deputy sheriff and had the Forest Service identify its stolen property. Both men later pleaded guilty to the illegal possession of deer and possession of stolen U.S. government property. Owing to previous records of theft, both drew three-year sentences for the theft charges and an additional six months and fines for the Fish and Game violations, plus loss of their rifles.

The instinct of the hunter really paid off in this case, which developed from one drop of blood and went on to pay even greater dividends. The deer killing that had plagued me for two years, the broken fences, the gut piles, and the spent casings in the road were no more. Just as soon as these lads disappeared into the penal system, my deer killing stopped. It took me several months to realize what had happened, but it finally began to dawn on me. Plain and simply, it was as if the poachers had dropped into a black hole. Out of curiosity, I had the seized 30-06 rifles and the many spent 30-06 casings I had gathered at the kill sites over the years sent to forensics in Sacramento, and they matched. These lads had been my deer killers in 1968 and 1969, the ones who had given me fits. It was fitting that it had taken me two years to catch the lads and that they had three years to ruminate over that fact. My lads, for whatever reason, had gotten careless or bold and changed their killing from weekdays to the weekend. They left the safety of the night and highways and tried Sullivan Canyon. Greed and ego will do you in every time. It might take a while, even two years, but the catch will happen, as it did in this case.

Well, the newsman got his story, and the people of Colusa County received a firsthand insight into how the hunter and prey really lived. But neither the newsman nor the good people of Colusa County got the *real* story, that is, how God loves little children and fools. Somehow, I think God blinked that fine day on a dusty road in Colusa County and included game wardens because he allowed me the opportunity to apprehend two lads who really needed catching. From that day forth, I have led a blessed and charmed life, catching many others who crossed over the line.

It probably doesn't seem fair to those on the "dark side" of the line that God is on our side. I guess they need to keep in mind that since He created all the critters, it is only fair that He should have a hand in the lessons of life we all share, especially when we deal with those critters.

17

Tinkle, Tinkle, Eeeeeee, Boom!

SEVERAL THOUSAND MALLARDS and pintail rose from the rice field in front of me, turned into the slight breeze from the northwest, and headed for Colusa National Wildlife Refuge for a day of rest. I could now relax my vigilance. It was early fall, 1968, and my location was a dry harvested rice field somewhere south of the refuge in Colusa County, California. My home for the moment was a rice check. My covers were a tarp and the marvelous cloak of night changing to day. My companion was Shadow, a 110-pound female black Lab whose snoring told me that at least one of the enforcement team was doing the right thing.

I was a California state Fish and Game warden doing what most of us did in the Sacramento Valley in that diminishing heyday of the commercial-market hunter. That is, I was "sleeping" with the ducks in the harvested rice to protect them from an untimely death from flying lead pellets and subsequent sale in the markets of large cities in California. The evening before, just at dusk, I had slipped into the field where I now lay against the rice check for cover to guard a feeding flock of ducks that numbered about ten thousand. The flock was not big enough to draw the protective attention of all the federal agents in the area (a recognized plus for the market hunter) but was not small enough to be overlooked by the state game wardens in pursuit of those trying to make a few dollars by feeding the commercial markets in Sacramento, Yuba City, or San Francisco fresh-killed, rice-fed ducks. Hence my presence in that field so long ago.

The contented flowing-water sound feeding ducks make was now gone. Little by little and then in larger flocks the ducks had gotten quiet and then lifted off for their favorite loafing sites. The rice field was still, as was the early morning. Lying there against the rice check, satisfied with my night's work, I became aware of the cold seeping into my body that comes just before the break of dawn after a long night of inactivity. The stiffness in my back from lying on the cold ground all night began to manifest itself as well. However, both elements of discomfort were quickly forgotten as God worked His eternal magic and created a sunrise for those who cared to notice. I felt that this morning He had created one just for me and my efforts to protect His creatures the night before. Game wardens think like that often during the many hours they lie in wait in their never-ending commitment to protect the natural resources we still have for those yet to come.

This morning was spectacular! Against the backdrop of the Sutter Buttes, He ran His paintbrush of many colors across the canvasgray sky. The reds, golds, and yellows, interspersed with background shades of blue, were truly what feeds the souls of those of us who serve Him and His. As if this magnificence were not enough, He wafted the unique smell of burning rice stubble across my nostrils and ran skeins of ducks and geese across the painted skies, looking for whatever they look for that time of the morning. Damn, it was a sight I had seen many times before and since, but I have yet to tire of that kind of spectacle. I could only hope this fine morning that those of us who serve the American people in an endeavor to protect their rapidly diminishing natural heritage would be successful in our quest, and that the people would wake up in time to learn that their heritage is limited and in danger.

Rolling stiffly to my side and rising to one knee, I surveyed my rice field one more time for anything out of place and then climbed to my feet to meet the rest of the day. Shadow, who was the very essence of that word, rose also and looked up at me for a command or body-language indicator to tell her what was up. This was one of the most remarkable dogs I ever knew, loyal to a fault, expecting nothing more than just to be with me and experience life as I knew it. She filled a time in my life when I needed the companion that she was. I only hope that wherever she is now, she feels I did the same for her. She was a gift to me from a wife not of this world.

Donna, my bride, knew she couldn't be with me herself for many reasons. But she made sure she was at least represented in spirit, and so she was. Anyone who has had such a dog as this will understand and forgive me for having a hard time continuing until my eyes clear.

It felt good to walk across the rice field that morning as I limbered up my stiff muscles and joints. The body heat that came from movement also felt good. It really was great to be alive. A pair of low-flying pintail, those greyhounds of the air, saluted that thought and brought a smile to my wind-burned face as they flew across the dawn toward the Sutter Buttes. Reaching my patrol vehicle, I pulled away the camouflage parachute covering it, repacked it in its protective container, threw it into the back of my pickup, loaded up Shadow, slid into the cold seat, started the truck, and drove down the muddy rice-field trail out to the pavement. Turning north on Lone Star Road, I headed for home, some of my wife's good home-cooked breakfast, and a few hours' sleep so I could start all over again.

In my tiredness as I drove about a mile north on Lone Star Road, I neglected to focus instantly on the suspicious muddy tracks coming from a fallow field to the east. When the tracks entered Lone Star Road, they also turned north. My mind might have been cluttered from lack of sleep and all the other ailments that afflict working officers, but the mind of a game warden is never still. The inner alertness that comes from hunting humans spun my mind into full alert when I finally did sight the evidence of a pair of muddy tracks that fine morning. In a moment the cluttered decks of my mind were cleared for action. The truck rolled to a stop while my eyes examined the tracks in the rearview mirror and my mind searched for answers. There were no rice fields in that area, which meant there was nothing a commercial-market hunter of ducks would want from that section of the land. What about deer poachers? No, there was inadequate habitat for such critters, much less animal activity. By now I had stopped and was backing up to the spot where the tracks had exited the field and entered Lone Star Road.

Squinting into the morning sun, my eyes followed the tracks over the trail they had left in the wet adobe Colusa County soil. They tracked eastward and out of sight into an area just south of the Colusa National Wildlife Refuge boundary. That was strange. There was nothing there except refuge boundary to the north and a creek to the east. There was nowhere to go, period. A fisherman maybe, but November was not a really hot time to fish, especially on that small creek. Staring into the unknown that came from too many questions and not enough answers, that unique instinct that comes to most of us in this profession began to make itself felt within my soul. There was something wrong here. The rush that comes from hunting your fellow human was again beginning to make itself felt. Sleep or my wife's home-cooked breakfast would have to wait, I thought as I wheeled my patrol truck off Lone Star Road and into the familiar adobe mud of the county.

Slipping and sliding, I dropped the GMC into four-wheel drive and followed the tracks out into the field along the southern refuge boundary and into the area adjacent to the creek. There the tracks curved southward behind a large mound of dirt, left in the area by a past farmer, and stopped. Stopping shy of the spot where the other vehicle had positioned itself, I carefully got out and began to examine the ground. I had one thing in my favor, and that was heritage. My dad, Otis Barnes, had been raised among California Indians as a boy. He had run with, hunted with, swum with, and loved these friends as he did his own brothers. They appreciated him as well (especially in schoolyard fights—Dad was a hell of a fighter!) and spent time teaching, as Dad did learning, their ways. As a result of these teachings, Dad became an excellent tracker and had the eyes and senses of an eagle. Throughout the years of our all-too-short relationship, he had taught me many of these ways, and now I was making use of that heritage.

Scanning the ground, I saw that the signs indicated a 4x4 pickup with an unusual off-road tread design. Identifying it as a four-wheel-drive was easy. When a 4x4 makes a turn, one of its front wheels will usually blur its track as the tire aids in pulling the rig forward. The tread was another matter. In Colusa County, I tried to make a mental note of every tread design used by my local outlaws.

That way if I ever ran across that tread mark and an illegal situation, I would have a place to start my investigation. However, this tread was very aggressive, with a pattern unfamiliar to me from my travels in the Colusa farming country. Making a mental note, I continued with my field examination. There were three sets of footprints, two small (about size 9 or 10) and one large, at least a size 12. The size 12 emerged from the driver's side of the vehicle and the smaller feet from the passenger side. The size 12 sank into the wet soil very deeply, indicating a pretty heavy man, considering the size of his foot surface. The other two footprints appeared to be as normal as day. All three were wearing vibram-soled boots, but the size 12 had what appeared to be a knifelike cut across the bottom of the left sole. This would be a good clue down the road, I said to myself. One of the men was a nervous heavy smoker. There were five cigarette butts left where the truck had been; all had teeth marks in them and were smoked down to the filter. Looking around for other clues, I noticed that where the truck had parked behind the dirt mound, it would not be visible from Lone Star Road. Moving closer for the first time, I walked to where the truck had been parked.

There were a lot of footprints where the tail end of the truck would have been had it still been parked there. This time I noticed that all the footprints in that area were sunk deeply into the soil as if they had been lifting a heavy load. In addition, all the footprints were not clear-cleated as they had been when they disembarked from the vehicle. The boot-sole cleats were obscured, probably full of rice-grass stems, leaves, and mud. Dropping to one knee, I ran my fingers over a thin stream of blood about one-eighth inch wide and a foot in length that crossed several of the deeper footprints. The fact that the blood had spewed over the footprints told me that a large animal had been loaded into the truck. It was obvious that a heavy part had been lifted, followed by the part leaking the blood last. Large and long was my estimate of the animal's size. The blood was bright red, which told me that no paunch shooting had occurred. It had probably been a head or neck shot, and this was just the clean blood that would occur from a normal opening and evisceration of the body cavity. It had to be an animal of value or they wouldn't have gone through the trouble of gutting and hauling it out. But what?

There were no cattle in the area and very few deer. When I smelled the blood, it had a faint odor I did not recognize. There was no hair on the ground and no other evidence such as bloody rags or paper towels, which told me the poachers had cleaned their hands elsewhere. The blood was still wet and sticky, which told me it was recent, and it had yet to blacken with exposure to the air. Intermingled all around these signs were the footprints of four dogs. They were all large-footed, so my guess was that they were black-and-tans, blue ticks, or walkers, and the tips of their toenails were blunted, telling me these were kennel dogs. Such dogs were normally bred to hunt raccoons, lions, bears, or other large animals. Other than skunks and coons, we sure as hell had little to offer these boys in the form of a good chase of a worthy adversary, I thought. Boy, was I wrong!

My tired eyes followed the footprints from where the pickup had been parked as they trekked northward toward the Colusa National Wildlife Refuge external boundary. The refuge, a zone closed to all hunting, had to be where they had come from. Now my mind was really racing. It took a lot of balls to hunt a totally closed area, and more than likely at night to avoid discovery. But for what? The refuge had few deer, and they would be difficult to get no matter how hard you tried. This refuge was only several thousand acres in size and had at one time been a rice farm. It still had vestiges of old rice dikes, interspersed with marsh development created by the U.S. Fish and Wildlife Service to establish habitat favorable to the wintering waterfowl. Still drawing a blank, I called Shadow out of the back of the patrol truck, and the two of us headed off into another adventure.

Backtracking the three sets of footprints, I could see that the dogs stayed uncommonly close to the size 12 footprint. Arriving at the refuge fence and boundary, I noticed that the tracks scarcely hesitated but went right over the fence and in as if they owned the place. Once inside, the dog tracks forged back and forth and from side to side of the size 12 but were never more than ten to fifteen yards away at any time. Boy, talk about trained dogs: this lad sure had them. The tracks walked down an old refuge road for about two hundred yards and then headed west across the refuge along a set of old rice dikes. Walking about one hundred yards into this area of marsh and rice dikes, it finally dawned on me what the quarry was: *pigs!* The refuge had a large wild hog population. The history was that during the Depression, a farmer was about to have his farm taken from him by the bank. In the heat of the moment, the farmer decided that the bank wasn't going to get everything and released his hogs into the wild. Since that day the hogs had done well in the area along the creek bottoms and marginal farmlands. In fact, they had prospered so well in numbers and in size that they were now a problem on the refuge and surrounding farmlands because of their rooting and the resulting soil displacement. During a hog drive to reduce their numbers on the refuge in 1967, I had killed one that weighed about six hundred pounds with my .44 magnum pistol. The damn boar had charged me after I shot one of his sows, and it had taken five solid hits from that magnum shooting 240-grain expanding bullets to drop him—at my feet, I might add! That is the only time I've had mud and water tossed into my face by a charging animal. Standing in that marsh, knee deep in slop and with nowhere to run, with a crazed six-hundred-pound animal bearing down on me sure made me understand mortality.

Continuing westward into the marsh about another fifty yards, I ran across muddy water and lots of hog tracks interspersed with dog and human tracks. It was apparent that the chase had started here! About forty yards farther to the west, I found where a single hog had made a stand, as evidenced by the surrounding dog tracks. There was snot, hog crap, and hair everywhere. From the size of the hog tracks, he had to be a big one. There was a spew of blood off to one side on the dike where the hog had made this last stand, with bone and muscle meeting modern humankind's inventions in the form of a speeding bullet. Adjacent to the blood lay a gut pile, mute evidence of the loser of that clash, smeared with blood that smelled like the blood I had found earlier at the truck. I began following the drag trail made by the men as they removed the hog carcass from refuge lands. They did not go out the way they had come in but took another route. Pretty damn clever of size 12, I thought. That way he was reducing his chances of being discovered. I was beginning to think that my gut feeling indicating I was looking at a real poaching ace was correct (a sense that was certainly confirmed over the subsequent times I pursued this lad). The drag trail led to the refuge's southern boundary fence, above where they had parked their vehicle. I could see that they had stood there for a while observing their pickup to make sure no one had discovered it or suspected their intentions. This wait was apparent by the number of footprints, knee impressions in the soil, and cigarette butts with tooth marks on them around where they had stood. They had also apparently redrained the blood from the hog carcass because there was a huge splash of blood all over the rice grass, with a lot of blood clots at the center. Finally satisfied that all was clear, they had moved to the truck and made good their escape.

Satisfied that I could do no more, I returned to my patrol truck and headed out to the highway en route to the headquarters of the Colusa National Wildlife Refuge. Driving in, I was met by Refuge Manager Ed Buria en route to pick up his government mail. I asked Ed if he had heard anything interesting on his refuge lately. He answered that all was quiet as far as he knew but, quickly realizing that my curiosity was not ordinary, asked for an explanation.

I told Ed of the morning's events, and he grunted. "We have a real good hog population, and I wouldn't care if they killed them all except for the issue of the law. Those guys don't belong out there, and I hope you catch every one of them."

Leaving Ed with instructions to keep an eye on the poachers' little hidden parking lot and to be sure and let the Williams game warden or me know if anyone showed up, we parted company. My wife had departed for school (she is a schoolteacher, and a damn good one) but had left me a lumberjack's breakfast (steak, eggs, spuds, homemade bread, and a slice of pie my size). She knew I was on the run, with a 107-day duck season and all, and always saw to it that I had fuel for the furnace.

Throughout the rest of duck season and into the end of January, I ran across various bits of evidence that my size 12 hog poacher was in the area. I also noticed that the tire tracks changed every time I discovered he had been in the area, as did the soles of his shoes. One time the original tire tread and the knife mark across the sole I had seen the first time would be in evidence. The next time, both would be different, and then the next time both would trade back to the ones used the first time. The one screw-up was the nervous person on the end of the cigarettes. That never changed. It was always three guys, they always parked in the same little hidey-hole, cigarette butts were scattered everywhere, and they always seemed to only be after the hogs. As far as I could tell, in 1968 and early 1969 my friend trod in this arena of interest at least eight times, as was evidenced by my discovery of gut piles on the refuge. I never found more than one gut pile at a time, and when I asked the Colusa County sheriff's office over the radio to watch the area for me, the bad guys never would appear. Surprise, surprise. Both the Williams warden (since it was his district) and I kept a keen eye out for these lads, but no brass ring was in the offing.

Summer came, and with it my madcap fishing season associated with the Sacramento Valley waterways. For a while I was too busy to worry about this hog killing going on in another warden's district, but as the fishing slacked off I began to take runs by the area just for grins. During one of those runs, I looked out the window of my slowly passing vehicle, and there it was! Muddy tracks coming from the refuge area. Damn it, that did it! The hunt was on, and my gut feeling told me I could soon be hunting one of my own kind, that is, a law enforcement officer. This would account for the fact that whenever I used the sheriff's office radio, the object of my attention would disappear for at least two weeks after the transmission. It just seemed to me that this fellow thought and did things like a cop. If that was the case, then I really had my work laid out for me. A "kill" in this arena would be earned with difficulty and richly deserved.

I worked days and nights with an average of four hours of sleep per night as the hunt went on. Twice I was so close that the mud on the highway was still wet and sticky where minutes before he had fled from the field of battle. But no matter how hard I tried, he was nowhere to be found. Numerous nighttime stakeouts on the refuge near hog concentrations netted me nothing but mosquito bites by the zillions. I never heard a dog bark, never heard a shot, nothing!

Then early one morning, several hours before daylight, it happened! My two guardian angels (I have two because of my size) were getting tired of only four hours of sleep per night and I guess had had enough. I was coming off a set-line case in the southern part of the county (108 hooks at $10 each—a good fine in those days) when my inner instincts along with my two angels, recognizable by the bags under their eyes, suggested I swing by the road I'd been watching. Parking in an adjacent field, I grabbed my flashlight, put on my hip boots, and cautioned Shadow to stay in the patrol rig. She didn't like that order but always minded and *never* left that truck. I knew that if I took her, size 12's dogs would wind her and the jig would be up. Moving carefully through the tall field grasses and weeds, I made my way to the hidey-hole where the lads always parked their vehicle. As I moved closer, the idea that the type of tread and boot soles should be the same as they were the first time ran through my mind. When I rounded the mound of dirt, my inner feeling that they would be there was so strong that I couldn't believe it. It was physical, that's how strong it was, and sure as shooting, there sat a 4x4 three-quarter-ton Ford pickup. I quickly fired off a prayer of thanks to the Great Game Warden in the Sky and then began the process of zeroing in on my prey.

Across the fence I went, angling for the center of the area where I knew the hogs would more than likely be. It was an area thick with tules where they could make nests and be secure from everything except humans. I stayed close to the much-used escape route these lads had followed in the past with an eye toward the area used by the hogs. My senses were very acute that morning as I moved carefully, step by step, through the marsh toward what I hoped would be contact with size 12. It is amazing how your senses sharpen when you are stalking a human and know you are about to get him. I could smell as if there were no tomorrow. I could hear dogs barking on ranches I knew were at least two miles away, and damn, did I ever feel part of the moment! I had gone maybe three hundred yards into the area where I suspected these lads might be when I caught it! The stinking smell of a cigarette! Not as if someone were smoking but the odor you smell when someone has recently smoked a cigarette and then walks by you. Freezing, I let my ears take over with the aid of hands cupped over them to amplify the sounds. The sound of mosquitoes, a bittern's croak, the *jug-a-rum* of several bullfrogs, more mosquitoes, and a tinkle.

A tinkle? There it was again, a tinkle like that clear sound that comes from a silver bell. Yeah, I know. What the hell do I mean, a silver bell? Well, next time you get the chance, listen to a bell that is made of pure silver. It has its very own sound unlike any other you will hear. I had found a silver bell by one of the hog-dog battle sites earlier in the year, one with bite marks in it made by a hog. I remembered picking it up and wondering, then listening to the clear, crisp sound it projected and, not having the rest of the pieces, thinking no more about it until the moment I now shared with the night. These rascals. They had trained their dogs to a T. They didn't stray far from their masters, they never barked, at least that I ever heard, and the poachers were tracking them through this trained closeness and the soft tinkle of a bell. What a way to poach! This lad was going to be a real catch if I could pull it off.

There it was again! The smell of cigarette, not as strong as before but definitely there. I stood frozen in time and space as the whirlwind of events passed through my senses for evaluation. Few if any sounds came forth, just the inky blackness of night, the sting of mosquitoes, the tinkle of several bells now, and the whir of two sets of tired angel wings overhead. Then I heard the splashing of animals running through the marsh. In a few moments it became apparent that these sounds of life, with the very real possibility of death attached, would come fairly close to where I stood. I could hear the grunting of pigs, the splashing as they moved through the marsh, not in disorder yet, and the tinkling of those soft trademark silver bells sounding as if they were behind the oncoming hogs.

Then for the first time I could hear heavier splashing like a larger animal moving clumsily through the marsh. No lights, just noises and my imagination. God, what an exhilarating moment. We're about to meet, for better or worse, but you can bet the hide will be set on someone's hind end before this event is finished, I thought. One on one, my ability against his for the trophy that comes with capture or escape. I now became aware of just how rigid my body was in anticipation of this moment. The splashing now picked up in tempo, as did the grunting of the hogs. Off in the distance I could hear one boar popping his tusks in anticipation of the meeting that was sure to come if the dogs continued to press their attack. Thinking back to my earlier episode with a similar tusker, I hoped that mad hog would be able to keep straight who was friend and who foe.

Finally I could see the dark silhouettes of streams of hogs going by me off to one side about twenty yards away as they ran down an old levee. It appeared to be the sows and little ones making their escape, while the boars stayed behind to take care of the business at hand. Soon I could hear the unmistakable sound of battle taking place between the hogs and the dogs. The noise gave me the cover I needed, and I moved to the pigs' defense as quickly and quietly as I could. Saying a fast prayer to my two tired but close-at-hand guardian angels to keep me out of the line of fire of the bullet that was inevitable for the hogs, off I went. The sounds of battle were now very real: the squealing of hogs, constant tinkling of bells, heavy splashing of humans running to the battle, and the sound of my racing heart as I made myself part of this dance with death. I had moved so close that I could smell wet dogs, cigarette smoke, and excrement from the hogs in terror as the dogs swirled around them and could hear the heavy breathing of humans close at hand for this moment of truth.

Tinkle-tinkle went one very clear, close silver bell. *"Eeeeeeeeeee,"* squealed a large tusker as one of the dogs found a soft spot, and *boom* went a gun with its accompanying ball of flame not ten feet from where I now stood. The sickening *whack* of a bullet striking flesh and bone was quickly followed by a fireball in the night from the muzzle of what I now recognized as a pistol. It was a large-bore and sounded a lot like my own .44 magnum going off. Now the battle got real as the dogs realized their adversary was down.

I heard a voice saying, "Shoot him again; he has one of the dogs down."

Boom went a gun again, and this time the fireball illuminated the small group of human predators—save one very large one wearing a badge expectantly standing off to one side. In that microinstant, I could see that the hog was down and covered by swirling dogs. Standing not six feet away were three men, two small (one of whom was holding a pistol in his hands) and one fellow weighing about 250 pounds. He was holding the gun that had just fired the last shot, and I decided right then and there that he was mine. They were so intent on their mission of destruction that they didn't even see the very large threat at hand. Soon the fight in the hog went out with the juice of his body through two bullet holes, and the men gained control of the dogs. Then there was the unbroken blackness of night and the sounds an animal makes as he leaves this life. The soft tinkling of the bells could still be heard, and it was evident that the men were listening for the sounds of discovery and pursuit.

Hearing none, one voice in the dark said, "Congratulations, Bill, you did it."

There was a pause and then another voice said, "I have never hunted hogs at night, and you were right, Bob, it's a thrill beyond compare, especially if you remember we're hunting on a national wildlife refuge."

Bill's voice continued, "This was worth every bit of the $1,000 fee I paid for this experience. I can't wait to tell my brother so he can go with you."

So that was the game. A commercial venture with the national wildlife refuge as their little proving ground. Well, that crap was coming to an end here and now if I could get the large lad with the field howitzer on his hip under control.

A small light went on, and with one man holding the four dogs, the other two started to gut a very large boar. Their backs were to me, so I waited for the explosion that would come once my presence was known. When the gutting of the hog was finished, Bill and the cigarette man started to drag the hog toward their distant vehicle. The dogs were released, and one came right over to me and started to smell this new addition to the group. I was amazed he didn't bark, but since he was there, I felt it was now or never! On went my flashlight with the beam going right into the face of the large man wearing size 12's.

He froze for an instant as the words, "Evening, gentlemen, state Fish and Game warden. You are under arrest," rang through the cool night air. Then he exploded!

"Run," he bellowed. He took off at a right angle to me as the other two men remained frozen in time. The angle size 12 took was perfect for a flying tackle. It was the kind of tackle you seldom get in football because the ones carrying the ball are so fast and elusive, but here it was, and I took advantage of it in a heartbeat. I hit the lad so hard I about broke my right shoulder, which hit the pistol on his hip. The impact knocked the wind out of him, and he was further incapacitated when we went into the marsh and he landed face down. I don't even remember handcuffing him, but I did in record time as he lay there almost knocked out.

Grabbing the pistol from his holster, I stuck it under my gunbelt, then jumped up, grabbed my still shining flashlight out of the mud, and, hitting the two lads with the beam, thundered, "Make a move and you die."

I knew I couldn't shoot them for running, but they didn't know that. The trick worked. Both remained frozen in their mind's worst moment as I approached. Asking for and receiving their driver's licenses and sidearms, I then asked them to go pull their buddy out of the mire. They did it meekly, and it was plain to see that size 12 wasn't going anywhere—at least not until he got the kink out of his ass from being tackled by a three-hundred-pounder flying at the speed of light (well, almost the speed of light). When he finally got his faculties back, I asked for and received his driver's license as well. As he dug the license out, I could see a police badge and ID card attached to the opposite side of his driver's license in his wallet. Ignoring that for the moment, I gathered up their loose gear, and then we headed for the refuge fence and their vehicle.

Making all three drag the hog, which went about five hundred pounds, took a lot out of them, and by the time we got back to their truck they were an exhausted lot. I took the car keys from size 12, who turned out to be a Sergeant Thomas from a San Francisco Bay area police department, and the distributor cap from the Ford to preclude thoughts of escape by the two left behind. I advised both men to remain with the pickup, and then the good sergeant and I walked back to where my patrol truck was hidden. Loading and seatbelting him into the patrol truck, I petted my much-excited horse of a Lab, Shadow, and told her (in a gruff voice, of course) to watch him.

I don't think the sergeant moved during the entire trip back except for the labored breathing caused by the kink from my flying tackle, which I rated a "ten." Once in my truck, I radioed the sheriff's office and had them send a unit out to transport the prisoners and a wrecker to tow away the Ford once I seized it. In short order, everybody was in jail, the Ford was impounded, and the dogs were detained in the animal welfare shelter in Yuba City. The hog was photographed and donated to a needy family with seven kids to avoid spoilage. Boy, were they glad to see that slab of bacon arrive.

As it turned out, the good sergeant, in order to fatten his income, had been guiding illegal hunts on the national wildlife refuge for years. He would quietly advertise among friends and associates, sneak them in one at a time, and charge them $1,000 for the experience. Bill, an attorney and the one who had fired that first shot that mortally wounded the big tusker that fateful night, broke like an egg and told all. Aware that I was armed with this information, the good sergeant came clean with the rest of the story in short order. Included in his explanation was the story of the dogs. He had trained them to stay very close to him throughout the hunt. Additionally, he had had a veterinarian in the Bay area fix them so they couldn't bark, only croak or growl. Those poor damn dogs. Humankind can really be the lowest form of animal there is with just half a thought and a little time.

Several weeks after this "hoorah" my three lads appeared in front of the federal judge in Sacramento and without a whimper pleaded guilty. Jack Downs, my future boss in the federal service, saw to it that they were charged with trespassing, possession of a firearm on a national wildlife refuge, removal of wildlife from a national wildlife refuge, and possession of dogs on a refuge without a permit. All three were found guilty and fined $2,000 each for the error of their ways. After that I never saw muddy tracks leading from that area onto Lone Star Road again.

As it turned out, the good sergeant and his trusty sidekick, the cigarette man, were both police officers from the San Francisco Bay area. In addition, the Ford turned out to be a police undercover vehicle that the sergeant would commandeer for these hunts, even charging the police department for the gas and oil. It was later discovered that he claimed on his vouchers that he was on a moving drug surveillance. Well, I don't know about a moving surveillance, but he certainly had a moving experience before this episode in his life was finished. He and the other man were both removed from the police force, and both dropped from view.

All the way through the episode my senses had kept telling me that the situation was something unusual, that the person being pursued was out of the ordinary. He was. He was very good at what he did and took a lot of life. Unfortunately for him, at that moment in time someone else was better than he at the hunt. That is usually the case in this world of wildlife. Someone always has the upper hand. I can only hope that for those of us enlisted in wildlife law enforcement, our moments are better than those of the people on the other side of the fence and in the business of extinction. If not, we'd better grab our asses because we and the passenger pigeon will eventually have a lot in common.

18

A Game Warden's Ears

ONE EVENING, after having worked most of the day checking waterfowl hunters in Colusa County, I grabbed a sackload of decoys and my dog, Shadow, and took off to do a little duck hunting myself. My little duck hunt turned into a typical enjoyable afternoon, with the opportunity to listen to the sounds of the marsh and the whistle of the ducks' wings as they sailed into my set and to smell the gunpowder from the freshly fired shells of my 10-gauge double-barreled shotgun. Taking my time, I made sure all my shots were well within the thirty-five-yard range and only took a shot if the ducks coming into the set were pintail drakes. The weather was cool but clear, which necessitated the liberal use of my mallard call and pintail whistle. For the most part, the air carried only single ducks and a few pairs at this time of the day, but before long, with the limit at eight, I had seven plump rice-fed drakes resting beside me in the blind. Shadow was having the time of her life bringing back the birds I killed, and the day was good. As the shooting slowed, I sat back in the blind to enjoy one of God's beautiful purple sunsets coupled with a cool but not cold breeze and topped off with a dying afternoon sky now filling with tens of thousands of pintail, mallards, wigeon, and everything else that quacks, seeking a safe place to feed. It was one of many beautiful marsh memories that are burned forever into the recesses of my mind. Today those hordes of ducks leaving the Butte Sink are nothing but a memory, a moment in time in which I was privileged to be a participant.

Forgoing the last duck of my limit because the onrushing sweep of the second hand of my watch announced the end of legal shooting hours was near, I left the blind, took one more look around to complete my memory of the afternoon, and started trudging toward my vehicle. Walking along a rice check with my ducks swinging from my duck strap, acutely aware of the two swollen fingers on my right hand from the recoil of the 10-gauge double-barrel and the soft *ploosh* of the footsteps of my tired but happy dog walking in the water at the edge of the dike, I awoke from my dream world to the sound of shooting farther to the west. Glancing at my watch, I saw that the end of legal shooting hours was rapidly approaching. When I reached my vehicle, I took the time to pick and clean all my ducks, all the while keeping an ear cocked to the distant sound of shots. Legal shooting hours had long since ended, but the shots didn't.

Damn, I was hoping the lads in the field would end their illegal activities and allow me to go home early for once with my great marsh memories. But it was not to be. It didn't take long to realize that the shots, rather than ceasing, were increasing in tempo to match the increase of the now hungry targets whirling through the skies. The air was absolutely full of skeins of waterfowl traveling every which way and looking for a place to eat in the thousands of acres of recently harvested rice fields. I could look in any direction and see literally thousands of birds moving in every direction of the compass. This was a special sight for those of us who took the time to look. Trying hard to relax during my time off and enjoy Mother Nature's sights of a lifetime, I continued to pick and clean my ducks, hoping these shooters would soon realize legal hunting hours were over and leave. They didn't and kept shooting while I fussed with my seven now not-so-interesting ducks.

Loading my gear, ducks, and dog into my pickup, I worked my way across the farmland on farm access roads, running without my lights until I was within one hundred yards of the place where the offending shots were coming from. Stopping my vehicle, I just sat there and listened so I could echo-locate my offending late shooting party. Off to my west sat four duck blinds, all within about four hundred yards of each other. From one blind in the middle, I saw two lads stand up and fire six shots into the air, killing two mallard ducks. The shooting was coming from one of many sections of leased waterfowl hunting lands known as the American Sportsman's

Club, an organization with a history of violation problems in my district. Gazing out over the evening shine of water on the flooded rice field, I said to myself, "Well, there sits your offending duck blind; now what are you going to do?"

Looking the lay of the land over one more time, I left my vehicle and dog and closed in on my duck shooters, who all the while continued to blaze away at the ducks crossing over their decoys. By now I was close enough not only to count the number of ducks they killed but to identify the species as well. The sun had set behind the mountains, the wind was picking up briskly, the birds were flying low and slow, and the shooting continued, increasing in intensity. I believed there were only two shooters in the blind, but they had dozens of dead ducks around them. Taking out my flashlight and binoculars, I moved in a crouch even closer to the gunmen, trying to figure out how best to approach and apprehend them as night rapidly descended on the marsh.

By the time I had worked in close enough to the blind to be effective as a "catch dog," darkness had really set in. I could see flame spurting from the barrels of the hunters' shotguns as they shot into the night sky at the thousands of pintail that were leaving the haven of their refuge in the Butte Sink in unbelievable numbers for the harvested rice fields surrounding them. I wasn't able to distinguish physically between the two men through my binoculars because they were so close in size (I later discovered they were brothers), so I had to rely on my ears to show me the difference between them. Most of their shot groups were in threes, which ruled out the possibility of a double-barreled shotgun. I couldn't hear the familiar *clackety-clack* of a pump shotgun, so I ruled out a pump as well. After listening for a while, I decided both were using semiautomatic shotguns, one a 12-gauge and the other a 16- or 20-gauge three-inch shotgun. This belief was reinforced by the knowledge that rarely did folks hunting on these wealthy duck clubs use junk for shotguns after paying many thousands of dollars for the privilege of hunting waterfowl on their "own" private shooting areas. There was no mistaking the signature hard thump of the 12-gauge shotgun. The other shotgun had a lighter thump that was clearly audible and definitely lighter in sound, and that gunman didn't shoot as often as his partner.

The shooting continued for one hour past the end of legal shooting hours until the sky was literally black and then stopped. Since I didn't have a notebook with me, I used a pen to record the number of shots, shooters, and birds killed on my fingers and hands. Don't laugh! You have enough space for ten entries on your fingers and many more on your hands. I couldn't use a light to illuminate what I was writing on or I would have given away my position, but I was aware, in the dark, of what I was writing on the soft flesh of my hands. Plus, it wouldn't wash off very easily, so if in crawling on the ground I got my hands wet, my notes would still be there. I have used this method many times in my thirty-two years in law enforcement, and it has always worked like a charm. The only time it doesn't is when the defense attorneys want to see your notes in a court of law. However, the lack of notes under these circumstances doesn't hurt your case and usually elicits a chuckle from the judge.

For the next twenty or so minutes, the lads remained in the blind, not moving and out of sight. I almost had the feeling they were sitting quietly to throw off any game wardens in the area. The pause was good because it gave me the opportunity to listen for other shooting that I might work after finishing up with these lads—or save for the next night because many times, if violators get away with something and are rewarded with game, they will return to the same battle ground to continue their successful poaching shortly thereafter. Keeping that fact in mind, many times I have gone to such a spot the night after hearing something suspicious and been able to apprehend some lads breaking the law. Whether they were the ones there the night before, who knows? All I would know was that the lads breaking the law that particular evening were now being attended to in a way they needed.

Hearing no other late shooting, I returned my attention to the chaps still motionless in the blind. Now I realized why these lads weren't moving, I thought. It was getting inky black out because of some cloud cover moving in from the northwest. These men were waiting until it got so dark that they would be hard to find.

However, these folks had walked out on a rice-check walkway, the easiest way to the blind versus walking across a flooded, sticky, adobe-bottomed rice field. Besides, walking through a flooded rice field would make a lot of sloshing noises. That idea convinced me they would come out the same way they had gone into their blind, along the easy-to-walk rice check. In those days, the fine was $2 per minute for every minute past legal shooting time, $25 for the base violation of late shooting, and loss of all your critters. It didn't take long, with that formula, to run up one hell of a bill. Little did these lads know they had just paid for my gas and oil for a week's hard work with their little sashay into the illegal world of late-night waterfowl shooting immediately adjacent to where the local game warden had chosen to kill a few ducks to give to a needy family.

Running the lay of the land through my memory bank, I realized that these lads had three ways to leave the marsh, and there was no easy way for me to approach them quietly in the field. If I approached in a direct line-of-sight pattern through a flooded rice field, they were only forty yards away but my passage would be very noisy, and hard going in the water and mud. Once they heard me sloshing across that flooded rice paddy, they could be off and gone out the back door, so to speak, on another rice check and outdistance me in short order. So that avenue was ruled out. If I walked down one rice check toward them, they would probably see or hear me coming and leave via the rear of the blind on another rice check radiating from the blind out into the inky darkness that now surrounded us. Splitting the difference, I stayed in between the two rice checks leading to their shooting area. That way I could move quickly to either side and intercept them as they came out no matter what rice check they chose to follow. Besides, I thought, the dirt roads behind me were as numerous as the clubhouses servicing this area. That meant that more than likely their vehicle was hidden behind me somewhere. That made my position even better because the lads would have to walk through me to get to their vehicle. After the many years I had played high school and college football, no one walked through me. Maybe my three-hundred-pound frame had something to do with that.

I noticed the lads were now standing up in the blind and quietly looking all around. They continued watching the skies as thousands of ducks whistled overhead en route to the rice fields to feed. After what seemed hours to me as I knelt in the icy water, they finally began to walk out on one of the rice checks toward where I was concealed. I crawled closer to their rice check, and as they approached a point where it would be pure folly for them to flee, I stood up, turned my flashlight on them, and identified myself. The men froze for a second in surprise, then continued walking toward me as if nothing were the matter. They were almost identical, and as luck would have it were both attorneys from Redding, California. I asked them if they knew when the legal shooting time had ended that evening. Neither had the foggiest idea, was their response. They continued to walk toward me and then passed me as if I had no business with them. I made sure they understood I wanted a few more words with them, and they halted in annoyance. They denied that they had been involved in any late shooting activity; it must have been someone else, they said. I asked them what time they had on their watches. Their times were only a few minutes different than my watch, which I set daily to avoid problems such as these in the field. One attorney told me that both of them had Rolex watches, and since my watch wasn't a Rolex, it could hardly be trusted to tell the correct time. Ignoring his obvious intent to belittle my Seiko, I told the two gentlemen that I had observed them late-shooting waterfowl from a very short distance away through my binoculars and had seen them kill six ducks (four mallards and two pintail) in the process. I informed them that taking migratory waterfowl after legal shooting hours was a state and federal wildlife violation and that they were each going to receive a citation for the offense.

They immediately objected, indicating that it hadn't been them but some other hunters farther to the west of their duck blind. "No way," I quietly told them. "I have been within forty yards of your position in direct line of sight the whole time and watched both of you shoot over an hour after legal shooting hours with my binoculars." They could argue all they wanted because as far as I was concerned, they had broken the law in plain view and both of them were going to get citations for late-shooting waterfowl. On top of that, I had observed them walking directly toward me after they finished shooting. There was no question in my mind about who had violated the law. Overexplaining, as game wardens will do, I pointed out that the man shooting the 16- or 20-gauge shotgun had quit shooting three minutes earlier than the one shooting the 12-gauge shotgun. The two hunters looked at each other and then really raised a fuss. It seemed that both were shooting 12-gauge shotguns, and now I was the one in error. I knew my ears had not deceived me, but when I examined their shotguns, I found that both men had Browning 12-gauge semiautomatic shotguns.

That turn of events put me in a little bit of a quandary. I knew my ears had not deceived me: there had been a sound difference between the two guns. The attorneys were now getting bolder, sensing a weakness in my case, and began to press me for the name of my supervisor, my badge number, and so on, as some attorneys are known to do, as a matter of course, to intimidate an officer. They again told me that the real culprits had been in a blind farther to their west and said that if I hurried, I might still be able to catch them, although they doubted it because of my large size and my inability to identify real culprits when I saw them. Equally determined (translation: hardheaded), I told them again that they would both receive citations for late shooting, and that was that! If they cared to argue the case further, the floor of the court was the place to carry on that activity, I added.

One of the lads told me that his shotgun had broken a few minutes before the other chap had finished shooting and that he would be damned if he was going to accept a citation for late-shooting waterfowl when he had a broken gun. Taking his shotgun, I examined it to verify his story. I was buying time until I could sort out the difference in what I was seeing and what I knew I had heard. Sure as shooting, he had a shell jammed in the chamber, which would have prevented any shells from feeding into the chamber from the magazine. I looked closely at the shell stuck in the chamber of his 12-gauge Browning shotgun and, to my glee, discovered that it was a 16-gauge shell! That is, the shell was one size smaller than his gun was safe to use. In shooting it, the shell case had expanded and stuck in the chamber of his shotgun. God, was I glad to see that stuck shell. A 16-gauge, when fired, makes a softer sound than a 12-gauge shell. This chap had been shooting shells of the wrong caliber in his shotgun and was very lucky he hadn't had an explosion and lost an eye in the process. Like a successful gunfighter of old blowing the smoke off the end of his pistol barrel before placing it back into the holster, I casually handed the shotgun back to the owner and pointed out why his shotgun had quit on him.

After an agitated examination, there was an abject and stunned silence and then a shaking of both heads in disbelief. Further examination of the game bag of the man who had been shooting the off-size shells produced numerous 16-gauge shells mixed in with his 12-gauge shells. A dangerous situation, to say the least. Thanks to his fine, strong Browning shotgun, he had avoided an accident that could have done a whole lot more damage than just a stuck shell. I took that moment to inform both gentlemen that I needed their driver's licenses so I could issue citations for the late shooting of waterfowl. The arguments refuting my accusations based on what I had heard with my game-warden ears faded away, and the following week the two attorneys paid a $145 fine each, without incident.

Conservation officers, like any other officers, rely on many facets of their senses to increase their efficiency and success. On that particular evening so long ago, a game warden's ears cocked and listening to the flight of thousands of ducks were also able to discern the difference between a 12-gauge shotgun shooting 12-gauge shells and a 12-gauge shotgun shooting 16-gauge shells from half a mile away, much to the chagrin of the hunters and much to the relief of the marsh inhabitants.

Even today, my joy in listening to the heartbeat of a marsh is warmed by the remembrance of yesteryear, two insistent attorneys, and a young man's ears.

19

Crazy Joe and the Drag

AFTER MY TRANSFER TO Colusa County, I spent many hours learning about the Sacramento Valley: its people, its wildlife populations, and its hunting subculture, especially as it related to illegal commercial wildlife-harvesting activity. One of my major problems in the Sacramento Valley at that time was trying to slow down the illegal commercial-market hunting of waterfowl. This activity consisted of hunters going at night into the rice fields, where the waterfowl, primarily ducks, were feeding, sneaking up on them, and shooting them on the ground as they fed in tightly packed masses, sometimes as many as fifty thousand feeding in a bunch. The hunters would then either haul the carcasses out or have their buyers go to the kill site the next day, taking all the risks of course, and haul them from the fields themselves. These rice-fed wild ducks would then end up in the commercial markets of some major west coast city or be shipped to commercial markets as far away as New York via rail or truck.

Many old-timers used to tell me that the tried-and-true method was to ambush the feeding ducks from behind a rice check as the ducks, in a compact mass, fed up to your place of concealment. They would use shotguns with homemade magazine extenders that increased the shell capacity from five to fifteen. With that kind of firepower, they would kill from three hundred to a thousand or more birds, depending on the number of shooters. After the shoot had been pulled, the shooters would either lie down and look to see if the game wardens were coming or run like hell and come back later to pick up their ducks after the area had cooled off. In such a situation there were always many crippled ducks, probably twice as many as the dead ones. The market hunter would move out among the carpet of dead and dying ducks, picking them up and placing them by twos between his fingers until he had eight in his hand. Any birds still alive and struggling would be bitten across the head, thereby crushing their skulls. Once the hunter had eight to ten birds in hand, he would hurriedly wrap a piece of butcher twine around the necks below the heads and above his fingers, cinch it tightly, and then drop the bundle to the ground. When all the birds that could be picked had been gathered, sometimes a rope would be tied to all of the bundles and the ducks would be dragged out of the field like some long daisy chain. This is how the term *drag* came into play when one talked about a duck shoot by commercial-market hunters in the Sacramento Valley, according to some of the old-timers I met over the years. To drag the ducks meant to slaughter them on the ground at night as they fed, killing large numbers for the market or one's own freezer. Those in the business of killing large quantities of ducks for either the market or their personal consumption were called *draggers*.

On one of my days off during the fall, I decided I had better spend some time getting my house ready for the winter storms that would soon appear. As I worked around the yard winterizing my sprinkler system, up drove an old beat-up pickup. The driver just sat there in the cab in front of my home and watched me work on the sprinklers. I thought that behavior somewhat odd, but I couldn't leave what I was working on just yet, so I continued with my task. When I finished what I was doing, I got up out of the mud that had water pipe going in every direction and walked over to greet the unknown driver and see who he was and what he wanted. Approaching the vehicle, I saw that the driver was not anyone I knew, so I said, "Good morning, may I help you?"

He said, "No, I just wanted to see what the dumbest son of a bitch in the valley looked like."

Somewhat taken aback by this very old man's boldness, I said, "Well, that is a matter of opinion."

"No, that is an accurate statement," he responded. "I have watched you bumble along in the rice fields at night, and you are walking right by too many draggers. Because of your inability to catch them or really understand what the ins and outs of the killing profession are, they're getting bolder."

He continued, "To be frank, they are my competition, and I need them out of the way. Since I have this problem and you really aren't part of the solution as yet, I have a proposition for you."

What he had said was pretty much on the money. I hadn't been able to get to the draggers in any way as yet because of my inexperience and my inability to get anyone in the valley to trust the new game warden and come forward with information on how to work these tight-knit groups of duck-killing sons of guns. In fact, my level of frustration was so high that at that time I would have teamed up with the devil if it meant some of these lads killing the ducks at night would fall into my pretty much empty hands. Something inside me told me this chap might be the ticket. To me, the eyes tell it all, and in this chap's case they did. His eyes were cold, calculating, intelligent, and a little bit crazy. Well, I thought, what have you got to lose, Terry? You still know right from wrong, so let's give it a whirl; you can always get off when you want. Little did I know that the rush I gained from this man in the form of knowledge would remain in my system until I retired some thirty years or so later.

"What is your offer?" I asked cautiously yet curiously.

"I'll tell you what," he answered, "I will teach you how to catch the draggers in the valley. If you pay attention to what I tell you, then maybe the fields won't be so cluttered by my competition. I am just getting too old to run with the younger men who are truly not worthy of this profession, and you can be of assistance to me, as I see it."

"Why don't you just quit if it's getting too hard for you? It's not like it's legal and all," I said. The look he gave me told me not to go there; that was not an intelligent question as far as he was concerned. The look in his light blue eyes told it all. This was something he had been doing for the better part of sixty years. When one is into the hunt for that long a time, it becomes a way of life. "Sorry," I said. The apology seemed to satisfy him.

I looked at him for a few more moments and then said, "What

about you? Where do you fit in this picture if I catch you doing the same thing you want me to prevent others from doing?"

He gave me a funny look, and his blue eyes snapped as he said, "You won't. If you are fortunate enough to catch me, then I will pay up just like a slot machine, no problem. But don't worry, that won't be an option you will have to live with."

Ignoring what he said and the way he said it because I had aspirations of my own regarding this chap as well as all the others, I said, "Well, that sounds pretty good to me. I'm always willing to learn." I stuck out my hand and added, "My name is Terry Grosz. You got a deal."

Refusing my hand, he answered, "I know who you are. You just call me Joe, and I will call you when I am ready." With that, he started up his clunker red Ford pickup and drove off, leaving me to memorize his license-plate number. Brother, I thought. Getting to know Colusa County and its people was going to be quite a challenge. Never in my wildest dreams did I think anyone in this county would step forward to help the game warden. Until then, hardly a single person had even offered a hand in friendship. Other than the Colusa County sheriff's officers, who were most helpful, the others in the county politely turned their backs on Fish and Game folks for the most part. People in Colusa County had a reputation of doing what they wanted and when, and they figured that tradition was just fine and would continue if they had anything to do with it. In addition, some of my Fish and Game predecessors had not really carried the cause too well in the eyes of the folks we were supposed to be serving. However, there was still the issue of the law of the land, and I was bound and determined to make the county safe for natural resources as well as preserving those resources for people yet to come. Boy, what a mouthful I had taken without yet knowing it.

My mind ran back to the meeting I had just had with Joe. Here it was, a nest on the ground if this chap came through. Going into the house, I called the sheriff's office and asked them to run Joe's license plate so I could find out who my "friend" really was. The plate came back registered to a local farming corporation, so I was no further ahead on this chap than before. However, I still had my friend Tom, who knew everyone in the valley, or so it seemed, so I made a call to him. Tom told me the fellow I had met, based on my description, was a very bad man and crazy to boot. Tom suggested that I be very careful around him because he would just as soon shoot me as look at me. Tom also informed me that this chap came from a family that had been in the valley for years and that had killed and sold to the San Francisco markets a lot of ducks. There was a long silence on the phone, and then Tom added, "Misser Grosz, if he wants to help you learn how to catch draggers, there is none better." Thanking Tom, I hung up and wondered what the hell I was letting myself in for.

I later found out about more about my mystery friend by nosing around, and as a result added a little bit more to my knowledge of him. Let's just call him Crazy Joe. He was an old man, probably in his middle to late sixties, of medium height and build, dark complected, with the bluest of eyes that spoke of a violence barely kept under the surface. He had a hair-trigger temper and was prone to shoot at anyone who crossed onto his small farm or the property of his employer. There were even those who claimed to have crossed into his hunting territory and had to lie in a rice ditch all day as a result of Joe's prowess with a rifle keeping them there. What a pair we would make, I thought, the law and the lawless. I had made up my mind a long time ago that I would take the outlaws out any way I could just as long as it was legal. Now, with Joe as my partner, the possibility of payback loomed large and a whole lot nearer than any time before. The thought of finally being able to run some of these duck-killing chaps to the ground gave me a damn good feeling, to say the least. I always worked hard, but many times I had to work harder just to offset my lack of knowledge. If I could work hard the way my body allowed and for once really know what I was doing, the critters might just have a chance, I thought. A large grin was starting to spread over my tired face—one of those "God really does love game wardens" types of grin.

For two weeks nothing happened, and I began to feel that Crazy Joe wasn't going to work out. If he really had a desire to slow down his competition, surely he would have called me by now, I thought. Then one evening as a light misty rain was falling, my phone rang. I had just sat down to a hurried supper so I could get back into the field when Donna said, "A Joe is on the phone." I picked up the phone and heard a voice say, "Let's go."

"Where?" I asked. He described a duck club north of Gunner's Field in the Lambertville complex. "I know where it is, but how do I find you in that maze?" I asked.

"I will find you; see you shortly." Then the voice was gone. Leaving the dinner table, I headed into my bedroom, grabbed a clean shirt, pinned on my badge, and headed for the door. As I went out, Donna knowingly handed me a thick meat sandwich. She had overheard part of the telephone conservation, realized I was on the run again, and swung into action. She was uncanny, and that is why one of her nicknames was Radar, after the character in the *M.A.S.H.* television series. Giving her a quick kiss for taking care of me the way she always did, I headed out the door into the evening's rainy mist.

Pulling into a bamboo thicket where Joe had asked me to meet him, I was relieved to see him come out of the brush with nothing in his hands but a flashlight. At that point I still wasn't sure who I had coupled up with and whether he could be trusted.

"Evening, Joe," I said.

He just gave me a hard look and said, "Get going south on 4–Mile Road; there's something down there I want to show you."

From that rainy-evening start, we worked together throughout that first winter, two odd ducks equally determined to achieve our goals. One of my goals, on a personal note, centered around Joe's left forearm. All across the bottom portion of that arm were terrible burn scars. After we had worked together for several weeks and I had gotten to know my stern taskmaster better, I found the courage to ask about the scars. He looked at me as if to say, What a dummy, and then pointed to the shotgun he now always carried when we worked together. He said the old Remington Model 11 shotgun was responsible for those burns. He called it Old Meat in the Pot. He said that when the market hunters put the extenders on their shotguns, which increased the shell capacity from three or five to sometimes as many as fifteen, they started burning their arms. He was quiet for a moment and then continued, explaining that when they went into the fields to blow up the ducks, they loaded their shotguns to their maximum shell capacities. As they began to shoot rapidly into the massed bunches of feeding ducks, the shotgun rose from the recoil of rapid repeated firings. The only way to hold the gun down so they could continue to deliver their shot-strings into the densest part of the flock was to throw their left forearms over the barrels and push them down. This worked fine until one approached shot number nine or ten. By that time the barrel was very hot, and leaving the arm over the barrel after that point would lead to burns. In the Sacramento Valley, repeated burns on the arms of many old-timers were considered their badge of courage. Conversely, apprehension of commercial-market hunters by the game warden was the warden's badge of courage and a stain most hunters fought hard to keep from their kilts.

Joe was a stern but good teacher. I guess desperation on my part to slow down the terrible carnage in the rice fields after dark made me a good student. He taught me how to read subtle signs left along the dirt roads after a drag. He taught me the details of duck behavior, how to read the weather, and how to read the ducks in conjunction with particular weather patterns. He taught me the factors that would lead to a duck slaughter, when to expect it, how to intercept those involved, and what parts of the valley the ducks favored during different times of the year. He taught me market-hunter terminology; where existing markets were located; names of buyers, shooters, and middlemen; favored methods of transport by the various clans in the valley; and the names of those storing ducks for mass pickups and where. He gave me personal insights into those I was hunting and told me how to be prepared for ambushes. Basically, he gave me an opportunity to look into the past with a set of eyes from the present. He also, not through words but through actions, allowed me access to himself. A hunter of humans does not really draw a line of distinction: a target is a target, and Joe was looming larger than life, something we both realized early in the relationship.

After one winter season of meeting clandestinely so people wouldn't know Joe was cooperating with the law, the training ended. He had taught me the commercial-market hunter's trade—how well only time would tell. Joe met me at our usual meeting place one evening and said, "We're through with the lessons. You have a handle on what needs to be done, and I suggest you get cracking."

About that time a small flock of graceful pintail went over en route to their chosen field for the evening, and as Joe followed their route, his eyes and voice softened.

"Terry," he said, "people are changing, the ducks are declining, and the history that was once mine is just that. I am getting too old to commercial-market hunt like I did when I was a young man fifty years ago."

There was a long pause before he spoke again, and I did not intrude. "Once a year from now on, I will drag enough ducks to fill my freezer for a year and keep me young. I will call you and let you know when I am going. If you catch me, fine. If you don't, that's your problem."

With that and a wave of the hand, off he went, basically out of my life because of who we were and what we each represented. Sitting there watching him drive off, I wondered. If he was getting too old to hunt commercially anymore, then why had he taught me the tricks of the trade? I began to get an unusual feeling that there was more to this than met the eye. Was I being set up, or was he setting himself up? I didn't have a sense of the answer but figured I would know when it came.

The following winter during duck season, I received a call from Crazy Joe. He said, "I think I will be going out this evening. Good luck."

He hung up before I could ask him a single question. Minutes later, out I went into the night. I was going out anyway because the time, ducks, and cycle of the moon were right for the draggers to do their thing. So Joe's call did nothing more than get me another sandwich for dinner as I left my home. Using his teaching and what I'd learned since then, I picked an area that suited a commercial shoot, hid my vehicle, walked into the area, and dug in for the evening's events. The area was one just loaded with bunches of ducks, mostly pintail, and all were hungrily feeding. I figured if anyone had any bad intentions, this is where they would expend those energies. About two in the morning, my hunch proved correct. Lying against my rice check, I saw three men walk right by me, heading in a crouched position toward my bunch of feeding ducks. They moved right up to my check, just a few feet north of where I lay, and then went to earth and commenced to crawl the rest of the distance, about forty yards, toward my feeding ducks. Rolling over on my right shoulder so I could mark their progress better, I thought with a grin, Well, lads, at least one of you will be mine tonight. Then a rattle of shots from the northeast shook the morning stillness, spooking the ducks feeding in my field. Up they went with a roar before the lads sneaking toward them could get a shot, and back to the Delevan National Wildlife Refuge immediately to the east they scampered. Damn, I thought, come on, God, give me a break here.

I could hear the soft roar of fleeing waterfowl from the shoot to the northeast. I counted about ten rapid-fire shots that ripped the morning quiet like the noise of a tearing sheet. I was too far away from that action to do any good and just lay there clenching my fists and teeth in frustration. Just too far away for me to catch that chap, I thought; only one gun doing the shooting, but just too far. I knew from past experience and from Joe's teachings that if I wasn't within forty yards or less of the shooters, I could kiss off any hope of fruitful action on my part. The shooters would just melt away into the night. A combination of shadows, knowledge of the area, and luck would allow them to escape as the ducks lay flopping and dying on the ground. Damn, two opportunities and I was not in the right place to be effective for either one.

At that time, the three lads who had been sneaking up on the ducks I had been watching walked by, heading back in the direction from which they had come. I recognized one of them by his shape and voice and said to myself, "Someday, Maxwell, you will not be so lucky. I don't care if your wife and mine are good buddies—someday, someday." I waited until daylight on my rice check and then moved northeast, using my knowledge of the area to find the kill site. Talk about frustrated: the kill site was on the north end of Delevan National Wildlife Refuge. A goddamned national wildlife refuge! That took the work of a master. Then the wheels began to turn. I had worked with the master; surely he wouldn't shoot the refuge, but then again ...

About three days later Joe called and said, "Where were you?"

I told him I'd been several miles from where I actually had been to see if that might draw a comment about where I should have been.

He said, "Well, I didn't shoot that area. Better luck next year."

You could almost hear the relief in his voice. He said, "See you next year," and hung up. That call provided an answer to my instincts about who might be my master shooter on the national wildlife refuge. I had heard no other shooting that evening for miles around, so it must have been him—but then again, was it?

The following year, just about the same time as the year before, Joe called and said, "It's a good night; I think I will be out and about."

In a teasing voice I said, "Where are you going this time?"

He said, "Good luck," and hung up the phone.

This time the birds were feeding over toward the west side of the valley, from Link Dennis's property all the way across the interstate. As I slowly moved through the dark, thick night on farm roads, I tried to echo-locate every bunch of ducks I could in order to make my choice for the night's activities. My selection had to be a good one this time or I would be rewarded again with dead and crippled ducks. I finally decided to sit to the east of the main flocks of ducks strung out across the valley and just south of a large bunch happily feeding on the north end of Delevan National Wildlife Refuge, Link Dennis's property, and the Newhall Farms property. About two A.M. somebody blew up the ducks immediately north of my stakeout location on what appeared to be the national wildlife refuge. Again, I was hidden just too far away to try to intercept the shooter. Dammit anyway, that was twice the same thing had happened to me. I sat there in my hiding place just off the south end of the refuge as many of the ducks nearest to me took to the air in alarm, trying to figure out how to work this problem more successfully in the future.

About an hour passed as I sat there in frustration, and suddenly I noticed that bunches of dead pintail ducks were floating past me in the canal that bordered the west side of the refuge. That canal ran under the Maxwell Highway and stopped at a small dam on private property. I watched in utter amazement as the bunches of pintail floated down the canal and under the highway and lodged gently against the headboards of the small irrigation dam. Looking back up the canal through my Starlight Scope, I could see more dead ducks coming down in what appeared to be an endless stream. Then it dawned on me! Whoever had shot the ducks on the refuge earlier that morning had tossed them into the canal for two reasons. First, it relieved him of the need to pack them any distance, and second, it relieved him of any evidence that might be held against him if he were stopped on his way out of the rice fields. Only an old master in the commercial-market-hunting arena would think of such a plan. It was now apparent that the shooter had planned this raid very carefully and would be along shortly to pick up his birds, carry them a short distance to the road, throw them into a waiting pickup, and be gone. The idea was as slick as cow slobbers, with one exception: the student in the ointment. I hurriedly hid right next to the check dam, using a thick patch of tule as my cover. Sitting down, I could look right at the headboard area of the dam and plainly see the bunches of ducks stacking up. I sat there quietly waiting.

By three-thirty A.M., I estimated that at least three hundred ducks had quietly floated down the canal and lodged against the check dam, with more still coming. Then I heard someone coming from behind me. I froze so as not to alert the person approaching and intently waited. Pretty soon the unmistakable shape of a man emerged from the darkness, examined the area around the check dam, then walked over to its edge and began to stuff bunches of ducks into a gunnysack. I let him collect about three bunches of ducks and then quickly stood up and stepped out from my hiding place. I said, "Good morning, state Fish and Game warden. You are under arrest."

Without showing any surprise or emotion, as if he had expected me to be there, the man kept stuffing ducks into the sack, and when he had filled it moved it off to one side. He then picked up another empty gunnysack lying by his feet and, in the unmistakable voice of Crazy Joe, said, "Terry, give me a hand with the rest of these, please."

I had caught my teacher, one of the best draggers in the country. I was speechless. Without a word, I dropped down by his side like an old friend and helped him load that gunnysack and others with dead ducks. Without any conversation we finished cleaning up the ducks around the dam. Walking over to my hidden patrol truck, I started the engine and drove it back to the check dam. Joe and I loaded eight sacks of dead ducks into the back of the truck, still without a word passing between us. When we finished loading our cargo, we got into the truck and drove in silence north along the canal bordering the refuge on the west, picking up the bunches of ducks that had hung up in the overhanging bushes as they floated down toward the dam. After completing that task, I turned to Joe and said, "Where is the kill site?"

He pointed toward a field to the northwest, about fifty yards from the canal. By now daylight was showing in the east. The dawn of another day for all of us, except the ducks in the bags and those dotting the field in front of us. The ducks in the field numbered another seventy-three, which were picked up by two rapidly tiring friends. When we got back to my truck, I said, "Joe, I'm going to have to cite you for all of this."

Looking me dead in the eye he said, "I know."

I said, "Well, I don't believe in that without a full stomach, how about you?"

Joe grinned and answered, "Let's go. I could go for some of that food I hear you cook."

With that, the game warden and the outlaw drove to the game warden's house and, side by side in the kitchen, cooked up spuds, steak, and eggs topped off with some of my wife's homemade bread

(which, by the way, is the world's best), coffee for Joe, and milk for
me. After breakfast I sat down at the kitchen table with my citation
book and issued citations to Joe for a monster over-limit, taking migratory waterfowl before legal shooting hours, wanton waste, and
use of an unplugged shotgun. Joe accepted the tickets without a
word and then asked for a lift home, which I was happy to give
him. When I got back home, I gutted all the ducks and placed them
in my evidence freezer, located on Sacramento National Wildlife
Refuge, for use in court. However, there was no need for courtroom preparation. Joe paid $500 per charge, or $2,000 total, and as
far as I was concerned he was square with the government and me.

Several days later I saw Joe in the field and told him no offense,
I had just done what I was trained to do.

He said, "I didn't expect anything less of you. If you had done
anything less than what you did, I would have been terribly disappointed in my student. However, I want you to understand that my
days as a dragger ended when you apprehended me at the check
dam. The days are gone when one can kill large numbers of birds
and expect large numbers of them to return the following year. I
have watched the demise of our waterfowl and am partly responsible. As self-imposed punishment, I will never again hunt ducks the
rest of my life." The look in his eyes confirmed what he had just
said. I could see something else in those eyes as well. It was like seeing a tremendous loss of personal history, almost as if a flame had
gone out.

I said, "Joe, that isn't necessary; you can hunt the rest of the days
of your life—just stay within the limits."

He looked at me with those hard blue eyes and said, "Terry, I
don't go back on my word. The ducks need a reprieve. I for one
have taken more than my share and now, seeing what that has
caused, will hunt no more. Seeing all the cripples the other morning just brought that point home, and that is it. No more." There
was a real finality in the way Joe spoke, a passing of an era—a
bloody era but historical as well.

Until his dying day, I never knew Joe to take a shotgun into the
field to smell the curing hay from the rows of rice straw left by the

combines, to hear the whir of wings overhead, to feel the tule fog on his face or the dampness in his feet as he crawled up on the ducks. He flat-out simply stayed home. He was an unusual man from a unique time in history. He was also a man who was smart enough to take the knowledge gained from that history and pass it on. To this day, I still use some of the tricks of the trade that Crazy Joe taught me. I grew up a lot in those formative years, but that night at the check dam, I learned to read history and perhaps became part of it myself.

Joe is dead now, and the personal diary he kept from age eleven until that fateful day on the canal, listing all the ducks he had killed and sold for over fifty years, was tossed into the trash by his unknowing daughter after his death. With it went a piece of history.

I went on to catch sixteen draggers in the valley over the time I remained there carrying a badge. All but five were locals, and all were very surprised that I was there when they pulled the trigger.

Thank you, Joe.

20

Two Strikes and You Are Out!

REACHING ACROSS AS slowly and quietly as I could, I placed my hand firmly but gently over Vince DePalma's mouth. We were lying in a rice-straw pile next to a farm-road berm, and Vince had been quietly sleeping until that moment. He awoke with a start, but the firmness of my hand kept him from moving or making any noise while telegraphing to his enforcement-trained mind the message, "Don't move!" Realizing what I was doing and why, he nodded and then froze as I slowly removed my hand, returning it to the cold steel butt of the Colt .45 on my hip. I assumed Vince was doing the same. Standing on the road were two quiet figures. They had walked right up to our position in the darkness of the Colusa County winter night, and I had not heard their footsteps or known they were there until that moment! For the longest time they said nothing, totally unaware of the presence of two state of California conservation officers lying at their very feet in the rice straw trying to keep still. They were so close I could have reached up and grabbed one of them by the leg!

It was three o'clock on a cold November morning in John Hardy's harvested rice field just a mile or so north of Williams, California. Vince and I had been working these Colusa County rice fields once the dark of night settled in, trying to put a stop to some of the illegal and very destructive commercial-market hunting, or dragging, of ducks that was an ever-present problem in the Sacramento Valley. Dragging was a time-worn tradition in this valley and, although past its prime, was dying hard in the souls of some the traditional shooters and their children. These lads for the most part waited until the mantle of night fell before they ventured out to conduct their bloody business. The same cover of darkness that allowed the ducks safety in feeding allowed human predators to feed upon the ducks. Once harvested by the practice of shooting them while they fed in great numbers on the ground, the birds would then be sold to nearby markets or stuffed into home freezers for excellent rice-fed-duck dinners throughout the year. The markets in San Francisco, Sacramento, Yuba City, and other Sacramento Valley and Bay area destinations demanded the wild, rice-fed, back-shot duck for the traditional duck dinner.

By the very nature of their trade, market hunters had developed a tradition and methodology that was uniquely their own. Using harvested rice fields as their slaughter grounds, their understanding of duck feeding behavior to close the shooting distance, and shotguns modified to shoot thirteen to fifteen shells each, they plied their trade for the ever-hungry markets. They traditionally sold only to those they trusted, many times the same people who had purchased ducks from their grandfathers and fathers. It was a cold, cruel business, and they were very good at what they did. It was not without risks, but, as with all wildlife law enforcement, the odds against getting caught were low enough to foster the effort for the rush and the monetary rewards it offered.

Vince, a deputy California state Fish and Game reserve warden from Yuba City, and I, a California state Fish and Game warden stationed in Colusa, California, had sneaked into this field some time after dark. From our hiding place we had watched thousands of ducks moving into this area to feed, arriving in a highly visible "tornado." This effect occurred when thousands of hungry ducks swirled into a rice field from hundreds of feet in the air like a vast living funnel cloud. The phenomenon was visible for miles to friend, foe, and duck alike.

Hiding our vehicle in a dry ditch under cover of darkness, we had crept to within forty yards of thousands of feeding ducks, then lain down and covered ourselves up in the rice straw to wait for any commercial-market hunter hoping to fill his freezer who might come along and liven up our evening. As I mentioned earlier, we waited in vain through most of the night until about three A.M., when our company arrived. Vince and I hardly breathed! I could see one of the lads out of the corner of my eye, and he was carrying a shotgun. I supposed the other lad was as well, but from where I was lying I couldn't see him. In front of our position were about ten thousand feeding waterfowl making their characteristic flowing-water sound as their bills hungrily searched the bottom of the field and stubble for spilled rice grains. I hadn't been paying much attention to the species composition as the birds traded in and out of the field all night but probably should have. What had started out as all mallards and pintail, two highly desirable commercial species, had dissolved into wigeon, a less desirable market duck because of its poorer eating qualities. Wigeon ate a high percentage of grass, which made them a stronger-tasting table meat. That, as well as the fact that they were smaller than mallards and pintail, meant they brought a lesser price.

"Do you want to punch 'em, Bob?" came a voice from the night.

There was a long silence and then the other voice said, "Nah."

"Why not?" came the first voice.

More silence; then the other voice said, "They sound like most of them are wigeon."

"Boy," the first voice said, "now is the time to do it; there isn't a game warden for miles."

I goddamned near split a gut at that one, and I could tell from the faint rustling in the rice straw that Vince too was having a hard time not laughing out loud. I badly wanted to reach up and grab that bastard by the leg just to show him how close those "miles" really were. But I knew that if I did, I'd surprise him so badly that he would probably shoot at the thing holding his leg, and I didn't think that would set too well with my constitution. Thinking better of my rash idea, I let well enough alone and kept my hands to myself. Presently the two dark figures moved off down the farm road toward the north in the direction of several other bunches of feeding ducks.

Once they were out of earshot, Vince and I moved up on the road and I turned on my Starlight Scope in order to follow the lads. The eerie light-green glow illuminated the two wanna-be draggers as they moved down the road, and I motioned for Vince to follow me as I followed them. Down the road we went, some forty yards or so behind the hunters, I with my eye fixed to the scope and Vince blindly following my rather large hulk. The two lads stopped again some distance from the next bunch of feeding ducks but, after some consideration, passed them by as well. Again, as they walked across the rice field toward another nearby bunch of feeding waterfowl, Vince and I tagged along like two bad dreams—bad because if the lads pulled a shoot on the feeding waterfowl, they would get a whole lot more than they had bargained for.

Passing the bunch of feeding waterfowl that our lads had just gone by, I determined from the sounds they were making that they too were mostly wigeon. The bunch the lads were now stalking was the real McCoy, that is, mostly mallards and pintail, premium market ducks. After a short discussion in the field of the night scope, the lads dropped to their hands and knees and started to sneak up on the feeding ducks, which were unaware of the approaching danger. Vince and I picked up the pace, I with my eye still on the scope keeping an eye on the lads' progress so we could move closer to the action if and when it began. If they shot the ducks, we would have to be no more than thirty-five to forty yards away if we wanted to have any chance of catching them. Once within thirty-five yards of the sneaking poachers, Vince and I also dropped to a crawling position, and when the lads crawled, so did we. This went on until the draggers got within about fifty yards of the feeding ducks in the pale quarter-moon light.

All at once the ducks stopped feeding and in unison roared into the air. All of us froze, those sneaking up on the ducks and those sneaking up on the sneakers. For a moment all was pandemonium. Ducks were flying everywhere, from zooming over our heads at rice-check level to milling just overhead in the air. Within moments the ducks got organized, and before long all had left the rice field and headed northeast back to Delevan National Wildlife Refuge. The lads silently rose up and examined the rice field in front of them as if to say, What the hell happened? I asked myself the same question. Something had spooked the ducks, and now the bad guys had nothing to shoot. Through the scope I watched them finally trudge back across the rice field to the farm road and quietly walk back to where they had come from. I didn't see any sense in following them because there weren't any ducks in the direction they were going, and I didn't want to spook them in the hope that they might return the next evening.

Vince and I let them leave and then moved slowly in the opposite direction across the now vacant rice field toward our hidden vehicle. Leaving the area before dawn, and before anyone could see us in the area, I headed home. I dropped Vince off so he could return to his home in Yuba City, and I went to bed for a couple of hours of much-needed rest. I knew I would be alone on the coming evening because Vince had to work at his regular job, so I figured I'd better get a couple hours of sleep because it was very hard to keep from going to sleep against a comfortable rice check in the fields when working alone. I thought, Working alone again, huh? That was pretty dumb. I had taken a load of number 4 shot earlier in my career trying to work these draggers by myself. You might think I would have learned my lesson by now about such lone-wolf activity. Nope! When you are young and immortal, crap like that doesn't bother you until you are knee deep in it, and then it is too late to worry about anything except getting out of it anyway!

❧

After getting four hours of sleep, I spent most of the day working the regular-season duck hunters in the northern clubs in my district and then cooked dinner for my bride, spending a few pleasant minutes with her after she came home from work. As soon as it got dark, I loaded up the patrol vehicle and Shadow, my retriever, and off we went to the wildlife wars.

Shortly after dark we slid into the same rice field Vince and I had occupied earlier, and stepping out of my hidden truck, I was rewarded with the flowing-water sound of thousands of feeding waterfowl happily gleaning what rice the farmer had left behind for them. Grabbing my Starlight Scope in one hand and my flashlight in the other, I headed off into the dark to see what the night had to offer the dog and her master. Not making the same mistake I had made the previous evening, I picked a bunch of feeding mallards and pintail away from the road. I positioned myself where I could easily watch the farm road in case it was used again by the shooters, yet close enough to the birds to be of help when the shooting started. Shadow and I dug into a pile of dry, sweet-smelling rice straw, propped our backs up next to a rice check, and watched the ducks mill around in front of us in their feeding frenzy. Correction—I watched the ducks. The dog was soon off into "dog land," dreaming of who knows what, but whatever it was, her snoring and foot movements told me she was having the time of her life.

Along about midnight the cold began to tell, and I unpacked a light tarp and wrapped it around me as I sat there on the ground listening to the ducks and sensing the chilly breeze from the northwest on my left cheek. The weather was changing. I could sense the arriving moisture in the air and also noticed an increased urgency in the feeding behavior of the ducks. They were moving around like a big feeding snake now, constantly adjusting their direction so they would always be heading into the wind. That way, if surprised, they could lift off into the air with a minimum of effort and be away from any danger in a heartbeat. All of a sudden I noticed they were feeding my way. Like a giant living vacuum cleaner with ten thousand bills, here they came. My tiredness from many previous long days had overcome my alertness, and now it was too late to move without alarming the birds into the air. So I just lay very still along that rice check, hoping not to spook the ducks. They came feeding right up to me in the dark and then went right over the top of me and the dog, all the while "talking" to anyone who would listen and gumming the hell out of any rice they found, not to mention pooping on everything under them.

God, it was the strangest feeling having the better part of ten thousand ducks walk over me, unaware of what they were doing. Shadow was awake now and shaking like a dog crapping peach pits! She knew better than to move unless told to, so she just lay there waiting for the command to "get 'em," quivering all the time in anticipation. This duck parade crawling over me went on for about ten or fifteen minutes, mallards and pintail first, followed by wigeon and the like. Damn, it was the first time this had ever happened to me, and it was an experience I will never forget. Turning around on my rice check after the ducks had moved into the adjacent rice field, I again watched their progress with my scope, all the while searching the perimeter for any draggers who might be in the country. Finding none, I began to let the cold comfort of the rice straw and lack of sleep from several months of long hours take over and drifted off into a light but comfortable sleep.

A drop of rain on my face woke me to the predicted change in the weather. The ducks were feeding much more quietly now, as they had a tendency to do when the weather turned, and the frequency of the raindrops foretold wetter conditions on the way. Taking leave of my field after one more look through the scope, which was becoming useless in the increasing rain, I headed for my truck. By the time Shadow and I reached it, the rain was falling heavily. Putting the dog in the front seat with me, I started out of the field and headed for home. I was more tired than I had originally thought and had great difficulty staying awake. Realizing that I was falling asleep at the wheel far more frequently then common sense allowed, I picked up my speed in order to get home more quickly. Not a smart move but, unfortunately, what I did. Finally a combination of the warmth from the heater and deep tiredness began to really manifest itself along with the reduction of adrenaline flowing through my system now that the detail was over. Damn, it was all I could do to keep awake. Speeding along a deserted backcountry dirt road toward home, I opened my window and hung my head out into the rain to help keep me awake. Across the land I zoomed, trying to get home for some much-needed sleep.

As I sped along in the very heavy rain with my head out the window, my foggy brain picked up a roaring sound. As tired as I was, it didn't register at first. The rain was coming down in sheets now, and I couldn't see too far ahead, but I knew the road was straight as an arrow and I kept the hammer down. The roar continued, only louder now. Damn, what was that sound? I kept thinking. Then it dawned on me. *Train!* I was approaching an unmarked railroad crossing, and that sound was being made by a fast freight moving south in front of my speeding path. I slammed on the brakes as the sight of a line of boxcars moved across my way! Skidding from the speed I had built up in my haste to get home, the truck finally plowed to a stop not three feet from the side of the moving train. I was so close to that train that the wind it generated in its fifty-mph-plus speed rocked the truck every time another boxcar passed in front of the pickup! Small rocks thrown up by the train were hitting the truck as it sat there, so close to the flying boxcars that I could read the small print on their sides as they zoomed by.

My very close call had done the trick. I was awake now! In fact, my eyes were the size of garbage-can lids, and sleep was the furthest thing from my mind. Noticing that my heart was beating at the staccato speed of a snare-drum roll, I waited for the train to pass. Damn, that was close! When the train had gone by, I just sat there for a moment thanking my guardian angels and then again headed for home. My speed was more acceptable now, and I had no trouble staying awake! After I reached home, it took an hour in bed before I settled down enough to drift off to sleep. Brother, I liked catching things—but not a speeding train!

❧

Because the ducks were still using the west side of my district, I decided to continue my night efforts on that side of the valley and my daytime enforcement efforts checking waterfowl hunters on the east side. Located along the west side of my district were the historical market-hunting towns of Willows, Maxwell, and Williams. I figured that since most of the lads inclined to kill more than their share and at night were living in those towns, it wouldn't take them long to recognize the shift in the feeding patterns of the ducks as well. Knowing what would come next in the form of killing fields if they were able to sneak up on the ducks, I decided it would be best if I put the blessing of a rather large "tule creeper" (a nickname for a game warden) into their baskets instead. I picked up Guy Bird, another deputy game warden, and a damn good one, I might add, and off we went to the west side to see if we could spin a little magic for the commercial-market hunters I suspected would be there.

Ditching my patrol vehicle and covering it with my brand-new camouflage parachute, we made our way into a likely-looking waterfowl feeding area inhabited by about fifty thousand feeding ducks scattered about in three large bunches. We quietly walked and crawled right into the middle of the noisily feeding ducks, picked a rice check for home base, and dug in to wait for any action that was to follow. On went my Starlight Scope, and boy, what a sight. Ducks were moving like bees in every field of view. The eerie green glow of the scope made the scene even more memorable as we took turns looking into the night made into day by the device's technology. I thought our use of the scope was ironic because its original function was to aid solders in the job of killing. Guy and I were using it to stop killing. Life in all its aspects is really a mystery, I thought.

Taking turns, we alternated scanning the feeding ducks surrounding us on all sides from our kneeling positions alongside the rice check, watching for any suspicious human forms to sneak into our field of view. This routine went on into the wee hours of the morning as the ducks continued to eagerly feed around us on the abundant rice grains. Once they filled their crops, they would leave as others were arriving, constantly homing in on the sound made by thousands of their feeding brethren. Finally tiring of the stake-out because of the lack of activity, Guy and I decided we would pull up stakes and save our energies for another time. We loaded up our gear and after one more scan of the area began walking toward our concealed vehicle. The ducks nearest us who spotted us as we walked across the field lifted into the air with a soft whirring of wings and headed for points unknown. However, the urge to feed was very strong in the remaining many thousands of ducks, and they continued to feed like there was no tomorrow. I was uncomfortable leaving them there without their bodyguards, but I had to pace my energies or I would run out of gas before the end of the hunting season—or before the illegal night shooters did.

When Guy and I reached the patrol vehicle, I uncovered it and started to drive out into the field occupied by the feeding ducks. Reaching a spot where I was sure I would get the ducks' attention, I turned on the headlights and siren. The lights illuminated a scene of thousands of feeding ducks scared witless at the approaching monster with two glowing eyes and a howl that could be heard clear up where God was sleeping. Up they went just as fast as they could clear each other and the ground. Up they climbed as Guy and I sat there watching them in utter fascination, and then the unexpected happened! Down they came right at the vehicle like dive-bombers of old! *Wham, boom, bang, bang, ka-thump* went the ducks as they hurled pell-mell into my parked vehicle. *Bang, bang,* out went the headlights as the flying bodies that were acting like living cannon shot broke them into hundreds of pieces! I had ducks flying through the open windows right through the cab as its two very surprised occupants tried to duck (no pun intended) to avoid injury. *Crash* went the windshield as several ducks exploded through it into our laps, and I could hear several more hitting the hood, roof, and bed of the truck. With the headlights gone, the onslaught of flying bodies slowly stopped. Guy and I just sat there in stunned surprise. A little pintail hen stood in the front seat of our truck with a look of amazement that had to match the expressions on our faces. Guy reached down and gently tossed her out the window, and she flew off as if nothing unusual had happened. Carefully getting out of the cab, covered with shattered glass, we surveyed the damage with our flashlights.

What a mess the ducks had made of my truck. There were dead ducks everywhere! Guy and I picked up eighty-three dead mallards and pintail that had killed themselves when they collided with the vehicle as it sat in that rice field. I always carried spare parts, and in a few moments I had replaced the broken headlights with spares. The windshield, mirrors, and dents I couldn't do much about. Damn, what a catastrophe! I will never do that again, I said to myself as I threw another bunch of dead ducks into the back of my now dented and beat-up patrol truck. Previously when I had pulled the same maneuver, the birds had just flown away from the lights and siren. That night for some reason they decided to crash-land on my truck, and needless to say, they did so with a vengeance!

We swept the broken glass out of the front seat and broke out the remaining windshield. I then headed the truck toward the state-controlled shooting area at the Sacramento National Wildlife Refuge just a few miles north. Since the next morning was a shooting day, I knew there would be a lot of hunters camping in the parking lot awaiting their chance to go hunting once the area opened up. When we got there, Guy and I located all the kids we could find who were too young to hunt and gave them each a limit of the ducks who had been foolish enough to run into my truck at a high rate of speed. This done, we headed home for a night's sleep.

❦

The next morning I had the Willow Garage in Colusa replace my windshield and then moved into the east side of my district to check hunters in the hopes of finding those breaking the law and honoring them with a visit from the world's largest tule creeper. That evening I hooked up with another deputy game warden trying to get in his monthly patrol hours. That lad will remain nameless for the duration of this story because he was worthless as tits on a side of bacon! I can't remember ever running across a person with less common sense than that fellow. In those days, when you needed help you took what you could get, even if it was a halfwit.

That day the ducks moved into the central part of my district, on Link Dennis's land. Link was one of the most honest men I knew, and I knew he wouldn't give me any problems in the illegal-duck-killing arena, but the market hunters would, regardless of who owned the property. They didn't hold any boundaries sacred, so Link's land was fair game, and that was where we positioned ourselves for the night. I hid my rig by Link's farm buildings, and my partner and I ventured forth into the harvested rice fields in quest of those who were there with less-than-noble intentions. We hadn't gone one hundred yards into the darkened field when we heard a rattle of shots indicative of a commercial shoot about 150 yards north of us. Trotting as best we could across the harvested rice field,

I worked at opening the carrying case for the Starlight Scope. Once I had the scope out, I stopped, turned it on, and scanned the area to the north. I picked up three individuals hurriedly picking up and stacking what appeared to be ducks. Every now and then I could plainly see the white breast feathers of a male pintail as they hurried to gather up their kill before any game wardens interrupted their little evening of illegal work.

Marking where we left our coats and scope case (so we could run faster), off we went as quickly as possible toward these lads. They didn't have the foggiest idea we were coming because of the mantle of night, but I knew we'd have a hard time catching up to them. After working with Crazy Joe, the dragger who had taught me the tricks of the trade, I knew it was a long shot, but damn, just walking away from a situation like this left me cold. I just had to try, and maybe with a little luck. … As we got close enough to try to run the lads down as they attempted to drag their kill across the fields toward a ditch, I stopped to gather my breath and form a plan. Observing them heading west across the field through the scope, my partner and I headed that way by running down a convenient rice ditch. Running until I figured we were about even with the lads but still forty yards out, I stopped and cautiously looked with the Starlight Scope over the edge of the ditch toward their last known position. The lads in question were only about thirty-five yards away and were looking hard in our direction. It was obvious they had heard us running down the ditch and were alert to the possibility of our presence. Slowly lowering myself back down in the ditch, I told my partner to be prepared to run like the wind because that would be the speed these lads would move once they saw us in pursuit. I told him about the lay of the land in front of us and to expect a long chase because market hunters hated getting caught more than anything else on account of the embarrassment it brought them in their home towns.

We looked over the ditch into the night in the hunters' direction and then put the scope on them again. They were still standing there, hoping against hope that the noise wasn't what they feared the most. They had a huge pile of ducks at their feet, and I was sure they would hold still for as long as possible in order to hang on to their hard-won but illegal gains. Turning to my partner, I told him we would move out of the ditch and crawl as close as we could get without being discovered. Once they took alarm, he was to turn on his flashlight and take the man on the right and I would do the same with the one on the left. We would just have to let the third man in their group escape. With that hasty plan, I took one more look at the lads, then shut off the scope and left it where I could find it in the morning. Over the top we quietly crawled.

Almost instantly my partner accidentally turned on his flashlight, giving away our position, and the race was on! My guy just happened to be a short, fast little fellow, and in about ten minutes he was out of the area of my light beam and gone. I tried to follow his tracks, but he was nowhere to be found in the dark and expanse of that thousand-acre rice field. I knew he was probably down and crawling off, but damned if I could see him, much less catch someone half my size who was scared as all get-out. With that maddening realization, I started the long trek back to my starting point, hoping my partner had done better. About twenty minutes later I was back at our ill-fated starting point looking over the pile of ducks the lads had left behind in their hurry to escape. There were about two hundred mallards and pintail lying there, ten ducks to a bunch, their necks tied together with butcher twine. A classic commercial-market-hunter hit! I had not recognized any of the lads when the lights went on and suspected that I may have had some of the Willows crowd in my field that night. I backtracked their footprints to where they had lain in wait for the ducks and picked up their empty shotgun shells. Looking out over where the shooting had occurred, I noticed that the ground was covered with feathers, cripples, and quite a few dead but abandoned females.

Figuring I would pick those critters up later, I started to track my partner to see where the hell he had gone, since he sure as hell wasn't in view. After walking about two hundred yards, I lost his track on the hard ground. I looked as far as my light beam would carry and could see nothing. Now I was beginning to worry. I waited a few yards from where I had lost his track, hoping to see his flashlight beam any moment, but no soap. I had lost his track by a series of ditches, so I returned to that area and figured I would try tracking from that position once again. Back at the ditches, I started my cold-tracking exercise again. I was passing a set of thirty-six-inch, vertically buried standpipe goose blinds when I heard a faint cry. Flashing my light to my right, I could see a pair of hands holding on to the sides of a standpipe!

What the hell? I ran over to the pipe, and there hung my partner. He had apparently, at a full run, dropped into the standpipe. He was hanging there with a smashed nose and gouged-up knees, not wanting to let the bad guys know he was helpless and hoping I would find him. Damn, he had to have been in the pipe for at least forty-five minutes. But without his flashlight, he couldn't look down into the dark to see how deep the pipe was, so he just hung there! He was exhausted but figured he was going to die if he fell any deeper into the pipe, so he was hanging on for dear life. A quick look revealed that the bottom was only six inches below his feet! He had hung there all that time for no reason at all! Helping him out, I could not imagine how anyone, at a full run, could get both feet into a thirty-six-inch-wide pipe! Well, this lad had certainly found the answer to that question. He was very embarrassed. But just as soon as he had been rescued, he was off and ready to fight like a real tough guy! All he could talk about was what he would do if he ever caught those chaps who had been the objects of our attention earlier in the evening. On and on he went until I had about had a gut full of how tough he was. We had just arrived back at the site where the ducks had been killed and were starting to pick up those we could salvage so they could be donated to a needy family when we both heard rustling in a large rice-straw pile about twenty yards away.

Before I could say anything, my partner put his finger to his lips and mouthed, "Shhhh." He then whispered, "The third shooter is hiding in the rice straw." Not sure where he had gotten that idea, I kept my light on the rice straw while my partner stalked the pile as if it held a bomb. When he got within about ten feet, he let out a primal yell and, running at full speed, dove onto the pile. He had no sooner landed on the pile of straw than he bounded straight up into the air as if he'd been shot out of a cannon! Before he could say anything, I smelled exactly what had happened. *Skunk!* He had landed directly on a skunk that had been hunting mice in the straw pile and had been duly rewarded for his attack. Good God almighty, he was dancing around making all kinds of choking sounds when out came the black-and-white object of his earlier attention and gave it to him again from about three feet away! By now the smell of skunk was becoming overpowering, and I moved out of the way to let nature work its course.

In about ten minutes my partner had recovered enough to speak. It's amazing what a little skunk spray can do to help one gain a little worldly perspective. It had helped my partner gain a whole lot of perspective! With the fire gone out him, we got back to the business at hand, namely, picking up and stacking ducks. Moving them over to the ditch we had run down earlier, we stacked the birds in a place where the shooters wouldn't easily find them, gathered up our previously discarded gear, and headed for the truck, since there was no use remaining here any longer after all the disturbances. When we reached the truck, my partner, realizing his smell was socially unacceptable, asked me how he was going to get home. I pointed with my light beam to the back of the truck. He looked at me for a moment and then climbed in for the ride back to his vehicle. When we arrived at my home, he stripped down bare-assed naked, got into his own car, and drove off. Somehow, I don't think removing his clothing helped a whole lot. He had really taken a shot from that surprised skunk and had to be a real joy to be around for the next week.

❧

Over the next couple of days, it stormed like the furies of hell, and the ducks reacted accordingly. They were scattered, spooky, and very difficult to approach. The night shooters left them alone, and I worked the standard "bomber-turn" late waterfowl shooters instead. During weather patterns heavy with storms, I could really make hay with the late shooters, and I did. Then the sky cleared, and for the next several days we had a "dragger's moon" (one that casts enough light to shoot the ducks but not enough for the game wardens to chase hunters successfully without using a light).

That evening my brother-in-law, Joe Galipeau, arrived from his home in Sacramento. Never did a scrappier lad live than Joe. He was a little stump of a man but had more nerve, common sense, and work ethic than any dozen other men. He came to pursue his much-loved sport of hunting birds. I always ignored his desires and took him hunting "yardbirds" instead. Joe always seemed to enjoy himself either way—hunting birds or his fellow human—and was equally good at both. He wasn't a credentialed officer, so he just rode backup for me. I never had any problems with Joe at my back. Not having the opportunity to look in his direction during altercations, I never knew what he was doing to keep my back clear, but whatever it was, it worked! On this particular night, after a good dinner, we loaded our gear into the truck and worked our way north toward the Butte City area. I explained how the birds were working and what to expect from the illegal night hunters and anything else of interest related to our night's activities.

The wind was blowing, which made the birds very spooky, so we staked out about seventy-five thousand birds feeding in several rice fields from quite a distance away. The place I chose was well hidden, and we could see for several miles across the flat farmland in every direction. Along about midnight I was beginning to tire again and, mindful of the train incident, vowed not to let my body wear down that far again. Looking over at Joe, I could tell he was tired too. He had probably worked a sixteen-hour shift at the air force base and then driven up to be with me so I could abuse his body some more. I said, "Let's go, Joe, I've had enough." Out from our hiding place we drove without headlights and up onto a road that passed through the thousands of feeding ducks. Wanting to scare the ducks and anyone sneaking up on them, I thought of turning on my lights and siren again, the usual game-warden tactic in those days. But remembering the mishap of the duck bombardment several nights earlier, I thought better of it.

Then I remembered the herding rockets I had in the back of the truck. We used these foot-long rockets to herd feeding ducks off the unharvested rice fields to keep the birds from destroying the crops. The rockets were little speed demons that went about a thousand feet and then blew up with a hell of a roar. Digging one out from the junk in the box in the bed of my truck, I slipped in a fuse and tried to light it, but the wind was blowing so hard I couldn't get it to light. I tried several times with wooden matches, all to no avail. Finally I stood the rocket on the ground on its legs and held Joe's lighter to the fuse while he held his cupped hands on the windward side. The fuse finally lit. As it sputtered into life, Joe moved off to the windward side and I to the lee side. *Whoosh* went the rocket, but instead of moving straight up into the air as they usually did, the damned thing headed right into the wind and hit Joe, who was standing upwind, right in the crotch!

Joe, mindful of the consequences of the rocket exploding, tried to brush the rocket away. But the rocket kept going full steam, stuck in the crotch of his pants. By now Joe was getting frantic, realizing the *boom* was not far off—and not nearly far enough from his manhood! Finally, in a last desperate act, Joe turned and started to run. This action threw the rocket off, and it hit the ground. Not to be denied, up came the rocket, and off it went into the wind again. Well, Joe was running upwind, and here came the rocket after Joe as if it had something against Frenchmen! Just before it got to Joe's last part over the fence, it ran out of gas and blew up. *Boom!* I thought for a second the rocket had blown Joe's hind end clear off. But what I saw fly off was not his ass but his handkerchief!

Joe returned to the truck amidst hundreds of thousands of flailing wings trying to get airborne and leave the rice fields before the *boom* got them. We started to laugh, and agreed that we should go home before anything else happened. On the way home I began to run the last few days' events through my mind, all failures as far as catching the night shooters was concerned. I took the next several days off and spent them with Joe, hunting ducks and incidentally making only about a dozen cases involving waterfowl violations as we tried to rest amidst God's creatures.

◦❧

Saturday found me with a dragger's moon and raring to go. The ducks were feeding just about everywhere, and it made no difference where I went—every place was just as good as the next. Moving out onto Newhall Farms between 2-Mile and 4-Mile Roads, I ditched my truck and crawled out into a pile of ducks whose numbers boggled the mind. There had to be at least 150,000 ducks feeding in that area adjacent to Delevan National Wildlife Refuge and on the Newhall Farms property. Typical—a ton of work and a one-seventh-ton man to do the job! I picked a beautiful hiding place right next to a mound of dirt alongside a ditch near about fifty thousand feeding ducks. There appeared to be a lot of feed in the area, and with a light wind the birds were pretty much staying put. A farmer had put a bunch of rice boxes by my dirt mound, and I fashioned them into a little fort from which I could look out but that would prevent anyone who didn't know I was there from spotting me. Throughout the night, the ducks fed right up to my feet in my location by the dry ditch and never did see me. It was great! I had enough moon so I didn't need my Starlight Scope, but I was sobered by the fact that the night shooters wouldn't need anything to help them with their plans either.

About two-thirty A.M., I sensed there was something behind me larger than any animal I expected to be in those fields—anything wild, that is! Freezing, I listened like the animal I wished I was. There it was again: something was coming my way. I slowly reached for my pistol and took it out of the holster, reassured by the cold-steel feel in my hand. I was sure someone could hear my heart if they were listening! There was the sound again, only, this time it was closer, *really* close. The damn ducks were again feeding near me, and their feeding noises made it hard for me to hear what was going on behind me. As the ducks moved closer, the noise behind me was drowned out by the clattering of thousands of bills.

The next thing I remember was a sudden feeling of a vacuum by my head, followed by the ear-splitting roar of a shotgun going off not two feet over my head. I burrowed into the ground, quickly covering my ears as numerous shots went off just above me. What made it even worse was the fact that I had surrounded myself with those rice boxes, and they were now acting as reflection boards to amplify the sound. I rolled on the ground in pain as the booming continued for what seemed like a century. Then it was quiet except for the ringing in my ears! Goddamnit, I could hardly hear. I had sense enough not to move, but those damned guns had gone off right over my head. It was a good thing I had not stood up in panic. The shooters would have unknowingly cut me in half with the charges of lead they had sailed into the feeding ducks in the field! Rolling over, I turned within my fort and looked back. Nothing. I waited for a few minutes and then could faintly hear men talking. They weren't more than four feet from me, just on the other side of the berm and my rice-box fort. At first I could make out only muffled sounds, but as my hearing returned, I could make out a few words over the ringing. "Got a lot," "See anyone," "Damn," and then "Shhhh."

I continued to wait for about thirty minutes, not moving, waiting for the lads in the ditch behind me to make their move so I could counter. In front of me flopped hundreds of injured ducks. Bastards! I thought. If I get half a chance, you folks are going to feel the sting of the long arm of the law, count on that!

Soon wounded ducks began crawling by me, trying to hide in the boxes next to my feet and in the adjacent weeds. One little pintail crawled right next to me and died alongside my leg. I reached over and held his warm body in my hand but didn't say anything. I didn't have to—he had said it for me. Then a human form surprised me by reaching into where I sat, grabbing another wounded duck, and wringing its neck. At that moment I reached out from my hiding place and "wrung" his. In my younger days I had the grip of a bear. That is exactly the grip I put on the back of that man's neck, jerking him into me! There was a groan, and he just went limp. I had scared the bastard so badly that he passed out in my hand.

In those days I was considerably stronger than I am today, especially after thirty years in the trenches. I remember during my early years testing my hand strength at the doctor's office on one of those devices that measured your strength in pounds. I could easily grip 220 pounds in my right hand! When I played college football, many times my teammates complained after I had grabbed them as they ran by carrying the ball during scrimmages. Suffice it to say that once I got my hand on you, your distance to run was 37.5 inches (the length of my arm). I could just imagine what had gone through this chap's mind, I thought as I crawled over his inert form looking for the rest of the bunch responsible for the mess before me. As I emerged from my hiding place, a voice in the dark hissed, "Grab these and stack them in the boxes." This was too good to be true, I thought—they thought I was one of them! Staying low so they wouldn't recognize the bearlike form as the local game warden, I pitched in to help with the chores at hand.

There were three more lads working at fever pitch picking up the ducks and a lone one standing guard on the ditch bank on the lookout for the game wardens. His job, as I had found out earlier in my career, was to shoot at the game warden if one was discovered moving in on the shooters as they picked up their ill-gotten gains. Moving closer to the two busy forms picking up dead ducks, I felt for the reassuring grip of my pistol, which I had replaced in the holster, and the heavy five-cell flashlight in the other hand that could do double duty as a club. With that confidence booster, I turned on the light and grabbed the two nearest chaps, one in each hand, taking them to the ground in a fashion that clearly meant business.

"Game warden, you are under arrest," I boomed.

Swinging around quickly over the two stunned lads on the ground at my feet, I yelled, "Freeze!" to the lad on the ditch bank, but he disappeared as if the ground had sucked him straight down into its bowels! There was no way he could shoot without hitting his two pals, and both of us knew it. I had hoped to freeze him with the surprise of attack, but to no avail. He was making off like a jackrabbit! The two lads on the ground were trying to get up and get away, so I put my knee on one's back, grabbed the other with my right hand, and jerked him hard back to the ground. Very hard, in fact, on behalf of the pintail that had died by my leg. I now had control of the two in the field and saw by looking back at the boxes that my other lad still had not regained consciousness. The lad on the bank and the other in the field were gone, but I still had a fair sample of the men doing the dirty work that evening. Grabbing handcuffs from my belt pouch, I cuffed the two lads on the ground and jerked them to their feet. I wanted to make sure they understood who was boss in the field that night. They got the message.

One of my handcuffed chaps I recognized right off as a farmer from Maxwell; the other was an unknown. Pushing the lads toward the boxes, I sat them down hard and reached in to retrieve the inert fellow who had grabbed and been grabbed. He was groaning a lot, and for a moment I thought I may have hurt his neck, but it turned out he was all right. I swung my flashlight beam all around and, satisfied that the others had run off for good, returned to my catch of the day for identification. One, as I said, was a farmer from Maxwell, a big raw-boned kid named Dave whose dad had a reputation for killing ducks in days past. Like father, like son, I guessed. The other two were visiting farmers from the Yuba City area up for a good time. Well, if you went by the poundage of the lad who had joined in their fun, then they had a great time!

I took all their driver's licenses and uncuffed my two subdued farmers. Then we all picked up dead ducks for the next hour. The tally for their night's work was 461 ducks, plus one game warden with still ringing ears. Stacking the ducks by the boxes, I made each man carry all he could, and I did the same. That way if the other lads came in behind me and took the rest, I would still have enough evidence to prosecute the lads I had caught. We walked to where my truck was hidden and loaded the ducks into the back along with the lads, and then I drove back into the field to pick up the rest of the night's kill. Once loaded, I drove Dave and his friends to Dave's home in Maxwell.

Moving into his garage, Dave turned on the light, and the four of us stood there looking at each other.

"Dave," I said, "you know better than to do this."

"Terry, write the ticket, will you? I really don't feel like talking about it right now. Maybe later, but not now."

Not wanting to rub his nose in it, I complied. Dave was issued a citation for taking an over-limit, wanton waste, use of an unplugged shotgun, and shooting after hours. The standard penalty in those days for such activity was a $2,000 ticket.

Once finished with him, I asked, "Who were your pals, Dave, who chose not to stand with you lads?"

He just shook his head, indicating he would not tell. I knew they would share in paying the fine, so I let it go at that, hoping Dave might talk to me later. I wrote the other two lads up for the same violations, and when I handed them their tickets, the fellow named Bob said, "That is the worst scare I've ever had in my life! You can't possibly imagine what went through my mind that instant I reached for that duck and you grabbed me by the neck. Mister, my heart still hasn't stopped beating like it's out of control! I'm here to tell you, I will never do that ever again as long as I live."

Somehow I could relate to his feelings and believed him when he said this was his first and last time for this kind of tomfoolery. All of us then field-dressed the ducks so they wouldn't spoil and I left to find my friendly duck picker, Angelo Jaconetti, so I could finish the process of preserving the seized ducks. I made sure before I left the garage that I shook the hand of all the lads I had just caught to show no hard feelings. I also made sure during each handshake that each and every one of them realized there was a man on the game-warden end of that handshake!

～

That evening found me again staking out several large bunches of ducks by myself. This time I was just north of Colusa on Beauchamp's farm, and the ducks were there in great numbers. It was a real pleasure to see thousands of waterfowl swirling in the air and landing in great hordes as they were doing that evening. I always considered that kind of viewing a treat, and a tribute to those officers who came before me. Along about midnight I heard a rip of shots, like the tearing of a bedsheet, a sound characteristic of a drag shoot on feeding ducks. Gritting my teeth, I tried to echo-locate the sound, finally placing it across the Sacramento River and about even with my location. There was a typical dragger's moon out, and the lads were making the most of it. Deciding to stay all night on the Beauchamp place because of the large numbers of feeding ducks, I put the shots out of my mind and snuggled down into the dry, sweet-smelling rice straw for the duration.

About two-thirty in the morning, I again heard the ragged sound of a string of shots characteristic of illegal shooting of the ducks feeding in the rice fields. This time the shots were again across the Sacramento River but far north, somewhere near the Princeton area. With those sounds I began to be a not-so-happy camper. I had long ago realized that I couldn't catch all the bad guys, but I sure liked to try! Damn. I knew where I was going to be during the night coming up. If those bastards carried off their illegal duck shoots without interference, they would usually be right back at it in the same place the following night. But if I had my way, this time there would be another guest in the field besides the ducks! Not sleepy now, I sat up in my straw hiding place and watched my ducks do their dance of life as they contentedly fed all around me.

There it was again! Another rattle of shots, this time a long one characteristic of at least five gunners! Damn, the lads were sure having the time of their life in the rice fields to my east at the expense of the ducks. I knew there weren't any federal officers in the valley to put a stop to this slaughter, only me, and I was tied down on the Beauchamp place. Large as I was, I began to realize just how thinly I was spread around! Those poor damn ducks. They came in for a mouthful of feed and ended up with a faceful of lead shot! Damn, damn, damn! My frustration was not offset by the beautiful sunrise God offered up to console His faithful servant lying in a straw pile in a rice field in Colusa County. That morning, after listening to that shootfest on the east side all night, did not make for anything more than a grouchy game warden. When that game warden was twice the size of a regular game warden, a man had better watch out—especially if he had plans to shoot ducks and was within that 37.5-inch grabbin' distance.

❧

That evening after it got good and dark, I slowly drove by the Garvin Boggs ranch house. There was no sign of lights or life in the house. Hurrying to a wide spot in the road, I spun a tight reverse turn, shut off all my lights, including brake lights (special switches in the vehicle enabled me to cut off all lights so I could sneak around in the dark), and turned down the dirt lane running alongside the darkened Boggs house. Moving as fast as I could go in the dark with eyes not yet adjusted to night driving, I hurried east toward Terrill Sartain's rice-farming ground, looking for a place to hide my truck before I was discovered. Catching market hunters demanded not only a lot of skill but a ton of luck. That luck started if one was able to get into a likely-looking area without being seen. As near as I could tell, I had done so.

I parked my truck in a wide ditch that was about a foot deeper than the height of the truck. It had originally been sloped so farm equipment could get into it for repair work. The slope made a perfect ramp for me to drive down into the ditch and be hidden, unless the night shooters planned to use the same ditch. If that was the case—and it had happened to me once—it really caused a case of the big eye and tight hind end on the part of the bad guys when they found the local game warden's rig parked there before them! That night my hiding place worked like a charm, and no one else showed. I quickly covered my truck with a camouflage parachute and scrambled up onto the ditch bank for a look-see at my world for the evening.

The air for as far as I could see with my Starlight Scope was full of ducks seeking a place to eat. I would bet there were at least 100,000 ducks milling around. I could see seven huge tornado-like funnels of ducks working down into different places all to the northeast of me in that thousand acres of rice around Sartain's. God, it was awe-inspiring! I was brought back to reality with the realization that about five hundred yards behind me was the place where I had been shot in 1967. I mentally vowed to never again let such a thing happen and then pushed that thought out of my mind so I could concentrate on that evening's events. There were several rice dike cross-checks smack-dab in the middle of those whirling masses of waterfowl, and I mapped out a route that would take me right to where I believed the shooters, if they struck again, would position themselves.

Working into my target area, I used the cover of another ditch bank to cover my progress. Every fifty yards or so I would stop, pan the area with my night-vision scope, memorize the lay of the land, and, using that mental picture, move forward some more in the inky blackness. Striking my cross-ditch, I moved east down it toward where I heard the greatest sound of feeding ducks. Damn, what a sound of music for the soul of a game warden. If that didn't recharge my tired batteries, nothing would! Sliding into the deep unharvested rice grass next to a small farm access road, I took a position from which I could watch four distinct flocks of feeding ducks. My position would also allow me a running chance at anyone who might try to shoot into any of the feeding bunches. Perfect, I thought as the adrenaline began to rise within me. The hunter and the hunted—what better a way to spend an evening than casting for your fellow humans!

Along about one A.M., the dragger's moon made its appearance. Less than half a moon. Perfect for those stalking the ducks, I happily thought. With that evening's hazy skies, there was just enough light for hunters to stalk and shoot the ducks but not enough for the game wardens to chase them effectively without using a light. I swept my field of view at one-thirty A.M. with the night-vision scope. Nothing. Every fifteen minutes I did the same, but no takers. Damn, that was not like the lads. When they scored like they had the morning I heard all the shooting in this area, they usually would come back unless they had killed all they wanted. Breaking out two sandwiches that I had previously sat on, I sat down on the ground and was starting to enjoy my wife's meatloaf in one of them when I had a visitor. Down my side of the roadbank ambled a striped skunk, heading right for me. By the time I spotted him, I was within his firing range. Freezing, forgetting the good sandwich in my hands, I watched this problem as he came right up to my outstretched boots. Stopping (as I was afraid he would do), he paused and then turned and came straight between my legs toward my crotch. This episode was now starting to have serious implications! I could get gunned down with nature's perfume, get bitten in what was definitely the wrong place, or both. I didn't see any options except to hold my ground (what the hell else could I do?) and hope for the best. In a heartbeat I could see what the object of his attention was. The other meatloaf sandwich I had tossed between my legs for safekeeping.

Moving right over the sandwich, my visitor began his dinner while I held onto the sandwich in my hand, hoping for a chance to eat it without being "skunked" in the process! My skunk had manners, and it took him about ten days to eat his damn sandwich. Finally, without a thank-you or anything, he ambled off. Boy, was I glad to see him go. I watched him to make sure he was gone, and once satisfied that he was, I took a bite out of my sandwich. Almost throwing up, I realized that his wonderful odor had permeated my sandwich, and it was no longer usable as my dinner! Checking myself over, I realized that after he left I had closed my legs. Apparently he had left some residual odor, and now the two of us had something in common after I had dragged my legs over the scent left on the grass. Damn, would my wife love me! Not having anything to eat, I was forced to get back to work and check out my ducks. Sweeping the fields of feeding birds, I was satisfied that all was well. Then, looking back toward the area I had come from, I was stunned to see two lads standing in the pale moonlight not thirty-five yards from where I sat. Jesus, my hair went straight up! They had crept to within a very short distance of my position and were intently watching the ducks. My thoughts went back to that morning in 1967 when I had been shot by someone I had not seen. These two lads had sneaked too close for comfort. I wondered if anyone else were with them.

Quickly scanning the area around me from my hidden position with the night-vision scope, I satisfied myself that there was no one else in the area. Easing even further into the ground and loose rice straw where I sat, I continued to watch the lads to see what they were going to do. Once they committed themselves, then I could make up my plan of action and with any luck catch at least one of them. They stood there for quite a while, then dropped down on their hands and knees and started crawling down the same road I was hidden on, but on the other side of the road bed. Since the little road was only about ten feet wide, I really dug in so they wouldn't discover me before my time. Fat chance! They crawled to a point just about opposite me on the other side of the road and then smelled the skunk scent on me.

"Whew," went one of the lads, "there's a skunk very close to us, Bob."

"I know," said the other voice. "Try not to rile him."

"Well, we know the game wardens aren't in the country with that little bastard around so close," responded the first voice.

Damn! Those voices were the same ones that had stood over Vince and me several days earlier in a rice field north of Williams, commenting on the lack of game wardens in the country! Man, did my heart ever race with the prospect of possibly catching these lads this time! A warden hardly ever got a second chance at bad guys like this, and I damned well was going to make the best of it this time. No three strikes and you are out on this one! Two strikes was fair, I thought.

As I watched, the lads continued crawling east toward about ten thousand feeding mallards and pintail. Watching the lads through the Starlight Scope, I could see that they were heading for what is known as a dogleg rice check, that is, a U-shaped one. This kind of approach can be bad news for the feeding ducks because they will jam into the constricted area in massive numbers before they move over that check into the next part of the rice field. If a market hunter or poacher plays his cards right, he will wait on the opposite side of the berm until the area created by the dogleg in front of him is chock-full of ducks and then pull his shot. Usually the shooters will wait until just moments before the feeding horde of ducks flows over the rice check out of the area created by the dogleg into the next section of the field. At that moment one of the poachers will whistle softly, whereupon all the duck heads will go up en masse to listen for the sound of danger. The first shot will go right into all the raised heads, which really makes for a killing-field situ-

ation that is unreal. Then, as the remaining ducks rise up off the
ground like a sheet being lifted, the shooter will continue to pour
round after round into the wall of ducks, killing a new portion of
birds leaving the ground at each shot. If it's done right, several
shooters without plugs in their shotguns, keeping their shot streams
low, can kill three hundred to four hundred ducks in one sitting!
This number does not take into account the hundreds of ducks that
take a few shot pellets as they attempt to flee and die moments or
days later as a result of those wounds. Suffice it to say, it's a very
deadly way to harvest a great number of ducks in short order!

My two lads headed for one side of the dogleg check, and the
unsuspecting feeding ducks, still thirty-five to forty yards away,
headed for the other side. A disaster in the making, I thought as I
watched events unfold. The two lads crawled to the point of the
check and then, after a hurried conversation, split, assuming positions on either side of the point of the rice check. I suspected they
had looked the area over and concluded they could kill more ducks
if they caught them in a slight cross fire. Later events would prove
that assumption correct. The lads dug into the side of the rice check
and all but disappeared from view.

Knowing they were not looking back, I lightened up my gear,
getting rid of my coat and Starlight Scope, and began to crawl toward them via a convenient muddy tire rut cut into the rice field
by a Hardy Harvester when the farmer had pulled the rice out of
these fields. The muddy rut allowed me to crawl to within maybe
thirty-five feet of the two lads without being seen. As I lay there in
the mud, gun side up, I was hoping the ducks would hurry up and
get there. It was November, and not all the mud in the rut had
frozen.

As wet as I was now getting, I could not lie there for too long
without affecting my ability to run because of the cold seeping into
my body. Hurry up, ducks, I said to myself through chattering teeth.
A coat would have been nice, and I was having second thoughts
about leaving it so I could fly like the wind in a chase. Well, maybe
not like the wind, more like a cattle truck. Then the din created by
ten thousand approaching feeding ducks became louder and the

adrenaline started to flow because of what was to come, so I partly forgot the cold. Pretty soon ducks were flying into the area at the head of the feeding swarm and landing all around me. Knowing I now had to lie perfectly still, I concentrated on my two lads and ignored the ducks landing and starting to feed just feet from my inert body. I noticed the horde of ducks starting to flow over a lower portion of the dike and figured the killing was about to start.

A few moments later I heard one of the lads whistle, and the ducks became instantly quiet. Then came the simultaneous roar of shotguns being rapidly fired into the masses of ducks. This sound was instantly followed by the roar of thousands of wings beating frantically in an effort to escape the terror in front. The happy feeding of a few moments before had turned into terror, and every duck, except those already lying inert on the ground, made frantic efforts to escape. The roar of the twin shotguns continued, as did the racket of fleeing wings. I almost got up at that point and went for one of the shooters, but I held my position in an effort to develop a battle plan that would enable me to catch both of them. The thought went through my mind as I lay there among flying shot and feathers that if I got too greedy everything would turn to crap!

After the barrage ended, the lads dropped out of sight next to the levee and began to look all around to see if the game wardens were after them. Realizing what they were doing, I held my position, all the while listening to the two lads hurriedly reloading their shotguns. Food for thought for any game wardens who attempted to take them for what they had just done, I said to myself. Ducks still flew every which way, including bunches other than the one the lads had just shot into. Cripples were walking by me by the dozens in an attempt to escape to some form of cover to avoid capture.

"Let's do it," came the command from one of the lads as they jumped to their feet and, laying their shotguns down on the levee, began to run around to pick up the dead and dying ducks. I waited until the lads were fully engrossed in this activity before I started to crawl toward the levee and the two shotguns left behind. When I reached the levee, I peeked over and confirmed that they were still picking up dead ducks as if there were plenty more to gather, and there were! The ground, though they had been collecting ducks for a few minutes, was strewn with the efforts of their illegal labors! Damn, I thought as I reached the shotguns, they wouldn't be using these to kill any more ducks if I had my way. Both guns were Model 11 Remington semiautomatic 12-gauge shotguns, a market hunter's weapon of choice, to say the least. Taking both guns, I removed the magazine caps and slid the barrels forward a short distance so that if they somehow got back to these guns they would not fire until the barrels were pushed back and locked into the blocks. Putting the magazine caps in my pocket, I inched my head up over the levee to see what the lads were doing. They were still picking up the ducks and appeared to have killed quite a few from the looks of the piles of broken bodies they had created. Stopping and looking around every few minutes, the lads continued their detail until they had picked up every duck they could see. With that, they both knelt down to rest and being only fifteen feet away, I was privy to their entire conversation.

"Why don't you go and get the truck, and while you're doing that I will drag them over to the road so we can load them up and get the hell out of here."

"OK, but keep your eyes peeled, and if you see someone coming, meet me at our meeting spot. Also, watch out for that skunk; I can smell him again."

Skunk! I thought. You haven't seen anything yet.

The tallest of the two took off toward the west. He soon was out of my sight, and I let him go. I still had at least one of the lads and both of their shotguns. That was a start, and with a little luck I would have them both if everything went according to plan. Getting back to the business at hand, I continued to watch the lad in the field picking up ducks, tying them together in bunches, and stacking them for hauling to the pickup site. When he was finished, he grabbed several bunches of ducks and rapidly walked over the rice check to the road I had previously lain behind and deposited them alongside the berm. He returned along the same route and repeated the operation for several more trips. On one of his trips to the road with a load of ducks, I crawled over to where he had been crossing the dogleg rice check and set up an ambush. When he came back, he stepped over the rice check en route to the pile of ducks and right into my arms as I quickly rose up from my hiding place.

"Ho-ho" was his scared response to being grabbed by another human he had never figured was that close to him.

"State game warden; you are under arrest," I boomed as I grabbed him even more tightly. I could feel him start to run and tripped him in an instant to preclude any such adventure. Down we both went, and my handcuffs went on the wrists of the struggling lad in about two heartbeats. Weighing over three hundred, when I got my hands on you and perched my weight on top, you were mine! This case was no different.

After the handcuffs went on, the man ceased to struggle and just lay there getting his breath back from the fright he had just suffered. Rolling him over, I was surprised to find that I had an Asian man in bracelets! Not recognizing the lad as being from my neck of the woods, I asked for his name. Silence. I asked again with a little more "umph" on my request, and "Kam Fong," came his reply.

"Where you from, Fong?" was my next question as I kept my eye on the road still dimly lit by the moonlight for the arrival of his partner.

"Yuba City," came the reply.

"What are the ducks for?" came my next rapid-fire question. I didn't get a rapid-fire response. In fact, I didn't get any answer to that question. The rule of silence now prevailed. I figured the ducks were for sale in a Yuba City market, probably the Tong Society. Later in the week I heard that several members of the Tong had contacted a white market hunter from the town of Sutter for ducks on a hurry-up basis. It seemed that their usual Asian market-hunting sources had been tapped by the long arm of the law in Colusa County a few nights earlier! My friend Tom Okimoto supplied the missing pieces about a month after my encounter with my two Asian shooters. He informed me that there were plans for a large gathering of the Tong in San Francisco to celebrate a historical occasion. Several members of that group had initiated the request for wild ducks for the traditional duck dinner via the shooters from Yuba City, another historical Tong center. It seems that a "bear" got in the way, though, and apprehended the Chinese duck shooters out to supply the basic centerpiece for this festive dinner. The only thing that got munched in that "hoorah" were those pulling the triggers!

Picking up my shooter by the shoulder, I requested his driver's license and in short order put it in my shirt pocket for safekeeping. Then I filled his hands with ducks, and the two of us hauled ducks to the pick-up spot near the farm road. Still not seeing the other lad returning with the vehicle, we returned for another haul of ducks. They had killed a bunch, 303 to be exact, and we had a way to go before all the ducks were moved to the road. Grabbing two more armloads, we moved back to the road area. I had Kam sit down in the tall grass alongside the road while I moved the piles of ducks to the center of the road to mark the spot for the vehicle to stop when it arrived. Retrieving my Starlight Scope, I panned the area, looking for the vehicle driven by the other lad responsible for the ever-growing pile of dead ducks. As I continued looking, I heard a rattle of about twenty shots to the west.

Beauchamp's property, I mentally noted, gritting my teeth! Well, I knew where I would be later this day doing my perpetual dance with the draggers! Damn, the ducks just didn't have a chance. Come to think of it, neither did the game wardens! About that time, I heard the rattle of a vehicle coming down the dirt road. The noise was behind me! Whirling around, I was surprised to find the vehicle being driven by my other shooter coming in from the side opposite the one on which they had originally entered the rice field. Damn, I had forgotten one of the rules of market hunting driven into my head by Crazy Joe: to avoid being caught, enter from one side, leave by another. Maybe that is why we Germans have never won a war since 1870! Locking on to the oncoming rig, I could see that I still had a few minutes before contact. Moving over to Kam, I told him to lie down and not to move or try to warn his buddy unless he wanted to spend a lot of extra time in jail for interfering with the duties of a peace officer.

Seeing that my message had more than registered in his memory banks, I hustled across the road and hid on that side in the tall road-berm grasses. That way, when my lad stopped in front of the pile of ducks barely observable in the pale moonlight, I would be on the driver's side. When he stepped out to load the ducks and his buddy, all he would get was a load of me!

Nearing the pile of ducks, the lad coasted to a stop using compression so he wouldn't disclose his position to anyone watching by using his brakes. I heard him use his emergency brake to stop the rig, shut off the engine, and open the door. Then I rose out of the tall grass right next to him. Hitting him with my flashlight beam, I said, "Good morning, state game warden; you are under arrest."

With that, the fireworks started! He instantly dove back into the pickup and tried to start the engine. That was really hard to do with the right hand of a three hundred–pound game warden on his neck and left hand on his left arm, pulling in a way opposite the way he wanted to go! It was amazing how fast the lad came out of that pickup with my little assist! *Whump* he went, headfirst on the ground, and being stunned by the velocity at which he had hit, he just lay there for a few moments getting his wits about him. I would imagine the first thing he saw after the stars was the huge shape of a game warden standing over him advising him that to resist further would add another charge to those he had already accrued during his evening's work. He lay there on the ground, rubbing his now very sore neck, while I identified myself again on the off-chance that he had not heard me properly the first time and then asked him some questions. As it turned out he was Bob Chu, also from Yuba City, and like his partner he had nothing to say after that.

That was OK; I had them with the goods, and before that night was over they would learn a lesson about our courts here in the valley that I was sure would stick with them for a long time. Dragging Bob to his feet, I asked for and received his driver's license and Social Security card. With those, and with just the one set of handcuffs, which were already in use by his partner, off the three of us went to haul ducks from the field to their truck. For the next half hour or so we hauled several hundred ducks from the field and spent some time catching cripples as well to avoid the waste associated with a shoot such as they had enacted. Loading all the ducks into Bob's vehicle, I loaded Kam in the bed of the truck and Bob in the front seat, passenger side.

Driving out of the field to where my truck was hidden, we transferred the ducks from their truck to mine. Locking up their truck in preparation for Joe Willow's wrecker, I loaded the lads into my vehicle for the ride to the Colusa County jail. Calling the Colusa County sheriff's office on the radio, I advised the dispatcher that I was on the way with two prisoners, identified them, and headed in. Upon arrival, I booked the two lads on the usual state charges and then got Joe Willow out of bed and sent him with his wrecker to fetch the lads' vehicle for impoundment in the sheriff's office impound lot. I then got Angelo Jaconetti, a commercial duck picker, out of bed and put him to work on the 303 ducks so they could be salvaged for later distribution to the needy. In those days Angelo charged only fifty cents per duck, but he was only too happy to get out of bed for the cash this effort would bring. Besides, he was a true sportsman and a damn good hunter-safety instructor. He didn't mind one bit doing his part to help the wildlife officers in their far-flung endeavors and was always there to assist in any way he could. Wherever he is now, may God rest his soul. He was a good man who came from a family with a unique history in the valley.

I spent the rest of the morning writing out the lads' citations for early shooting, use of unplugged shotguns, taking over-limits of waterfowl, wanton waste, and illegal possession of an over-limit of waterfowl. I figured those charges would relieve them of plenty from their wallets, not to mention the shame of being apprehended. Then I went home for breakfast, showered, and went back into the field where the lads had pulled off their shoot with my dog, Shadow. After several hours of combing the ditch banks, clumps of grass, and other possible hiding places for wounded ducks, the dog and I picked up ninety-six more ducks as mute testimony to the destructiveness of such night-shooting practices! These too were turned over to Angelo for picking and preservation.

❧

About two weeks later my lads had their day in court, both pleading guilty to the charges as read. Old Judge Weyand was not usually known for being a hanging judge, but on that day he held each lad accountable for $500 per offense, or $2,500 apiece. After a really swell tail-end chewing, the judge told them that this time he would not send them to jail, but if they were apprehended in the future they could expect to spend a long time behind bars as guests of Colusa County. The judge then asked the lads if they could pay right then. Both lads dug out their wallets, took out hundred-dollar bills, and paid right on the spot. I didn't say anything, but that was one of the first moments in my career that I began to realize I was fighting a losing battle and that ultimately the poacher would have his way with the resources of the land. As long as money is involved, wildlife will lose.

It is not often that a law enforcement officer in my business is able to catch a real outlaw more than once. Even more rare is the opportunity to have an informed second chance at someone as I did with these chaps after missing them that first time with Vince. They didn't get the usual three strikes before being put out this time. I kind of like the notion of "two strikes and you are out." Only one other time in my career have I had an opportunity like this one, and I took that lad out in two strikes as well. After all, the only voice the world of wildlife has is that of the wildlife law enforcement officer. If that person isn't really raising hell with the outlaws, then the officer is nothing more than part of the problem and no better than the poacher.

Suffice it to say that over thirty-two years as an enforcement officer in the world of wildlife, I have run down every son of a bitch I could find who crossed that line. As you can probably tell, I don't believe in waiting for that third strike.

As far as I know, the Tong Society did not get its rice-fed wild ducks for the historic dinner because the long arm of the law got in the way. I guess they had to eat "flaming filet of yak, Peking style" instead—or was that "crow"?

About the Author

TERRY GROSZ EARNED his bachelor's degree in 1964 and his master's in wildlife management in 1966 from Humboldt State College in California. He was a California State Fish and Game Warden, based first in Eureka and then Colusa, from 1966 to 1970. He then joined the U.S. Fish & Wildlife Service, and served in California as a U.S. Game Management Agent and Special Agent to 1974. After that, he was promoted to Senior Resident Agent and placed in charge of North and South Dakota for two years, followed by three years as Senior Special Agent in Washington, D.C., with the Endangered Species Program, Division of Law Enforcement. While in Washington, he also served as a foreign liaison officer. In 1979 he became Assistant Special Agent in Charge in Minneapolis, and then was promoted to Special Agent in Charge, and transferred to Denver in 1981, where he remained until retirement in June 1998 (although his title changed to Assistant Regional Director for Law Enforcement). He has earned many awards and honors during his career, including, from the U.S. Fish & Wildlife Service, the Meritorious Service Award in 1996, and Top Ten Award in 1987 as one of the ten top employees (in an agency of some 9,000). The Fish & Wildlife Foundation presented him with the Guy Bradley Award in 1989, and in 1995 he received the Conservation Achievement Award for Law Enforcement from the National Wildlife Federation. Terry Grosz lives in Colorado with his wife, Donna, who teaches 4th grade and makes the best pies in the world. They have three grown children.